Transcultural Picture
Word List

Judy P. Donaldson

Transcultural Picture Word List

For Teaching English to Children from Any of 35 Language Backgrounds

Second Edition

Judy P. Donaldson

Learning Publications, Inc.
Holmes Beach, Florida

ISBN 1-55691-132-7

Learning Publications, Inc.
5351 Gulf Drive
P.O. Box 1338
Holmes Beach, FL 34218-1338

Printing: 5 4 3 2   Year: 3 2 1 0

Printed in the United States of America

Contents

Preface

Until you've "walked the walk and talked the talk," you can't begin to understand the frustration caused by the inability to communicate with people in your native language — unable to comprehend what is spoken, written, or read — you can't follow directions, yet you have the same needs as those around you.

Experience how it feels to be a foreigner and in the minority, rather than the majority, of your environment. Regardless of your age, education level, fluency in your language, or former level of social prominence, you are now illiterate and unable to communicate. Functionally, once you step out of your home, you're as helpless as a preschool child!

I was prompted to write this book because of my first teaching assignment at the eighth grade level in a school where English was a second language for 90 percent of the students. I spoke only English.

This book will become an invaluable asset for anyone who is working with non-English people. It has been written in an easy to use and understandable format, uncluttered with the usual dreaded grammar verbiage extending adfinitum.

Most categorical programs have a component that requires parent involvement. The **Letters to Parents** section is the first step in meeting that requirement. The letters enable the school to build a bridge of friendship, trust, and understanding to expedite the acquisition of English fluency, while encouraging use of native language.

Dolch Word Lists* are included because they are high-frequency-use, basic-sight vocabulary words that comprise 70 percent of all English in print.

Syntax variants are designed to enable the teacher or reader to understand, in a basic way, how English and the other languages compare. The comparison regards word order in sentences, and in some cases the use of omissions of various parts of speech. Alphabet comparisons and pronunciations are close approximations due to many varying factors too numerous to list.

Word pairs and **vowel** and **consonant transpositions** are included to help identify the individual who is having phonological interference with English and the native language. A person who has this problem will have difficulty determining whether the spoken word pairs or letter pairs, sound the "same" or "different." This problem is common with persons who are still "hearing" in their native language: w/v, we ve; l/r, light right; th (voiced) t/d, those does; ch/sh, chips ships; y/j, yellow jello; etc.

While there are often better choices of word explanations that could have been used, the translators were instructed to use the most simplified, most easily understandable level of language. This was done in order to reach all people. Some cultures have levels of speaking determined by the age or social ranking of the persons who are speaking or to whom the speaking is directed. This is a Linguistic Caste System. In many countries, education is for the wealthy.

---

*Some monolingual speakers of English are also confused. Many are the "youth at risk." Those yellow ships are right there. = Does jello chips are light dare. Reading, writing, and speaking comprehension levels are contributing to Attention Deficit Disorder Syndrome (ADDS). The students do not qualify for ESL-funded assistance because English is their **only** language. Many are therefore being considered for placement in Special Education programs.

There are few who have had the opportunity for formal learning in schools. If there is opportunity for schooling, the males are given priority as they are the workers outside the home, and the females are kept home, bound to the "mother tongue."

Translators were chosen with utmost care. English literacy and fluency were a prerequisite. In addition, they had to be able to read and write their native language fluently. They were not only bilingual, but biliterate as well. Each translator's work was later examined by one or more of his or her peers. In addition, the use of professional translators, translations were done by educational, governmental, and religious personnel. More than 100 translators were involved in this project. More than seven years were spent compiling the text with people from 38 different cultural and linguistic backgrounds. Their lives were often filled with wealth that is found in the palaces of kings and queens — some were from these palaces! Some spoke of "man's inhumanity to men, women, and infants" in terms that are beyond our imagination. All spoke of courage, hope, faith, love, and a desire to bring peace and security with them to share with each of us.

These are useful in adult and secondary education as well as required texts for future teachers.

Acknowledgement

This book is dedicated to those involved in the vital process of language learning with its complex cultural implications and to their teachers in the belief that communication among the peoples of the earth is all-important to a peaceful universe.

I wish to express my deep gratitude and sincere appreciation to each of you, wherever you may be, for the time and effort you have so generously given for the purpose of helping us to communicate more easily and to further the cause of humanity, love, and understanding.

Without your help, this work would not have been accomplished.

Introduction

The *Transcultural Picture Word List,* with more than 600 entries, was created for the purpose of helping teachers to help the students who have English as a second language, to learn English more rapidly and at the same time reinforce the knowledge of their native language.

Letters to the parents are included in the various languages, in order that parents can reinforce at home, what the students are being taught in school; this will minimize fragmented learning by allowing the vocabulary of the students to be built on concrete knowledge of the words in both languages, based on the premise that a person can only utilize a vocabulary that he understands. This will help to narrow the degree of difference between the student's oral and silent reading comprehension level.

Information on the syntax variants and letter transpositions, such as "p" for "v" "wif" for "with," are included to give the teacher a synopsis of characteristic difficulties that students of a specific language background, that is different from English, may exhibit. This information is given with the hope that a teacher who is prepared, in advance, to meet the learning difficulties of students, may help to make acquisition of English a pleasant experience.

The next four sections of the book contain basic transcultural picture word lists of things (nouns), opposites, place or position (near-far), actions, colors, numbers, and shapes with the English word for the object, action, etc. printed under the picture.

The final section of the book is made up of the *220 Basic Sight Word List** by Edward W. Dolch in the various languages. The list, when learned, will serve as a springboard into more rapid progress in your reading program.

Flashcards, in any language, can be made either from the "Dolch List," and/or from the various entries found in the *Transcultural Picture Word List.* The teacher would make the cards, to assure uniformity of size. The teacher or the student would then write the word in English on one side of the card. The student or parent would then write the word in his native language on the reverse side.

Implementation of these ideas and materials will greatly assist those teachers and schools where a bilingual teacher or program is not possible. Bilingual teachers and their programs can also utilize these ideas and materials as valuable supplements.

---

*Reprinted by permission of the publisher, *220 Basic Sight Word List,* Edward W. Dolch, © Garrard Publishing Company.

Section 1
Letters to Parents

This section includes letters in the following languages:

English	German	Navajo
Arabic	Greek	Norwegian
Bengali	Hebrew	Persian
Cambodian	Hindi	Polish
Chinese	White Hmong	Portuguese
Croatian	Hungarian	Russian
Czech	Indonesian	Samoan
Danish	Italian	Spanish
Dutch	Japanese	Swedish
Filipino (Tagalog)	Korean	Thai
Finnish	Laotian	Tongan
French	Blue Mong	Vietnamese

English

Dear Parents of _____ Date _____

Please help the school to be able to help your child learn to read and write in English more easily. At different times during the school year, your child will bring home word lists or pictures with the names of objects written in English and a blank line beside or under them, for you to write the meanings on the blank lines, in your own language. If your child can hear you say the word in your language, and see how it is written, he will be able to understand what the meaning is in English also; and at the same time, be studying his own language. Any help you can give your child will be appreciated.

_____
Teacher

Arabic

Dear Parents of _____ Date _____

    Please help the school to be able to help your child learn to read and write in English more easily. At different times during the school year, your child will bring home word lists or pictures with the names of objects written in English and a blank line beside or under them, for you to write the meanings on the blank lines, in your own language. If your child can hear you say the word in your language, and see how it is written, he will be able to understand what the meaning is in English also; and at the same time, be studying his own language. Any help you can give your child will be appreciated.

_____

Teacher

المُدَرِّس _____ _____ اعزائي و الدي

ارجو مس حضرتكم التعاون مع المدرسة في

مساعدة ابنكم/ابنتكم لتعلم قراءة وكتابة اللغة

الانكليزية بسهولة ، ولذا سيقوم ولدكم/ابنتكم

بعودته للدار خلال السنة الدراسية احضار

كلمات انكليزية او صور ما داخل الصور لكي يكتبوا

له معانيها باللغة العربية بجانبها ، وبذلك يتمكن

ولدكم من سماع الكلمة ومشاهدة كتابتها باللغة العربية

وبهذه الخطوة تساعد الطالب على معرفة معاني الكلمات

باللغتين العربية والانكليزية .

و نشكركم لاهتمامكم

_____

معلمة/المعلم

Bengali

Dear Parents of _____ Date _____

Please help the school to be able to help your child learn to read and write in English more easily. At different times during the school year, your child will bring home word lists or pictures with the names of objects written in English and a blank line beside or under them, for you to write the meanings on the blank lines, in your own language. If your child can hear you say the word in your language, and see how it is written, he will be able to understand what the meaning is in English also; and at the same time, be studying his own language. Any help you can give your child will be appreciated.

_____
Teacher

মান্যবরঃ অভিভাবক, _____ তারিখ _____

জনাব,

আপনার ছেলে মেয়ে সহজভাবে যেন বেশ ইংরেজী পড়তে ও লিখতে পারে সেই দিকে স্কুল তাকে উৎসাহ পূর্বক সাহায্য করছে। স্কুল চলাকালীন বিভিন্ন সময়ে আপনার ছেলে মেয়েরা যে বস্তুসমূহ ও ছবির সহ ইংরেজী বই সমস্তগুলো স্কুলে বা নিচে ধরণ বাড়িতে সঙ্গে নিয়ে যাবে তাহার মানে যেমন এ নিচে খালি, তাহাতে নিজভাষায় লিখিয়া রাখবে, যাহা আপনার ছেলে মেয়েরা শুনতে পারে তাহা ইহার লেখা। তাহলে সে সহজেই ইংরেজী মানে সহজে করবে। এই আপনার আপনার ছেলে মেয়েকে সাহায্যকরে তার ছেলে আপনার ছেলে _____ কৃতজ্ঞ থাকবে।

_____
বিনীত

Cambodian

Dear Parents of _____   Date _____

Please help the school to be able to help your child learn to read and write in English more easily. At different times during the school year, your child will bring home word lists or pictures with the names of objects written in English and a blank line beside or under them, for you to write the meanings on the blank lines, in your own language. If your child can hear you say the word in your language, and see how it is written, he will be able to understand what the meaning is in English also; and at the same time, be studying his own language. Any help you can give your child will be appreciated.

_____
                                                        Teacher

Chinese

Dear Parents of _____ Date _____

Please help the school to be able to help your child learn to read and write in English more easily. At different times during the school year, your child will bring home word lists or pictures with the names of objects written in English and a blank line beside or under them, for you to write the meanings on the blank lines, in your own language. If your child can hear you say the word in your language, and see how it is written, he will be able to understand what the meaning is in English also; and at the same time, be studying his own language. Any help you can give your child will be appreciated.

_____
Teacher

親愛的 _____ 家長   日期 _____

　　請助救校以協助您的學童在學習英文閱讀及書字方面較易些. 在學期中不同時間中, 貴子弟將學寫滿了英文字的單子或者圖片 (有英文解釋) 回家在這些字或圖片的旁邊或者下面留有空白的一行以便留給貴家長在家中以本國語言填寫. 如果貴子弟能聽您以本國語言說同時看他怎麼寫, 貴子弟也將會暸解英文的意思. 更進一步也能使其學習本國語言. 我們非常感謝您給予貴子弟的協助

_____ 教師

Croatian

Dear Parents of _____ Date _____

Please help the school to be able to help your child learn to read and write in English more easily. At different times during the school year, your child will bring home word lists or pictures with the names of objects written in English and a blank line beside or under them, for you to write the meanings on the blank lines, in your own language. If your child can hear you say the word in your language, and see how it is written, he will be able to understand what the meaning is in English also; and at the same time, be studying his own language. Any help you can give your child will be appreciated.

_____

Teacher

Dragi _____ Roditelji   Datum _____

Molim vas da pomognete školi da pomogne vašem djetetu da lakše nauči čitati i pisati engleski. Tokom školske godine dijete će donositi popise riječi ili slike sa imenima predmeta na engleskom i praznom crtom pored ili ispod njih, da ispunite značenje riječi na vašem jeziku. Kada dijete bude čulo kako izgovarate riječ na vašem jeziku, i vidi kako se ona piše, razumjet će što znači na engleskom; istouremeno će učiti materinji jezik. Zahvalni smo vam za svaku pomoć vašem djetetu.

S poštovanjem

_____

Učitelj

Czech

Dear Parents of _____ Date _____

Please help the school to be able to help your child learn to read and write in English more easily. At different times during the school year, your child will bring home word lists or pictures with the names of objects written in English and a blank line beside or under them, for you to write the meanings on the blank lines, in your own language. If your child can hear you say the word in your language, and see how it is written, he will be able to understand what the meaning is in English also; and at the same time, be studying his own language. Any help you can give your child will be appreciated.

_____

Teacher

Vážení rodiče _____ Datum _____

Prosíme Vás, abyste pomohli škole snadněji naučit Vaše dítě číst a psát anglicky. Vaše dítě bude občas nosit listy se slovíčky nebo obrázky s názvy předmětů v angličtině a vedle nich nebo pod nimi bude prázdná linka, na kterou napíšete česky výraz. Jestliže Vaše dítě uslyší jak se předmět čte a píše česky, bude také lépe rozumět jeho významu v angličtině. Současně se tím bude také učit svému rodnému jazyku. Uvítáme každou pomoc, kterou svému dítěti poskytnete.

_____

učitel

Danish

Dear Parents of _____ Date _____

   Please help the school to be able to help your child learn to read and write in English more easily. At different times during the school year, your child will bring home word lists or pictures with the names of objects written in English and a blank line beside or under them, for you to write the meanings on the blank lines, in your own language. If your child can hear you say the word in your language, and see how it is written, he will be able to understand what the meaning is in English also; and at the same time, be studying his own language. Any help you can give your child will be appreciated.

_____
                                                                                                Teacher

TIL _____   FORAELDRE _____   DATO _____

   VIL DE VAERE SAA VENLIG AT HJELPE OS, SAA DERES BARN KAN LETTERE LAERE AT LAESE OG SKRIVE ENGELSK. IGENNEM SKOLEAARET, VIL DERES BARN BRINGE EN LISTE AF ORD OG BILLEDER HJEM, NAVNENE VIL BLIVE SKREVET PAA ENGELSK, DER VIL OGSAA VAERE EN LINGE HVOR DE KAN SKRIVE ORDET OG MENINGEN AF BILLEDERNE PAA DANSK, PAA DEN MAADE, NAAR DE LAESER DET HOJT, WIL DERES BARN LAERE HVORDAN DET UDTALES, OG VIL SAA VAERE I STAND TIL AT LAERE BEAAE SPROG. VI VIL PAASKONNE ENHVER HJAELP DE KAN GIVE OS.

_____
                                                                                                LAERER

Dutch

Dear Parents of _____ Date _____

Please help the school to be able to help your child learn to read and write in English more easily. At different times during the school year, your child will bring home word lists or pictures with the names of objects written in English and a blank line beside or under them, for you to write the meanings on the blank lines, in your own language. If your child can hear you say the word in your language, and see how it is written, he will be able to understand what the meaning is in English also; and at the same time, be studying his own language. Any help you can give your child will be appreciated.

_____

Teacher

Beste Ouders van _____ Datum _____

Wilt u zo vriendelijk zijn om met de school mede te werken, zodat uw kind beter in het Engels zal leren lezen en schrijven.

Verschillende malen tijdens het schooljaar zal uw kind een lijst met woorden of afbeeldingen mee naar huis brengen, met de betekenissen van de voorwerpen er op in het Engels en daar naast open plaatsen voor u, om in te vullen in uw eigen taal.

Wanneer uw kind deze woorden in uw taal hoort spreken en kan zien hoe ze geschreven worden, is het mogelijk dat hij dan ook zal begrijpen wat de betekenis is in het Engels en tegelijkertijd zijn eigen taal leert.

Alle hulp die u uw kind kan geven wordt zeer op prijs gesteld.

_____

De onderwijzer

Filipino -- Tagalog

Dear Parents of _____ Date _____

Please help the school to be able to help your child learn to read and write in English more easily. At different times during the school year, your child will bring home word lists or pictures with the names of objects written in English and a blank line beside or under them, for you to write the meanings on the blank lines, in your own language. If your child can hear you say the word in your language, and see how it is written, he will be able to understand what the meaning is in English also; and at the same time, be studying his own language. Any help you can give your child will be appreciated.

_____

Teacher

Petsa _____

Mahal na mga magulang ni _____

Inihihingi namin ng tulong sa inyo na turuan ang inyung anak na matutong magbasa at sumulat sa Inglés ng madalian. Sa iba′t-ibang panahon sa loob ng taon sa paaralan, ang inyung anak ay mag-uuwi sa bahay ng mga listahan ng mga salita o larawan na may mga pangalan ng mga bagay na nakasulat sa Inglés at sa may patlang sa tabi nito, inyung isusulat ang mga kahulugan nito sa inyung sariling wika. Kapag naririnig ng inyung isusulat ang mga salita at nakikita kung paano ito isinusulat, maiintindihán din niya ang mga ibig sabihin nito sa Inglés at kaalinsabay nito, matutuhan din niya ang kaniyang sariling wika. Anumang tulong ang maibibigay ninyo sa inyung anak ay taos-puso naming pinasasalamatan.

_____

Gurô

Finnish

Dear Parents of _____ Date _____

Please help the school to be able to help your child learn to read and write in English more easily. At different times during the school year, your child will bring home word lists or pictures with the names of objects written in English and a blank line beside or under them, for you to write the meanings on the blank lines, in your own language. If your child can hear you say the word in your language, and see how it is written, he will be able to understand what the meaning is in English also; and at the same time, be studying his own language. Any help you can give your child will be appreciated.

_____

Teacher

Päiväys:

Arvoisat vanhemmat,

Pyydämme kohteliaimmin apuanne, jotta voisimme auttaa lastanne oppimaan lukemaan ja kirjoittamaan englantia mahdollisimman helposti. Aika ajoittain lukuvuoden aikana lapsenne tuo kotiin sanaluetteloja tai kuvasarjoja, joissa on englanniksi esineitten nimiä sekä tyhjiä rivejä, joille voitte kirjoittaa samat sanat suomeksi. Jos lapsenne voi kuulla teidän sanovan sanan suomeksi ja nähdä, kuinka se kirjoitetaan, hän pystyy ymmärtämään englanninkielisen sanan merkityksen — ja oppii samanaikaisesti suomea. Olemme kiitollia avustanne lapsenne hyväksi.

Kunnioittaen,

_____

Opettaja

French

Dear Parents of _____ Date _____

Please help the school to be able to help your child learn to read and write in English more easily. At different times during the school year, your child will bring home word lists or pictures with the names of objects written in English and a blank line beside or under them, for you to write the meanings on the blank lines, in your own language. If your child can hear you say the word in your language, and see how it is written, he will be able to understand what the meaning is in English also; and at the same time, be studying his own language. Any help you can give your child will be appreciated.

_____

Teacher

Aux Parents de _____ Date _____

Nous vous demandons de bien vouloir nous donner votre concours de façon à ce que nous puissions aider votre enfant à apprendre à lire et à écrire en anglais, plus facilement. A des occasions différentes pendant l'année scolaire, votre enfant apportera à la maison avec lui une liste de mots ou gravures avec le nom des objets écrit en anglais et un espace souligné à côte, ou dessous chaque mot, de façon à ce que vous puissiez écrire le mot dans votre propre langue. Si votre enfant peut vous entendre dire le mot et voir comment il s'écrit dans votre langue, il lui sera plus facile de comprendre le mot en anglais, et ceci tout en étudiant sa propre langue. Nous apprécions vivement l'aide que vous pourrez donner à votre enfant.

_____

Instituteur

German

Dear Parents of _____ Date _____

Please help the school to be able to help your child learn to read and write in English more easily. At different times during the school year, your child will bring home word lists or pictures with the names of objects written in English and a blank line beside or under them, for you to write the meanings on the blank lines, in your own language. If your child can hear you say the word in your language, and see how it is written, he will be able to understand what the meaning is in English also; and at the same time, be studying his own language. Any help you can give your child will be appreciated.

_____
Teacher

Liebe Eltern von _____ Datum _____

Bitte helfen Sie der Schule, Ihrem Kinde zu helfen, besser Englisch lesen und schreiben zu lernen. Verschiedene Male wärend des Schuljahrs wird Ihr Kind Wortlisten oder Bilder mit nach Hause bringen, auf denen die Namen von Dingen auf Englisch geschrieben sind mit einer freien Linie darunter, damit Sie die Bedeutung in Ihrer eigenen Sprache auf die freien Linien schreiben können. Wenn Ihr Kind von Ihnen das Wort in Ihrer Sprache gesprochen hört und sehen kann, wie es geschrieben wird, dann kann es auch verstehen, was es auf Englisch bedeutet und zur selben Zeit seine eigene Sprache lernen. Wir danken Ihnen für jegliche Hilfe, die sie Ihrem Kinde geben können.

_____
Lehrer

Greek

Dear Parents of _____ Date _____

Please help the school to be able to help your child learn to read and write in English more easily. At different times during the school year, your child will bring home word lists or pictures with the names of objects written in English and a blank line beside or under them, for you to write the meanings on the blank lines, in your own language. If your child can hear you say the word in your language, and see how it is written, he will be able to understand what the meaning is in English also; and at the same time, be studying his own language. Any help you can give your child will be appreciated.

_____

Teacher

Ἀγαπητοί γονεῖς τοῦ (τῆς) _____ Ἡμερ. _____

    Παρακαλῶ βοηθήσατε τό σχολεῖο νά μπορέση νά βοηθήση τό παιδί σας νά μάθη νά διαβάζη καί νά γράφη πιο εὔκολα. Μερικές φορές κατά τό σχολικό ἔτος τό παιδί σας θά φέρνη λέξεις ἤ φωτογραφίες μέ ὀνόματα ἀντικειμένων γραμμένα στην Ἀγγλική καί μία κενή γραμμή δίπλα ἤ κάτω διά νά γράφετε ἐσεῖς τήν σημασίαν των στήν δικήν σας γλῶσσα. Ἐάν τό παιδί σας σᾶς ἀκούει νά λέγετε τήν λέξιν στήν γλῶσσαν σας καί βλέπει τῶς τήν γράφετε θά μπορέση νά καταλάβη τήν σημασίαν της καί στήν Ἀγγλικήν. Συγχρόνως μελετᾶτε τήν γλῶσσαν τον. ὅ,τι βοήθεια μπορεῖτε νά προσφέρετε στό παιδί σας θά εἶναι ἐκτιμητή.

_____

Ἡ Δασκάλα

Hebrew

Dear Parents of _____ Date _____

Please help the school to be able to help your child learn to read and write in English more easily. At different times during the school year, your child will bring home word lists or pictures with the names of objects written in English and a blank line beside or under them, for you to write the meanings on the blank lines, in your own language. If your child can hear you say the word in your language, and see how it is written, he will be able to understand what the meaning is in English also; and at the same time, be studying his own language. Any help you can give your child will be appreciated.

_____

Teacher

תאריך _____ להורים של _____ _____

אודה לכם מאוד אם תוכלו לעזור לבית הספר ללמד את ילדכם לקרוא

ולכתוב אנגלית ביתר קלות. בזמנים שונים במשך השנה, ילדכם יביא

הביתה אוצרות- מילים או תמונות עם שמות של העצמים כתובים באנגלית

ושורה ריקה בצדם או מתחתם. אבקשכם לכתוב את התרגום בשפתכם במקום

הריק. אם ילדכם ישמע אתכם אומרים את המילה בשפתכם ויראה איך היא נכתבת

הוא יוכל להבין את המשמעות גם באנגלית: ובאותו זמן ילמד גם את שפתו.

נודה לכם מאוד על כל עזרה שתוכלו לתת לילדכם.

_____

מורה

Hindi

Dear Parents of _____ Date _____

   Please help the school to be able to help your child learn to read and write in English more easily. At different times during the school year, your child will bring home word lists or pictures with the names of objects written in English and a blank line beside or under them, for you to write the meanings on the blank lines, in your own language. If your child can hear you say the word in your language, and see how it is written, he will be able to understand what the meaning is in English also; and at the same time, be studying his own language. Any help you can give your child will be appreciated.

_____
                                                                                    Teacher

तारीख _____

_____ के प्यारे अभिभावकों;
     आपके बच्चे को अंग्रेजी सुविधापूर्वक पढ़ाने और लिखवाने में स्कूल की मदद करें। कभी-कभी आने वाले साल में आपका बच्चा स्कूल से कुछ पन्ने ला लाएगा। इन पन्नों के ऊपर कुछ अंग्रेजी शब्द या तस्वीरें होंगी। आप खाली स्थान पर हर अंग्रेजी शब्द का मतलब हिन्दी में लिखें। अंग्रेजी शब्दों को हिन्दी में लिखते वक्त जोर से उसका उच्चारण करें ताकि आपका बच्चा उसको सुने और वह भी देखे कि आपने हिन्दी में क्या और कैसे लिखा है। इससे वह अपनी भाषा भी सीखेगा।
     जो भी मदद आप अपने बच्चे की करेंगे वह प्रशंसनीय है।

_____
शिक्षक / शिक्षिका

White Hmong

Dear Parents of _____ Date _____

Please help the school to be able to help your child learn to read and write in English more easily. At different times during the school year, your child will bring home word lists or pictures with the names of objects written in English and a blank line beside or under them, for you to write the meanings on the blank lines, in your own language. If your child can hear you say the word in your language, and see how it is written, he will be able to understand what the meaning is in English also; and at the same time, be studying his own language. Any help you can give your child will be appreciated.

_____

Teacher

Nyob zoo txog niam txiv ntawm _____ tim _____

Thov pab koom tes nrog tseem fwv (xwb fwb) los yog kws qhia ntawv, kom muaj cuab kav pab nej cov me nyuam, kawm nyeem thiab sau ntawv askiv (English) yooj yim. Nyob rau hauv lub sij hawm txawv txav nrab xyoo kawm ntawv ntawd, nej cov me nyuam yuav nqa ntawv (tsiaj ntawv) los yog duab uas muaj npe sau nrog los ua npe ntawv askiv thiab tseg tej kab kos nrog, uas nyob ib sab los yog hauv qab ntawd los tsev. Cia rau nej sau yam tseeb ntsiab rau ntawm txoj kab kos ua nej yam lus. Yog li, nej tus me nyuam hnov nej hais cov lus ntawd ua nej yam lus thiab ho pom tias sau li cas ntawd, nws yuav muaj cuab kav kawm tau mws yam lus nrog. Txhia yam pab cuam uas nej muaj cuab kav ua pab rau nej cov me nyuam, kuj muaj lus zoo siab kawg.

_____

KWS QHIA NTAWV

Hungarian

Dear Parents of _____ Date _____

Please help the school to be able to help your child learn to read and write in English more easily. At different times during the school year, your child will bring home word lists or pictures with the names of objects written in English and a blank line beside or under them, for you to write the meanings on the blank lines, in your own language. If your child can hear you say the word in your language, and see how it is written, he will be able to understand what the meaning is in English also; and at the same time, be studying his own language. Any help you can give your child will be appreciated.

_____
                                                                              Teacher

Kedves Szülök _____ Dátum _____

Segítségüket szeretnénk kérni abban, hogy gyermekeik minél könnyebben megtanuljanak irni és olvasni. Az iskola év folyamán gyermekük idönként egy kép vagy szó listát fog hazavinni amelyen a tárgyak angol neve fog szerepelni, egy üres vonallal alattuk vagy mellettük. Kérjük, hogy irják be a megfelelö szavakat anyanyelvükön. Ha a gyermek hallja a kimondott szót az önök nyelvén és ugyanakkor látja is leirva, az angol jelentést is, megfogja érteni. Emmellett saját nyelvét is tanulni fogja. Hálásan köszönünk minden segítséget, melyet gyermeküknek nyújtani tudnak.

_____
                                                                   Tanár (or) tanárnö

Indonesian

Dear Parents of _____ Date _____

Please help the school to be able to help your child learn to read and write in English more easily. At different times during the school year, your child will bring home word lists or pictures with the names of objects written in English and a blank line beside or under them, for you to write the meanings on the blank lines, in your own language. If your child can hear you say the word in your language, and see how it is written, he will be able to understand what the meaning is in English also; and at the same time, be studying his own language. Any help you can give your child will be appreciated.

_____
Teacher

Yang terhormat orang tua dari _____ Tanggal _____

Tolonglah sekolah ini untuk menolong anak saudara membaca dan menulis dalam bahasa Inggeris dengan lebih mudah. Dalam waktu yang berbeda selama tahun^2 pelajaran sekolah, anak saudara akan membawa pulang daftar kata^2 atau gambar^2 dengan nama^2 yang tertulis dalam bahasa Inggeris dengan garis kosong disamping atau dibawahnja, untuk saudara menulis artinya didalam garis^2 kosong itu, didalam bahasa saudara sendiri. Kalau anak saudara dapat mendengar apa yang saudara katakan dalam bahasa saudara sendiri, dan lihat bagaimana menulisnya, dia akan mengerti juga apa artinya didalam bahasa Inggeris; dan dalam waktu yang sama, belajar dalam bahasanya sendiri. Pertolongan apa saja yang dapat saudara berikan pada anak saudara akan kita hargai.

_____
Guru

Italian

Dear Parents of _____ Date _____

Please help the school to be able to help your child learn to read and write in English more easily. At different times during the school year, your child will bring home word lists or pictures with the names of objects written in English and a blank line beside or under them, for you to write the meanings on the blank lines, in your own language. If your child can hear you say the word in your language, and see how it is written, he will be able to understand what the meaning is in English also; and at the same time, be studying his own language. Any help you can give your child will be appreciated.

_____
Teacher

Cari Genitori di _____ Data _____

Per favore, aiutate la scuola ad essere in grado di aiutare il vostro bambino ad imparare a leggere e scrivere in Inglese piùfacilmente. In periodi differenti durante l'anno scolastico il vostro bambino porterà delle liste di parole o di figure con i nomi degli oggetti scritte in Inglese ed un' altra riga in bianco affinchè voi possiate scrivere il significato nella vostra lingua – Se il bambino puó sentirvi dire la parola nella vostra lingua, e vedere come è scritta, egli potrà capire anche quale è il significato in Inglese; e contemporaneamente studierà la sua lingua. Qualsiasi aiuto potrete dare al vostro bambino sarà apprezzato.

_____
Maestra/Maestro

Japanese

Dear Parents of _____ Date _____

Please help the school to be able to help your child learn to read and write in English more easily. At different times during the school year, your child will bring home word lists or pictures with the names of objects written in English and a blank line beside or under them, for you to write the meanings on the blank lines, in your own language. If your child can hear you say the word in your language, and see how it is written, he will be able to understand what the meaning is in English also; and at the same time, be studying his own language. Any help you can give your child will be appreciated.

_____
Teacher

父兄の皆様 _____ 日付 _____

　　学生達が もっと たやすく 英語の よみ、かきが 出来る様、父兄様の 助力を お願い いたします。　これからの 学期中、生徒達が もちかへる 答案に 図を 通されて、一所に 発音したり 意味を 知る様 日本語、英語で 学ばれる ことを 願って やみません。

父兄の皆様 の 協力を 感謝します。

_____

先生.

Korean

Dear Parents of _____ Date _____

Please help the school to be able to help your child learn to read and write in English more easily. At different times during the school year, your child will bring home word lists or pictures with the names of objects written in English and a blank line beside or under them, for you to write the meanings on the blank lines, in your own language. If your child can hear you say the word in your language, and see how it is written, he will be able to understand what the meaning is in English also; and at the same time, be studying his own language. Any help you can give your child will be appreciated.

                                                      _____
                                                                                    Teacher

친애하는 _____ 의 학부형께   날짜_____

귀댁의 자녀로 하여금 영어를 쉽게 읽고 쓸수있도록 학교 당국에서 실시하는 방침에 적극 협력해주시기 바랍니다. 재학시에 귀댁의 자녀는 여러번에 걸쳐 영어의 낱말이 나열된 것이나 물건의 이름이 영어로 적힌 것을 갖고 올것입니다. 이 낱말과 그림의 옆이나 아래에는 빈칸이 있아오니 그림의 이름이나 낱말의 뜻을 한글로 적어주시면 감사하겠읍니다.
귀댁의 자녀가 부형께서 한국어로 발음하는 것을 듣고 어떻게 쓰는가도 알면, 영어로도 그뜻이 무엇인지를 쉽게 알게될것이며, 아울러 한글을 계속해서 배울수있는 기회를 갖게될 것입니다. 여하한 방법으로나 귀댁의 자녀들에게 영어를 배울 수 있도록 도와주시면 감사하겠읍니다.

                                                      _____
                                                              교   사

Laotian

Dear Parents of _____ Date _____

　　Please help the school to be able to help your child learn to read and write in English more easily. At different times during the school year, your child will bring home word lists or pictures with the names of objects written in English and a blank line beside or under them, for you to write the meanings on the blank lines, in your own language. If your child can hear you say the word in your language, and see how it is written, he will be able to understand what the meaning is in English also; and at the same time, be studying his own language. Any help you can give your child will be appreciated.

_____

Teacher

ວັນທີ _____

ເຖິງພໍ່ແມ່ຂອງ _____ ດ້ວຍຄວາມ

ກະລຸນາຊ່ວຍ ທາງໂຮງຮຽນໃຫ້ ສາມາດຊ່ວຍສ່ວນໃຫ້ເດັກ ນ້ອຍຂອງ ທ່ານ ຮຽນ ອ່ານ ແລະຂຽນ ພາສາອັງກິດໄດ້ງ່າຍ ຂຶ້ນ. ເວລາຕ່າງ ກັນ ໃນ ລະຍະ ປີທີ່ມຽນ ເດັກນ້ອຍ ຂອງທ່ານ ຈະເອົາ ຍົມ ຄວາມ ເອົາ ຫຼາຍ ຫຼື ຮູບ ຕ່າງໆ ກັບ ທັງ ຊື່ຂອງ ຂອງຕ່າງໆ ຂຽນ ເປັນ ພາສາອັງກິດ ມາ ທ່ານ ຈະໄດ້ ຂຽນ ຄວາມໝາຍ ລົງໃນເສັ້ນ ຕ່າງ ຂອງ ຫ່າງ ທ່ານ ຈະ ໄດ້ ຮຽນ ຄວາມໝາຍຂອງ ມັນ ເປັນ ພາສາ ຂອງ. ຖ້າວ່າ ລູກ ຂອງ ທ່ານ ໄດ້ ຍິນ ທ່ານ ເວົ້າເປັນ ພາ ສາ ຂອງ ທ່ານ, ພວກ ເຂົາ ຈະ ໄດ້ ຮູ້ ແລະ ເຫັນ ວ່າ ມັນ ຂຽນ ແລະ ສາມາດ ເຂົ້າໃຈ ຄວາມໝາຍ ຂອງ ພາ ສາອັງກິດ, ພວກ ກັນ ນັ້ນ ພວກ ເຂົາ ຈະ ໄດ້ ຮຽນ ພາ ສາ ຂອງ ໄປ ພ້ອມ. ໃນ ການ ທີ່ ທ່ານ ຊ່ວຍ ໃຫ້ ທ່ານ ສາມາດ ຊ່ວຍ ລູກ ຂອງ ທ່ານ, ພວກ ຂ້າພະ ເຈົ້າ ຈະ ຍິນ ດີ ຫຼາຍ.

_____

ຄຮູ.

Blue Mong

Dear Parents of _____ Date _____

Please help the school to be able to help your child learn to read and write in English more easily. At different times during the school year, your child will bring home word lists or pictures with the names of objects written in English and a blank line beside or under them, for you to write the meanings on the blank lines, in your own language. If your child can hear you say the word in your language, and see how it is written, he will be able to understand what the meaning is in English also; and at the same time, be studying his own language. Any help you can give your child will be appreciated.

_____
Teacher

Nyob zoo txug nam txiv ntawm _____ tim _____

Thov paab koom teg nrug tseem fwv (xwb fwb) los yog kws qha ntawv, kuas muaj cuab kaav paab mej cov miv nyuad, kawm nyeem hab sau ntawv aaskiv (English) yooj yim. Nyob rau huv lub noob nyoog txawv txaav nraab xyoo kawm ntawv ntawd, mej cov miv nyuad yuav nqaa ntawv (tsaj ntawv) los yog dluab kws muaj npe sau nrug lug ua npe ntawv aaskiv, hab tseg tej kaab kus nrug, kws nyob ib saab ntawd los yog huv qaab lug tsev. Ca rau mej sau yaam tseeb ntsab rua ntawm txuj kaab kus; ua mej yaam lug. Yog le, mej tug miv nyuad nov mej has los yog nyeem cov lug ntawd ua mej yaam lug hab ho pum tas sau le caag ntawd, nwg yuav muaj peev xwm nkaag sab thoob tsib yaam ntawd huv ntawv aaskiv tuab yaam; hab noob nyoog ua ke ntawd yuav muaj cuab kaav kawm tau nwg yaam lug nrug. Txhua yaam paab cuam kws mej muaj cuab kaav ua paab rua mej cov miv nyuad, kuj muaj lug zoo sab kawg.

_____
KWS QHA NTAWV

Navajo

Dear Parents of _____ Date _____

Please help the school to be able to help your child learn to read and write in English more easily. At different times during the school year, your child will bring home word lists or pictures with the names of objects written in English and a blank line beside or under them, for you to write the meanings on the blank lines, in your own language. If your child can hear you say the word in your language, and see how it is written, he will be able to understand what the meaning is in English also; and at the same time, be studying his own language. Any help you can give your child will be appreciated.

_____

Teacher

_____ Bimá dóó bizhé'é   Ji' _____

'Ólta' bikáa 'aandaaɫgho'go na'aɫchíní' bilag'aana bizaad dóó nantɫ'ahgo yee yadaalti'dóó dayooɫtaah dooleeɫ. Dii kwii daná' aɫchíní 'olta'déé' naaltsoos saad dóó 'e'elyaa bilag'aana k'ehjí bikáago nee dooɫtsoz, t'áá ninizaad bikáá 'ádííl'iiɫ biniiy'e. Na'aɫchíní t'áá ninizaad k'ehjí dei diits'aa' dóó dayooɫ tahgo bilag'aana k'ehjí 'aɫdo yidahooɫ'ááh, 'indídaa t'áá bibizaad yidahooɫ'ááh. Nina' aɫchíní bika' 'anaaniɫgho'go baa 'ahééh daniidzin.

Bá'ólta'í _____

Norwegian

Dear Parents of _____ Date _____

Please help the school to be able to help your child learn to read and write in English more easily. At different times during the school year, your child will bring home word lists or pictures with the names of objects written in English and a blank line beside or under them, for you to write the meanings on the blank lines, in your own language. If your child can hear you say the word in your language, and see how it is written, he will be able to understand what the meaning is in English also; and at the same time, be studying his own language. Any help you can give your child will be appreciated.

_____

Teacher

Kjære foreldre av _____ Dato _____

Vi trenger deres hjelp på skolen slik at deres barn kan lettere lære å lese og skrive på Engelsk. Barna vil bringe hjem ord lister og bilder, av og til, igjennom dette skole året. Vær så snil å jhelpe barna med å oversette de Engelske titlene til Norsk. Hvis barna kan hørre ordene på Norsk ville de forstå meningen mye bedre. Vi setter stor pris på all hjelp og stotte som de kan gi deres barn.

_____

lærer, lærerinne

(Persian) Farsi

Dear Parents of _____ Date _____

Please help the school to be able to help your child learn to read and write in English more easily. At different times during the school year, your child will bring home word lists or pictures with the names of objects written in English and a blank line beside or under them, for you to write the meanings on the blank lines, in your own language. If your child can hear you say the word in your language, and see how it is written, he will be able to understand what the meaning is in English also; and at the same time, be studying his own language. Any help you can give your child will be appreciated.

_____
Teacher

والدین گرامی

تمنای دلیم بتطور کست به فرزند تا دندسنه آگگیری بتهربردر خواندن وذرشتن ازبان انگلسی بابدوسۀ جمعاری نمائید. دطول سال تحصیلی، فرزندشها تربۀ ای ازاده مشتمل مولیست که با تصاویری با سامی مختلف وترزبان انگلسی درسدرآنها میاشت بنبرل خواهد کرد تا شما آنها را ازبان فارسی ترجمه نموده ودرحل خالی بنویسید. همۀ میلیه نوشتنی ای زندرشه مستول میا شده خیانی فرزندشها بشنود که خیلۀ این اسمی را تلفظ نموده، چگونه آنها مرجان فارسی می نویسید آی انها با ود که خواهد کرد تا ضمن آگگیری زبان مادری خودمانی لنت ط لهارا مرجان انگلسی نیز بشربردست نماید.

هرگونه کمکی که دراینمورد به فرزند تانمائید موجب زنا مننۀ شروست.

_____
آموزگار

Polish

Dear Parents of _____   Date _____

Please help the school to be able to help your child learn to read and write in English more easily. At different times during the school year, your child will bring home word lists or pictures with the names of objects written in English and a blank line beside or under them, for you to write the meanings on the blank lines, in your own language. If your child can hear you say the word in your language, and see how it is written, he will be able to understand what the meaning is in English also; and at the same time, be studying his own language. Any help you can give your child will be appreciated.

_____

Teacher

Do Rodziców _____   Data _____

Szanowni Państwo! Prosimy o udzielenie szkole pomocy w nauczaniu dziecka Państwa lepiej czytać i pisac po angielsku. W trakcie roku szkolnego, dziecko przynosić będzie do domu listy wyrazów lub obrazków z podpisami w języku angielskim. Prosimy bardzo, aby Państwo napisali obok, w swoim slasnym języku, ich znaczenie lub odpowiedniki. Dziecko, slysząc dane slowo wypowiedziane w swoim języku i poznając jego pisownię, latwiej przyswoi sobie jego znaczenie po angielsku, jednocześnie zaz-najamiając się lepiej ze swoim językiem. Będziemy Państwu wdzięczni za wszelką pomoc udzieloną dziecku.

_____

Nauczyciel(ka)

Portuguese

Dear Parents of _____   Date _____

Please help the school to be able to help your child learn to read and write in English more easily. At different times during the school year, your child will bring home word lists or pictures with the names of objects written in English and a blank line beside or under them, for you to write the meanings on the blank lines, in your own language. If your child can hear you say the word in your language, and see how it is written, he will be able to understand what the meaning is in English also; and at the same time, be studying his own language. Any help you can give your child will be appreciated.

_____
                                                                           Teacher

Queridos Pais de _____   Data _____

Por favor ajudem a escola poder ajudar seu filho (sua filha) a aprender a ler e escrever em ingles com facilidade. De vez em quando, durante o ano, seu filho devera trazerá listas de palavras com os nomes dos objectos escritos em ingles e uma lihna em branco ao lado para voces escreverem o significado nas linhas, na sua própria lingua. Se seu filho puder ouvir dizer a palavra na sua própria língua, e ver como está escrita, poderá entender o significade tambéin em ingles e, ao mesmo tempo, estará estudando a sua própria lingua. Qualquer ajuda que puderem dar a seu filho(a) será apreciada.

Sinceramente,

_____
                                                                 Professora/Professor

Russian

Dear Parents of _____ Date _____

Please help the school to be able to help your child learn to read and write in English more easily. At different times during the school year, your child will bring home word lists or pictures with the names of objects written in English and a blank line beside or under them, for you to write the meanings on the blank lines, in your own language. If your child can hear you say the word in your language, and see how it is written, he will be able to understand what the meaning is in English also; and at the same time, be studying his own language. Any help you can give your child will be appreciated.

_____

Teacher

Дорогие родители_____Число_____

Школа просит вашей помощи в обучений Вашего ребёнка лучше писать и читать по-английски. В разное время учебного года Ваш ребёнок будет приносить домой лист со словами или картинками с названиями предметов, написаниями по-английски для того чтобы Вы написали значения этих слов или названия этих предметов на Вашем родном языке. Если ребёнок будет понимать значение слова на родном языке, а также увидит как оно пишется, он сможет понимать значение этого слова и по-английски, не забывая в то же время и своего родного языка.

Любая помощь, какую вы могли бы оказать вашему ребёнку, будет принята с благодарностью.

Учитель_____

Samoan

Dear Parents of _____ Date _____

Please help the school to be able to help your child learn to read and write in English more easily. At different times during the school year, your child will bring home word lists or pictures with the names of objects written in English and a blank line beside or under them, for you to write the meanings on the blank lines, in your own language. If your child can hear you say the word in your language, and see how it is written, he will be able to understand what the meaning is in English also; and at the same time, be studying his own language. Any help you can give your child will be appreciated.

_____

Teacher

I Matua o _____ Aso _____

Faamolemole lava se'i oulua fesoasoani mai i le taumafaiga a le a'oga e aoaoina lo oulua alo e tusitusi ma tautala i le gagana faa-Peretania. O nisi aso o le a aumaia ia te oulua e lo lua alo ni lisi o upu faa-Peretania po o ni ata ma igoa faa-Peretania ina ia lua tusia i ai uiga faa-Samoa. A faailoaina i lo lua alo le faa-Peretania ma uiga faa-Samoa, ona ia iloaina lea o gagana e lua. Ou te faafetai atu i lo oulua fesoasoani i lenei mea.

_____

Faia'oga

Spanish

Dear Parents of _____   Date _____

Please help the school to be able to help your child learn to read and write in English more easily. At different times during the school year, your child will bring home word lists or pictures with the names of objects written in English and a blank line beside or under them, for you to write the meanings on the blank lines, in your own language. If your child can hear you say the word in your language, and see how it is written, he will be able to understand what the meaning is in English also; and at the same time, be studying his own language. Any help you can give your child will be appreciated.

_____
Teacher

Estimados Padres de _____   Fecha _____

Por medio de la presente, nos permitimos solicitar su ayuda a la escuela a fin de que ésta pueda ayudar a sus hijos a leer y escribir más eficazmente el idioma inglés.

En diferentes ocasiones, durante el año escolar, sus hijos llevarán a casa, listas de palabras o dibujos con nombres en inglés, para que ustedes escriban el significado de ellas en su propio idioma.

Si los niños escuchan la pronunciación de palabras y ven cómo se escriben también ellos podrán entender el significado en inglés, estudiando al mismo tiempo su propio idioma.

Agradecemos de antemano la ayuda que puedan brindar a sus hijos.

_____
Maestra(o)

Swedish

Dear Parents of _____ Date _____

Please help the school to be able to help your child learn to read and write in English more easily. At different times during the school year, your child will bring home word lists or pictures with the names of objects written in English and a blank line beside or under them, for you to write the meanings on the blank lines, in your own language. If your child can hear you say the word in your language, and see how it is written, he will be able to understand what the meaning is in English also; and at the same time, be studying his own language. Any help you can give your child will be appreciated.

_____

Teacher

Kärä Föräldrar till _____ Datum _____

Vill ni vara snälla och hjälpa ert barn med skolarbetet så att det lättare kan lära sig skriva och läsa på engelska. Vid olika tillfällen under årets lopp kommer ert barn att ta hem listor eller bilder med namn på olika saker skrivna på engelska, vid sidan om bilden, eller under den, finns en tom rad för dig att skriva detsamma på ert eget språk. Om ert barn hör ordet uttalas på sitt eget språk, och ser det skrivet, så kommer han/hon att förstå vad det är på engelska på samma gång som det studerar sitt eget språk. Vi uppskatar all den hjälp som ni kan ge ert barn.

_____

Lärare/lärarinna

Thai

Dear Parents of _____ Date _____

    Please help the school to be able to help your child learn to read and write in English more easily. At different times during the school year, your child will bring home word lists or pictures with the names of objects written in English and a blank line beside or under them, for you to write the meanings on the blank lines, in your own language. If your child can hear you say the word in your language, and see how it is written, he will be able to understand what the meaning is in English also; and at the same time, be studying his own language. Any help you can give your child will be appreciated.

_____

Teacher

เรียน ท่านผู้ปกครอง _____ ทราบ วันที่ _____

ทางโรงเรียนขอความร่วมมือจากท่านช่วยให้เด็ก เรียนอ่านเขียนภาษาอังกฤษง่ายขึ้น โดยบางครั้งเด็ก ของท่านอาจจะนำรายชื่อหรือรูปภาพของสิ่งของ ซึ่งจะมี ชื่อเป็นภาษาอังกฤษเขียนกำกับ และมีช่องว่างเว้นใกล้ๆ หรือใต้คำศัพท์สำหรับให้ท่านเขียน คำแปลเป็นภาษาไทย ในช่องว่างนั้น ถ้าเด็กได้ฟังและเรียนเขียนในภาษาของ ตัวเองก็จะช่วยให้เข้าใจทั้งสองภาษาไปด้วยในตัว ขอ ขอบคุณในความร่วมมือเพื่อช่วยให้เด็กของท่านเข้าใจ ภาษายิ่งขึ้น

_____

ครูประจำชั้น

Tongan

Dear Parents of _____ Date _____

Please help the school to be able to help your child learn to read and write in English more easily. At different times during the school year, your child will bring home word lists or pictures with the names of objects written in English and a blank line beside or under them, for you to write the meanings on the blank lines, in your own language. If your child can hear you say the word in your language, and see how it is written, he will be able to understand what the meaning is in English also; and at the same time, be studying his own language. Any help you can give your child will be appreciated.

_____
Teacher

Ki Si'i Ongo Matu'a 'a _____ 'Aho _____

Mo kataki mu'a 'o tokoni mai ki he ako ke nau lava 'o tokoni'i 'a ho'omo tama ke ne poto ange 'i he lau tohi mo e tohi 'i he lea fakaPilitānia. 'I he ngaahi taimi kehekehe 'i he lolotonga 'a e ta'u fakaako, 'e 'oatu 'e ho'omo tama ha lisi 'o ha ngaahi fo'i lea pe ko ha ngaahi fakatātā, ke mo hanga 'o tohi'i 'i he ngaahi funga laine 'a e 'uhinga 'o e ngaahi fo'i lea faka-Pilitānia pe ko e ngaahi fakatātā, 'i ho'omou lea fakafonua (faka-Tonga). Kapau 'e fanongo 'a ho'omo tama ki ha'amo lea'aki 'a e ngaahi fo'i lea ko ia 'i ho'omou lea fakafonua totonu, pea ne sio ki he anga 'o hono tohi'i, 'e mahino lelei ange kiate ia 'a hono 'uhinga 'i he lea faka-Pilitānia; pea 'i he taimi tatau, te ne lava ai 'o toe ako 'a e lea fakafonua totonu 'o 'ene fanga kui. Te mau fakamalo'ia lahi kiate kimoua 'i ha fa'ahinga tokoni pe te mo lava 'o fai ki ho'omo tama.

Faka'apa'apa atu,

_____
Faiako

Vietnamese

Dear Parents of _____ Date _____

    Please help the school to be able to help your child learn to read and write in English more easily. At different times during the school year, your child will bring home word lists or pictures with the names of objects written in English and a blank line beside or under them, for you to write the meanings on the blank lines, in your own language. If your child can hear you say the word in your language, and see how it is written, he will be able to understand what the meaning is in English also; and at the same time, be studying his own language. Any help you can give your child will be appreciated.

_____

                                        Teacher

Phụ huynh học sinh _____ thân mến. Ngày _____

Xin vui lòng giúp nhà trường, để có đủ khả năng giúp đỡ con em của quí vị học đọc và viết Anh ngữ dễ dàng hơn. Trong niên khoá, một đôi lần con em của quí vị sẽ mang về nhà, những trang chữ hoặc hình có chua tên những hình ảnh đó bằng Anh ngữ. và bên cạnh hay bên dưới có một khoảng trống, để quí vị viết nghĩa của những chữ hay hình đó bằng ngôn ngữ của quí vị.

Nếu con em của quí vị được nghe quí vị nói những danh từ bằng ngôn ngữ của quí vị và thấy chữ viết, chúng sẽ hiểu cùng một lúc nghĩa của các chữ đó bằng Anh ngữ và học được tiếng của mình nó nữa.

Mọi sự giúp đỡ mà quí vị để có thể cho con em của quí vị đều được hoan nghênh.

_____

giáo viên

Section 2
Explanation of Syntax Variants

This section includes explanations for the following languages:

	German	Navajo
Arabic	Greek	Norwegian
Bengali (not available)	Hebrew	Persian
Cambodian	Hindi	Polish
Chinese (Cantonese & Mandarin)	White Hmong	Portuguese
Croatian	Hungarian	Russian
Czech	Indonesian	Samoan
Danish	Italian	Spanish
Dutch	Japanese	Swedish
Filipino (Tagalog)	Korean	Thai
Finnish	Laotian	Tongan
French	Blue Mong	Vietnamese

Linguistic Interference with Arabic/English

Syntax Variants

Direction of reading is right to left. For example, **cat** would be written **tac** (using the actual word in Arabic, of course). Sentence structure differs from English, as shown in the following sentences.

English:	I see the black dog.
Arabic:	I see the dog the black.

English:	The old black dog is running down the road.
Arabic:	Running the dog the black down the road.

Three Levels of Language:

1. One kind of language use is for the king. It is very respectful.

2. One level of language is the "country" language. It is the main language, but uses a different accent in every Arab country.

3. The third level use is for servants and Bedouins. It is almost the same as the "country" language.

Letters and Blends That Are Often Confused

The letter R as used in the word VERY is often pronounced as a W = VEWY.

The letter T as used in the word ITALY is often pronounced as a D = IDALY.

Final ING as in BEING is often pronounced as BEINN.

Initial TH, as in THE is often pronounced as D or DE.

In English, the blend CH, as CHAIR is pronounced SH as in SHARE.

In English, the sound of J as in JUMP is pronounced ZJUMP.

There is no "P" sound in Arabic. P = "B."

Confusing Word Pairs

small – smole	frog – frag
hall – hole	hot – hut
track – truck	thought – that
ship – sheep	forth – ford
ball – bowl	comfortable – comftable

Vowels

The vowels are not written separately. They are included in the characters by certain accent marks as used in the Arabic alphabet.

Alphabet in Arabic with English Pronounciation

ا	alef	د	dāl	ض	ḍād	ك	kāf
ب	bā	ذ	dhāl	ط	ṭāh	ل	lām
ت	tā	ر	rā	ظ	ẓāh	م	mīm
ث	thā	ز	zāy	ع	ain	ن	nun
ج	jīm	س	sīn	غ	ghain	ه	hā
ح	ḥā	ش	shīn	ف	fā	و	wāw
خ	khā	ص	ṣād	ق	qāf	ي	ya
						ء	hamza

Linguistic Interference with Cambodian/English

Syntax Variants

Reading and writing is done horizontally left to right. Sentence structure differs from English, as shown in the following sentences.

English: I see the black dog.
Cambodian: I see the dog black.

English: The old black dog is running down the road.
Cambodian: The dog old black is running down the road. Or, the dog black old is running down the road.

In Cambodian writing, commas are not used. Instead of commas, spaces are left in the line of writing where commas would occur in English. At the end of the sentence, this mark ᧛ is put in place of a period. The other marks of punctuation, such as the question mark, and exclamation point are used the same as in English.

There are five levels of speaking Cambodian.

- Level 1 is used for the King, or very high government officials.
- Level 2 is used for Monks, Bishops, or other religious people.
- Level 3 is used for people of higher status, such as your boss or teacher, or the governor.
- Level 4 is used for friends.
- Level 5 is used for children and servants. The phrase "to eat" would be pronounced as follows: 1) *sauie* (king), 2) *tcham* (religious people), 3) *pesaw* (government official or boss), 4) *ngaam* (friends), 5) *see* (children and/or servants).

Head

Don't touch the head of a Cambodian student, as is frequently the custom for praise. The Cambodian people have such great respect for the brain and the head, that this is considered disrespectful to the person and — to the brain.

Letter Blends and Sound Transpositions

G, in words with the "soft" sound of j, as in George = Gorgay. F is often pronounced as V. X = S, Z = S, W = V, U = aw (as in paw). The middle R is usually omitted: bird = bud, birth = buts, girl = gull, storm = stom, born = boen, torn = toen, arcade = acade. The final R is dropped; star = sta, car = caw. Th (voiced) as in the = dh, the = dha, that = dhat, those = dhose. Th (unvoiced) as in think = tsink, thick = tsick, three = tsree.

Word Pair Comparisons

worry – vorry   storm – stom
work – vork   Dick – thick

star – sta   thousand – sousand

girl – gull   shirt – chirt

torn – toen   arcade – acade

Vowels

There are 24 vowels in Cambodian. The English pronounciation for the vowels of Cambodian are as follows: aw (as in paw), aw (as in ah); I (as in it); E (as in feet); uh (as in up); ur (as in occur); oo (as in look), oo (as in school) or (as in poor); er (as in there); ir (as in skirt), ir (as in ear); A (as in ate), A (as in cat); ai (long i as in tie); ow (as in cow); ou (as in out); om (as in comb); um (as in gum); am (as in jam); as (as in ask); os (as in ghost); S (as in U.S.A.), os (as in foster).

Alphabet as Pronounced in Cambodian

A = aw

B = baw

C = saw or kaw

D = daw or doe

E (There is none in their alphabet.) Use aw + a vowel that makes an e sound.

F (There is none in their alphabet.) Use ha + vo(v) = fve.

G (There is none in their alphabet.) Use ha(h) + kaw(k) = gha. The G is always a "hard" g.

H = haw

I = (There is none in their alphabet.) Use aw + a vowel that makes the I sound.

J = dja (It is used for the soft g or j.)

K = kaw or koe

L = law or loe

M = mo

N = no

O = aw + a vowel that makes an o sound.

P = paw or poe

Q (There is none in their alphabet.) Use kaw or koe (K).

R = roe

S = saw

T = taw or dta

U (There is none in their alphabet.) Use aw + a vowel that makes U.

V = vo

W (There is none in their alphabet.) Use ha + vo ((H) + (V)).

X = saw

Y = yoe

Z (There is none in their alphabet.) Use: saw + haw ((S) + (H)).

Linguistic Interference with Chinese/English

Syntax Variants

There are three styles of writing and directions of reading in Chinese. The old style is done in vertical columns and is read from top to bottom, right side to left side. Story books are still written like this. The new style is written horizontally and read from left to right. The third form is used for advertisements and to make special notice. It is written horizontally, right to left, and read from right to left also. The most frequently used method is left to right, horizontally.

When speaking or writing in Chinese, the sentence structures are very similar to those of English. There are, however, some noticeable differences.

English: The old black dog is running down the road.

Chinese: The old black dog run the road. Or, old black dog run road.

English: I see the black dog.

Chinese: I see black dog.

The use of articles is optional in many sentences. Also, words such as *is, am,* and *be* are not used. Instead of these words, the speaker or writer uses a certain word to preface the thought so as to explain the tense of the sentences.

The written language of China is Mandarin. There are, however, many spoken dialects.

Vowel and Consonant Transpositions

A speaker of Chinese will often pronounce English vowels: A = e, as in pet; E = e, as in pet; I = e, as in pet; O = a, as in pa; U = u, as in up.

The letter R = L (run = lun). Ng is difficult to say. It is usually pronounced N. The final blend, th, as in tooth = f (toof). Girl = gull, pearl = poll, lion = lon, wash = vash, sh = s, ch = s, shoes = soos, choose = soos. Words ending with X, such as ax, and tax, are pronounced ast, and tast, X = st. The letter V is often pronounced as W. Very = werly, or verly (the r = l). Victory = wictory. Z is pronounced as S. Zipper = sipper, soup = zoup, zoo = soo, shirt = surt (sult), sheet = seet. The letter J is often used as a substitute for the letter Y. Year = jear, yes = jes, yard = jard, yellow = jeow. The double L is pronounced as R. Yellow = jerro, or yerro.

Chinese is monosyllabic. A word like "elephant" which has three syllables in English, would sound like three words to a speaker of Chinese because all words in Chinese have no more than one syllable.

Word Pair Comparisons

with – wif

teeth – teef

thick – tick

that – tat

them – tem

these – tease

those – toes

zoo – soo

soup – zoup

shirt – surt

yes – jes

ax – ast

Alphabet Comparisons

In Cantonese, there is no letter equivalent for the following letters as we have in English: H, N, Q, R, S, T, (th), V, W, X, Y, Z. In the spoken Mandarin, there are no letter equivalents for the following letters: N, P, Q, S, T, (th), V, W, X, Y, Z.

Linguistic Interference with Croatian, Serbian, and Yugoslav/English

Syntax Variants

English:	I see the black dog.
Croatian:	See black dog.

There are no articles (a, the) in Croatian and they are often dropped or omitted. Pronouns are built into verbs and are dropped also.

Gender, masculine, feminine, or neuter, shows in nouns, pronouns, and adjectives. Inanimate things and nature phenomenons are of masculine, feminine, or neuter genders: sea — it (neuter), mountain — she (feminine), hill — he (masculine).

Denotations of time and place are placed in the sentence according to their importance to the context.

English:	I went to school yesterday.
Croatian:	Yesterday I went to school, or to school I went yesterday, or yesterday to school I went, depending on what the speaker wants to stress.

There are four main Yugoslav languages. They are written in two alphabets: Latinic for Croatian and Slovenian, Cyrillic for Serbian and Macedonian. These languages have numerous dialects that vary greatly in vocabulary and pronunciation.

There are mainly two levels of language: Written and spoken. Spoken language is often a blend of written language and local dialect or pure dialect.

There is a difference in addressing friends, children, adults, and acquaintances, or strangers, as in German (*du* and *sie*). In some areas, even parents would be addressed respectfully (sie) and a child would use third person plural when speaking of a parent or teacher. "Them (my mother) said, . . ."

Irregular verbs present difficulty, and have to be memorized, and their uses practiced. Since "to have" is not used as an auxiliary verb, there is a tendency to use past tense instead of perfect. While English speakers would say, "We have been married for years," Yugoslavs would phrase as, "we were married for years," meaning they are still married.

"At" is often used in the meaning of "by" and "in" in the meaning of "at." ("We'll meet at school" would mean somewhere around the building. In Croatia children are "in school" if they are attending classes.)

Uses of idioms could be confusing. "I am going down the road" would mean that you are going downhill. To "go straighten things up" would mean that you will walk or ride to some place in order to do it; the stress would be on the going, not on the doing.

Word Pairs

whale – veal	them – dem
that — dat	ship – sheep

steam – stem   man – men
three – tree   bird – beard
think – tink   you – jew

In dealing with parents, it would be useful to remember that addressing an adult by their first name without his or her permission has been considered rude. However, if a parent addresses a teacher by their first name, he or she is just trying to apply what strikes him or her as a particular American habit.

Alphabet sounds in Latinic and Cyrillic are pronounced in the same way.

A – fast	A, a (A)
B – bee	Б, б (B)
C – tc, like German Zurich	В, b (V)
Ć – tj, fast together, like Italian *ciao*	Г, г (G)
Č – choke	Д, д (D)
D – dog	Ђ, ђ (Đ)
DŽ – James, harder	Е, е (E)
Đ – James, softer	Ж, ж (Ž)
E – pet	З, з (Z)
F – fist	И, и (I)
G – grade	J, j (J)
H – hut	К, к (K)
I – ship	Л, л (L)
J – juma	Љ љ (lj)
K – cone	М, m (M)
L – lake	Н, h (N)
LJ – lf, fast together	Њ њ (NJ)
M – man	О, о (O)
N – nice	П, π (P)
NJ - new	Р, p (R)
O – corn	С, с (S)
P – pen	Т, т (T)
R – run, harder	Ћ, ћ (Ć)
S – son	У, у (U)
Š – shoe	Ф, ф (F)
T – top	Х, х (H)
U – loose	Џ џ (Č)
V – veal	Ч, ч (C)
Ž – zebu	Џ џ (DŽ)
Ž – like French *je*	Ш ш (Š)

Students who can read and write in Cyrillic would be confused about letters V-B, R-P, C-S, X-H, W-V, Y-J. The language is quite phonetic and every sound has its corresponding letter. For example, New York would be spelled as pronounced: Nju Jork (J is pronounced as Y); fish as "fis"; jam as "den"; city as "siti"; cat as "ket." Consequently, when learning to read and write, students do not depend on spelling as is done with English. The teacher would dictate "blue" as "b-l-u-e." This makes memorizing the way words are spelled rather easy for a student who has already mastered writing in Croatian. However, small children who have just started to recognize letters and put them together would find English spelling a hindrance when trying to read Croatian. The principle of a sound for a letter makes reading in English rather difficult. While reading, the student would pronounce a sound for every letter, as New York for "N-e-v Y-o-r-k" or fish as "f-i-s-h" or Judy as "J-oo-d-i."

Vowel and Consonant Transpositions

Pronunciation difficulties arise with voiced and unvoiced, "th," "w," and "q" which do not exist. There are local dialects in which "h" is not pronounced at the beginning of a word. Students would tend to pronounce (and write) "ard" instead of "hard," "evy" instead of "heavy." There are difficulties with "r" as in "run," which could be much harder and more rolling than in English. Similarly with "j" as in "jam," which would be pronounced much softer or harder, depending on the student's native dialect. There could be confusion with broad and soft "e" as in "men" and "pen." Also depending on the native dialect, as well as with long and short "i" (sheep and ship) or long and short "u" (school tends to be pronounced in a short way). The indefinite article "a" (a tree) would be pronounced as in "fast." Voiced and unvoiced, "th" is often pronounced as "d" or "t," and with as "wid," and them as "tem" or "dem."

Linguistic Interference with Czech/English

Syntax Variants

English:	The old black dog is running down the road.
Czech:	Old black dog running down road.

English:	I see the black dog.
Czech:	See black dog.

The Czech language does not use articles (a, an, the). There are three genders, masculine, feminine, and neuter. The letters used at the end of the word indicate the gender as well as person and tense.

Basic Vowels

ä as in at

A as in ah (as in father)

E as in eh

I as in ee

O as in saw

U as in school

Y ee (as in feet)

Double Vowels

IA

IE

IU

Ô

OU

Vowel and Consonant Transpositions

I = an e sound

O = as aw (as in saw)

Y = an ee sound (as in feet)

W = v

J = yĕ

Alphabet Pronunciation

A = ah (as in father)
B = bay
C = tsay
D = day
E = eh
F = eff
G = gay
H = hah (as in father)
CH = like *nacht* (in German)
I = ee (as in feet)
J = ya
K = ka
L = la
M = ma

N = na
O = as in s<u>aw</u>
P = pay
Q = kway
R = air
Ř = no English translation
S = ess
T = tay
U = oo (as in school)
V = vay
W = dvoy - tey vay
X = iks
Y = ipsilon = $\overline{e}$
Z = zet

Confusing Blends and Transposition

Initial voiced "th" as in <u>the</u> = da, <u>this</u> = dis

Initial unvoiced "th" as in <u>th</u>umb = tum

"Th" as in <u>th</u>ank = tank

"Th" as in <u>th</u>ree = tree

Final unvoiced "th" as in tee<u>th</u> = teef or tees
bo<u>th</u> = boat

Final G and K bag/back, dog/dock

Word Pair Comparisons

this – dis	led – let
that – dat	teeth – tees
mother – mudder	both – boat
winter – vinter	both – bof
work – vork	bag – back
bed – bet	dock – dog

Linguistic Interference with Danish/English

Syntax Variants

The sentence structure of Danish is practically the same as English. However, the Danish do not use verb forms such as "is running."

English: The old black dog is running down the road.
Danish: The old black dog runs down the road.

Gender is the same as English.

Difficult Word Pairs:

very – vary	just – yust	window – vindow
we – vee	teeth – teet	thirty – dirty
worm – warm	south – sout	through – true
ship – sheep	wish – vish	

The English "th" sound should not be a problem as it is just as it sounds in bill*ede* and s*øde*, common Danish words. There are some persons who do have difficulty with the unvoiced "th" as in teeth = teet, south = sout.

Danish Alphabet

The Danish alphabet has nine vowels and 20 consonants:

A as in ask

B as in begin

C as in celebrate

D as in deliver

E as in enlighten

F as in efficient

G as in gander

H as in hope

I as in infant

J as in joke

K as in corn

L as in elevate

M as in employee

N as in endure

O as in door

P as in pen

Q as in coop

R as in err

S as in estimate

T as in television

U as in do

V as in veteran

W (double v) There are no Danish words spelled with this letter. Pronounced like world, wine.

X as in extra

Y as in physics

Z as in set, zet

Æ equals ae, pronounced like egg

Ő equals oe, pronounced like u in murky

å (formerly aa) as in goal, hall

Danish Vowels

A as in b<u>a</u>t

E as in <u>e</u>ternal

I as in <u>e</u>at

O as in b<u>oo</u>k

U as in d<u>o</u>

Y as in l<u>y</u>mph

Æ as in <u>e</u>gg

Ø or Ö as in b<u>i</u>rd or m<u>u</u>rky

å as in goal

Linguistic Interference with Dutch/English

Syntax Variants

English: The old black dog was running down the street.
Dutch: The old black dog ran fast down the street.

Letter Blends

Sc = shk, ch = sh, sh = sh, th = ti (initial position). When L and K come together in the final section of a word (i.e., walk, milk, talk), another syllable is pronounced walk = wallick, milk = millick, talk = tallick.

The final position D is often pronounced as T, for example: good = hgoot. The final T is often pronounced D, for example: wrote = rode. V = F.

Word Pairs in English that Often Confuse

thick – tick	through – true
teeth – teet	shoes – choose
that – dat	wrote – rode
these – deeze	put – putt
just – yust	under – onder

Vowels

A vowel followed by a double consonant creates a short sound, for example: tack - taak. Vowels: A, E, I, O, U.

Dutch Alphabet and Pronounciation

A = ah	I = e	P = pay	W = way
B = bay	J = yea	Q = cu	X = ix
C = say	K = ka	R = err	Y = aie
D = day	L = l	S = s	Z = zet
E = aye	M = m	T = te	
F = ef	N = n	U = oo	
G = hgay	O = o	V = vay	

Linguistic Interference with Filipino (Tagalog)/English

Syntax Variants

Tagalog is written and read horizontally, from left to right. Tagalog uses three tenses: present, past, and future. Tagalog uses nouns, pronouns, adjectives, verbs, and adverbs, the same as used in English. A Filipino student can often pronounce written words in English quite well, but may have poor comprehension. The following are examples of sentence structure.

English:	The old black dog is running down the road.
Tagalog:	The old black dog is running down the road.
English:	I see the black dog.
Tagalog:	I see the black dog.
English:	I am going to work tomorrow.
Tagalog:	I am going to work tomorrow. Or, work, tomorrow I am going.

Letter Transpositions and Confusing Blends

The voiced th, in the initial position, as used in the, them, those, these, thy, has a D sound; the = da, them = dem, those = dose, these = deeze, thy = die. The unvoiced th, in the initial position, as used in think, thought, thin, thick, three has a T sound. Think = tink, thought = tought, thick = tick, thin = tin, three = tree. Final th as in with, teeth, both = wit, teet, bot.

The following letters are often transposed: D = j, jump = djump; P and F are often confused due to the use of PH in Phillipines and F in Filipino. The Z and S are pronounced as S. Zipper = sipper. V and B are interchanged. Very = berry, victory = bictory. Words that end in "tain" such as mountain, fountain, contain, certain, captain, are all pronounced the same as in "contain" with the long A sound. Y and J, jump = yump, jello = yellow, juice = yuse.

Difficult Word Pairs

very - berry	zipper – sipper
victory – bictory	sip – zip
jump – yump	thought – tought
jello – yellow	these – deeze
use – juice	think – tink

Vowel and Consonant Transpositions

English Vowels		**Tagalog Vowels (always the same)**
Long	**Short**	
A as in say	A as in cat	A as in ah
E as in feet	E as in pet	E as in yes

I as in ice   I as in it   I as in long e of feet

O as in go   O as in pot   O as in go

U as in cute   U as in up   U as in oo of school

Filipino Alphabet Letters and Pronounciation

A as in pa	Na
Ba	Ng as in song
Ca as in ka	O as in go
Da	Pa
E as in get	(No Q)
(No F)	Ra
Ga (hard g as in got)	Sa
Ha	Ta
I (ee as in feet)	Oo as in school
J as hw (used in Juan)	Wa as in water
(No K - use Ca)	Ya
La	(No Z)
Ma	

Linguistic Interference with Finnish/English

Syntax Variants

English:	I see the black dog.
Finnish:	I see black dog. (No articles)

English:	The black old dog is running down the road.
Finnish:	Old black dog runs road down/down road.

English:	Do you sing?
Finnish:	Sing you?

English:	The color of the house is blue.
Finnish:	House's color is blue.

Finnish is an agglutanative language. Instead of using prepositions, endings are added to the stem. They are called cases, and there are 14 of them in use currently.

Talo (house), *talossa* (in the house), *taloon* (into the house), *talosta* (from the house), *taloni* (my house), *talosi* (your house).

The verbs are conjugated by adding personal endings to the root of the verb: *saan* (I get), *saat* (you get), *saa* (he gets), *saamme* (we get), *saatte* (you get), *saavat* (they get).

The adjectives must agree with case and number with the noun they modify.

Word Pair Comparisons

wine – vine	bee – pea
then – den	pig – pick
both – bof	the – da
chair – share	zipper – sipper
shoes – choose	teeth – teet
with – wit	shall – sal
then – ten	fat – fad
want – van	big – bick
jeep – cheap	with – wif

Alphabet Pronunciation in Finnish (underlining indicates length)

A = ah	G = g<u>ay</u>
B = b<u>ay</u>	H = h<u>oh</u>
C = s<u>ay</u>	I = ee
D = d<u>ay</u>	J = yee
E = <u>ah</u>	K = k<u>oh</u>
F = ef	L = el

M = em   V = v<u>a</u>h
N = en   W = kaksios-v (pronounced like w)
O = <u>o</u>h   X = eks
P = p<u>a</u>h   Y = euh
Q = koo   Z = tset
R = trilled err   A = <u>a</u>h
S = es   Ä = hat
T = t<u>a</u>h   Ö = ∾ as in the
U = oo

All vowels can be doubled, that is their length is doubled. Vowels can be combined in the following diphthongs:

ai = i
ui = oow<u>e</u>
ai = ahie
yi = euhie
ou = go
iu = <u>e</u>oo
uo = oowo
ie = <u>e</u>ah
oi = boil
ei = bay
öi = ∾uie (the first sound like e in th<u>e</u>)
au = cow
eu = <u>a</u>oo
äy = <u>a</u>oo
öy = ∾uh (the first sound like e in th<u>e</u>)
yö = euh + (the sound like e in th<u>e</u>)

All consonants, except b, c, d, q, x, z, can be doubled, that is, their length is doubled:

kuka = who

kukka = flower

The English sounds "th" / ∾ , ∾ /, /z/, sh/ S /, b, g, j, / 3 /. and w do not exist in Finnish.

Linguistic Interference with French/English

Syntax Variants

English:	I see the black dog.
French:	I see the dog black.

English:	The old black dog is running down the road.
French:	The old dog black runs down the road.

In French, the adjective follows the noun. In French, the *pronoun* "it" is not used; instead, the words "he" or "she" are substituted for all objects and nouns — animate or inanimate. The reason for this designation is due to the particular gender as shown in the word ending — feminine or masculine. For example: "she" rains or "he" eats. Rain is of feminine gender. Therefore, "she" rains often in the mountains. The boat floats in the water. The word *boat* is written with a masculine form. One would not say, "It floats in the water." When referring to the floating of the boat in the water, it would be proper to say, "He floats in the water."

Articles are also determined by gender and whether or not the object is a specific or generalized object. A = un, un = a nonspecific object or noun. For example: While looking at a group of boys, someone might say, "I see *a* boy." *Un* is used for nonspecific masculine gender. *Une* is used for nonspecific feminine gender. The word apple is feminine. Therefore, the article *une* would preceed apple in this sentence: I see *"une"* apple. The plural form, *les* is used for masculine or feminine nonspecific nouns.

Specific nouns and articles: "Le" is used for masculine and "la" for feminine. *Chiens* = dogs. *Chiens* is masculine. I see the dog = I see "le" dog. The plural form "les" is used for masculine or feminine words. For example: The (les) dogs like the (les) apples.

There are two forms of French for writing and conversation. One is more formal, the other is more familiar and used for close association. For example, the familiar form is used with friends and family, the formal with the boss or professor.

Confusing Letters or Blends

The initial R is frequently pronounced as W. Run = won. The medial R is very difficult. Borrow = bowoe. Grow = gwo. I is often pronounced as long E. Fit = feet. Words beginning with Y are pronounced as if the Y is an E. Year = ear, Yard = eard. The letter W is frequentlyy pronounced as V. The initial th as in the (voiced) = za. The letter G is pronounced "jay." Therefore, when spelling the word "jump," a student might spell "gump." The letter G can also have the hard g sound as in gate.

The final S is not pronounced. The final T, when preceeded by a vowel is not pronounced. The last sound would be that of the vowel. For example: pots = pos, pet = pay, pot = po, pit = pee, put = pu, got = go, carpet = carpay.

Word Pair Comparisons

borrow – boewoe	worry – wurry
run – won	tomorrow – tomorwoe
rabbit – whabbit	row – woe
horror – hower	girl – gurl
harem – hirem	window – vindow

Vowels

A = ah, as in pa

E = uh, as in up

I = e, as in feet

O = o, as in go

U = u, as in cute (the U is not a long U – it's in between)

Alphabet Pronounciation

A = ah	N = en
B = bay	O = o
C = say	P = pay
D = day	Q = cu
E = uh	R = air
F = ef	S = es
G = jay	T = tay
H = ash	U = u, as in cute
I = e, as in feet	V = vay
J = g (jee)	W = double vay
K = ka	X = icks
L = el	Y = eegreck
M = em	Z = zed

Linguistic Interference with German/English

Syntax Variants

When asking some types of questions in German, the word order is changed. For example: What are you doing? = What doing you? The inflection equivalent to the English *ing,* does not exist in German. It is therefore difficult for a German to learn in English. The various tenses must be practiced and memorized. For example: go, went, gone, drink, drank, drunk. The various forms of the helping verb "to be" (be, am, is, are, was, were, being) are built into German verbs. Therefore, a German who is learning English will sometimes delete them in English sentences. For example: Where you going?

Word Pair Comparisons

where – wear	well – wail
then – den	shall – shawl
jeep – cheap	do – too
few – view	lit – lid
ran – rain	thumb – dumb

Vowel and Consonant Transpositions

W = v sound in English

S when followed by a vowel = z sound in English

OO represents a long o sound, *not* the vowel sound in the English words of boot or hoot

S when followed by P, T, or L is pronounced like an English sh sound

G in the final position (sing) is pronounced like K (sink)

D in the final position represents a T. Did = dit

EU = oi as in oil

V = f

EI = long i as in ice

IE = long e as in piece

Z = ts as in hits

R = in the final position after long vowels, represents a sound similar to the one at the end of the word sofa

J = y as in yes

Th does not exist in German. Most Germans would pronounce "things" as "tings," or "dings."

Alphabet with German Pronounciation

A = ah		N = en	
B = bay		O = oh	
C = tsay		P = pay	
D = day		Q = koo	
E = ay		R = air	
F = ef		S = ess	
G = gay		T = tay	
H = hah		U = oo	
I = ee		V = fow	
J = yot		W = way	
K = kah		K = iks	
L = el		Y = ipsilon	
M = em		Z = tzet	

Linguistic Interference with Greek/English

Syntax Variants

Sentence word order is the same as for English with exception to the personal pronoun position.

| **English:** | My car is brown. |
| **Greek:** | The car my is brown. |

There are three genders in Greek: masculine, feminine, and neuter. The gender is determined by the article (which always agrees with the gender) and the terminal letter of the word. The masculine ending is often an O. The feminine ending is often an E with the long e sound. The neuter is preceded by the article to (with a long o sound).

Blends and Transpositions

vt = nd	v = n
tz = j	n = long e
f = v	r is rolled
x = k	; = ?
p = r	b = v

Word pairs

sheep – ship	shown – sewn
chop – shop	hurt – herd
shoe – chew	sit – set
hot – hut	pin – pen
her – hair	

Names of Letters in Greek Alphabet

Note, the name is the initial sound of the letter (i.e., alpha = a with the short a sound).

A = alpha	N = ne, nu (long E) = N
B = veta, beta	Ξ = xe, xi (long E), pronounced Kse = X
Γ = gamma = G, n	O = omicron (long O) = O
Δ = thelta = Th, d, delta	Π = pe, pi (long E) = P
E = epsilon = E (short sound)	P = rho (rolled R, long O) = R, rh
Z = zeta = Z	Σ = sigma (long E) = S
N + h = eta (long E)	K = kappa
Θ = theta (unvoiced th, thief)	Λ = lamtha, lambda = L
I - yota (long E)	M = me, mu (long E) = M

T = tuf, tau = T   X = he, chi = H, Ch

Y = epsilon, upsilon (long E) =   Ψ = pse, psi (long E)

Φ = phe, phi = F, Ph   Ω = omega = $\overline{O}$

Linguistic Interference with Hebrew/English

Syntax Variants

Hebrew books are written and read from right to left — or as we who speak and read English would say, from the back of the book to the front of the book, with the title page at the "back" of the book.

The following are examples of differences in sentence structure:

English: I see the black dog.

Hebrew: I see * dog black. (*There is an untranslatable word in Hebrew that goes between a verb and the word "the." The adjective is after the noun.)

English: I see a black dog.

Hebrew: I see * dog black. (*There are no articles — a, an, or the.)

English: The old black dog is running down the road.

Hebrew: *The dog the old and the black runs along (or, in) the road. (*All adjectives as used in this sentence are preceded by "the" because the noun, dog, was preceded by "the." The word "down" is always opposite of "up" in Hebrew; therefore, along or in the road has been substituted for the phrase, "down the road."

English: The dog is black.

Hebrew: The dog * black. (*There is no "is" in Hebrew.)

English: The black dog.

Hebrew: The dog the black. Adjective, black, is preceded by the, because the noun, dog, is preceded by "the."

Prefixes: As used in Hebrew, the words, *the, in, to, from,* and *and* are like prefixes used with the following English words: Pre = prenatal, un = unlock, to = tonight, in=inside.

Idioms: English phrases such as follows are very confusing to the Hebrew-speaking people: "down the road" = "into a hole, or deep place in the road." "I'm going downtown" = You are going "under the city."

Punctuation: There are no capital letters in Hebrew, except as used for the names of people. There are, however, many marks of punctuation that are used to determine the pronounciation of words and to indicate a different vowel sound. Commas, periods, and other familiar marks of punctuation are also used.

Blends and Transpositions

Voiced th (as in the) = ze or de, that = zat or dat, those = zose or doze, them = zem or dem, these = zees or dees. Unvoiced th = s, think = sink, thigh = sigh, three = sree, through = srue. Final th = s or z, with = wiz, teeth = tees, both = bos. There is no sound for the double O as in book. Instead, the double o is pronounced as the double o in school. All Rs are rolled, whether at the beginning of a word or elsewhere. The rolling is different than that of the Spanish R in that it is most usually done in the back of the throat. One syllable words such as goes and does, are usually pronounced: go es and doo es.

Word Pairs

think – sink	teeth – tees
sigh – thigh	both – bos
three – sree	them – zem
those – doze	through – srue
with – wiz	that – dat

Vowels

There are actually only two "official" vowels. However, depending on the type of punctuation that is used, there are five vowel sounds, but more than five ways to write them. The Hebrew vowels are pronounced as follows: ah, as in kamatz; e, as in feet; a, as in gate; o, as in go; oo and/or u, as in school; e, as in pet.

Alphabet Comparisons

A = alef

B = bet or vet, B or V

C = (There is no C)

D = dalet

E = (There is no E)

F and P = pey (F or P)

G = gimel, as in good

H = hey

I = (There is no I)

J = (There is no J — use the character for gimel (g) + accent = J)

K = kaf

L = lamed

M = mem

N = noon

O = (There is no O)

P and F = pey (P or F)

Q = the K

R = reysh

S = Sh or S (as in yes) depending on the punctuation marks (samech) as in Bach.

T = taf

U = (There is no U)

V = vav

W = (There is no W — it is written as a double v character)

X = (There is no X)

Y = yud

Z = zayin

Ts = tsadi, the sound of ts as in hats

A = ayin

K = koof

	HEBREW		Print	Cursive
	A	alef	א	ן
ב (B) or **ב** (V)	B or V	bet	ב	ב
	G (good)	gimel	ג	צ
	D	dalet	ד	ך
	H	hey	ה	ה
	V	vav	ו	ו **
	Z	zayin	ז	ן
	(Bach)	chet	ח	ח
	T	tet	ט	ט
	Y (year)	yud	י	' **
כ (K) or **ב** (ch) CH (Bach) or	K	kaf	כ ך *	ך ך *
	L	lamed	ל	ל
	M	mem	מ ם *	א מ *
	N	nun	נ ן *	נ ן *
	S	samech	ס	ס
	A	ayin	ע	ע
פ (P) or **פ** (F)	P, F	pey	פ ף *	פ ף *
	(hats)	tsadi	צ ץ *	צ ץ *
	K	koof	ק	ק
	R	reysh	ר	ר
ש (Sh) or **ש** (S) / S (side) or (shade)		sheen	ש	ש
	T	taf	ת	ת
J, G (George):				
Ch (Churchill):				
J (Jaques) soft J:				

*Different shapes for letters at the end of words.
**The only letters that are vowels too.

Linguistic Interference with Hindi/English

Syntax Variants

English:	The old black dog is running down the street.
Hindi:	One old black dog on the street is running.

English:	I see the black dog.
Hindi:	I a black dog am seeing.

Hindi is written and read from left to right.

Helping verbs such as is, am, are, will, shall, and would are nonexistent in Hindi, as are the forms of "to be," am, are, be, been. There is one *pronoun* for the words, he, she, and it.

Letters and Blends That are Transposed

The voiced and unvoiced (th) as in the and things, is sounded as T. P = b, pick = bick, th = tr (sometimes), thick = trick, this = tis, three = tree, w = v, we = vee. The final consonant is often omitted: don't = don. Words with "ng" are difficult to pronounce: ring = rin. Ch and sh may cause confusion also — shoes may sound like choose.

Word Pairs

pick – bick	big – pig
choose – shoes	very – wery
thick – trick	we – ve
this – tis	things – tings
three – tree	

Vowel Comparison

Generally speaking, in English there are five vowels with 10 sounds. Five are "long vowels" that "say" the letter name (a, as in say; e, as in eat; i, as in line; o, as in go; u, as in cute). Five are "short" vowels having the following sounds: a, as in at; e, as in pet; i, as in it; o, as in pot; u, as in up. There are 36 consonants and 12 vowels. The vowels in Hindi are called Akars. The vowels of Hindi are pronounced in English as: uh, as in up; ah, as in fall; e, as in eat; ee, as in feet; oo, as in who; oo, as in school; a, as in age; aa, as in wait; o, as in go; oe, as in go o; um, as in hum; ugh, as in the ughh (very tired sound). The vowels of Hindi may be used as initially written or as symbols when they are joined with any consonant. One form of Hindi uses only certain parts of a given character for a consonant and combines it with parts of selected other ones.

Alphabet Comparisons

In the Hindi alphabet there is no independent character for the following letter equivalents in English, with possible exception as used in the Akars: A, C (k or s are substituted), E, F, I, O, Q, U, V, X, Z.

Hindi Alphabet with English Pronounciation

Hindi	Pronunciation	English
क	K	K as in Calcutta
ख	Kh	Kh as in Khatoum
ग	G	G as in Glass
घ	Gh	Gh as in Galighar
ङ	Nga	(No English equivalent)
च	Ch	Ch as in Cheeta
छ	Tcha	(No English equivalent)
ज	J	J as in Jump
झ	Jha	(No English equivalent)
ञ	Nga	(No English equivalent)
ट	T	T as in Turn
ठ	Tha	(No English equivalent)
ड	D	D as in Drum
ढ	Dda	D as in Dummy
ण (ड़)	Nra	(No English equivalent)
त	T	T as in Tajmahal
थ	Th	Th as in Thanks
द	D	Th as in The
ध	Dha	(No English equivalent)

न	N̄	N as in American
प	P̄	P as in Pot
फ	P̄h	F as in Photograph
ब	B̄	B as in But
भ	Bha	(No English equivalent)
म	M̃	M as in Volume
य	Yo	Yo as in Mayor
र	R̄a	Ra as in Rah
ल	L̄a	La as in Sellah
व	Wa	Wa as in Water
श	Sh	Sh as in Sheila
ष	Sch	Ch as in Chalet
स	S̄a	Sa as in Sauce
ह	h̄a	Ha as in Hatari
ज्ञ	gya	"Geya"
क्ष	Tcha	(No English equivalent)
श्र	sra	(No English equivalent)

A	ए		N	एन
B	बी		O	ओ
C	सी		P	पी
D	डी		Q	क्यू
E	ई		R	आर
F	एफ		S	एस
G	जी		T	टी
H	एच		U	यू
I	आई		V	वी
J	जे		W	डबल्यू
K	के		X	एक्स
L	एल		Y	वाई
M	एम		Z	जेड

Linguistic Interference with White Hmong/English

Syntax Variants

English: I see the black dog.
Hmong: I see the black dog.

There are three tenses for the Hmong language. However, only the present tense is used. For example, *I go* is used for the past, present, and future. This morning I go to the store. No use of past tense. Never use *was* or *were*. The morning is already gone, so no need for *went*. Plurals are made by adding a number and using the singular word form: boys = one boy, or two boy; several men = many man.

The forms of *to be* are different. For example, in English, *I am, you are*. In Hmong, *I am, you am*. The third person also used *am*. They *am*, it *am*. The word "is" is not used. For example, he sick; he fat; he old.

Direction of reading and writing is left to right. There are seven voice tones or language markings. The use of the following letters at the end of a word denotes this: M, S, G, D, V, J, B. *Maum, maus, maug, maud, mauv, mauj, maub*. The voice tones give meaning and expression to the word. For example, *maum* = sister, *maus* = to buy, *maug* = sale, *mauj* = have, *maub* = give.

Difficult Blends or Sound Transpositions

th
r
x
b/p
d/t
ch
sh
k/ng

Word Pair Comparisons

choose – shoes	think – thing
bed – bet	three – tree
pay – bay	thought – though
wear – were	wrist – rest
let – left	race – raise
dot – dog	letter – ledder
laugh – leaf	lift – left

Vowels

The vowels are always pronounced the same way:

a as in f<u>a</u>ther
e = a as in g<u>ay</u>
i = e as in f<u>ee</u>t
o = o as in <u>o</u>ff
u = o as in do
w = oo as in flu
oo = o as in phone
au = as in out
ua = ōwa
ia = ēya
ai = i as in nice
aw = er as in fath<u>er</u>
ee = ing as in r<u>ing</u>

Hmong Alphabet and Pronunciations

A = ah
B = np = (ba)
C = jau
D = daw
E = a
F = fa (fah)
G = g
H = how
I = e
J = j
K = k<u>o</u> as in c<u>o</u>t
L = 1
M = m
N = n
O = ou as in <u>o</u>ff
P = p as in s<u>p</u>ot
Q = (no English sound)
R = djau
S = s
T = t
U = oo
V = vā
W = er + w
X = zaw
Y = yaw
Z = zjaw

Linguistic Interference with Hungarian/English

Sentence structure: Most of the time, sentence word order is the same as used for English. There are, however, some exceptions.

English:	I see the black dog.
Hungarian:	I see the black dog.

English:	The old black dog is running down the road.
Hungarian:	The old black dog is running down the road.

Hungarian Alphabet	(English Pronunciation)	English Alphabet	(Hungarian Pronunciation)
A	a as in jaw	A	éj
A	a as pă		
B	bey	B	bi
C	tsey	C	szi
Cs	chā		
D	day	D	di
E	e	E	i
É			
F	ef	F	ef
G	gay	G	dzsi
Gy			
H	ha as in hah	H	éjcs
I	ee as in feet	I	áj
Í	eeee (longer e)		
J	ya as in yes	J	dzséj
K	ka (kah)	K	kéj
L	el	L	el
M	em	M	em
N	en	N	en
Ny	eñya (like Spanish tilde)		
O	O (as in go)	O	ou
Ó	Ó (as in go)		
Ö	Ö (like the e of father)		
Ő	Ő (no English equivalent)		
P	pēa	P	pi
no letter Q		Q	kjú
R	air (trilled r)	R	ár
S	esh	S	es
Sz	ess		
T	tay	T	ti
Ty	tchă		
U	U (as in use)	U	jú
Ú	U (as in use)		
Ü	no English equivalent		
Ű	no English equivalent		

Hungarian Alphabet	(English Pronunciation)	English Alphabet	(Hungarian Pronunciation)
V	vey	V	vi
no letter W			dabolju
X	iks	X	eksz
Y	ipsilon	Y	aj
Z	zay	Z	zi
Zs	sjay		

Confusing letters or blends: E/i, y/j, w/v, th/d, tr/th, th/s, th/z.

Confusion with the "th" blend: unvoiced th/tr (three/tree), th/s (thick/sick).

Confusion with the "th" blend: voiced th/d (the/dee, this/dis, that/dat), th/z (that/zat, these/zees, this/zis).

Word Pairs

that – zat	water – vater
these – zees	work – vork
this– zis	three – tree
this – dis	thick – sick
that – dat	trick – sick
they – day	

Linguistic Interference with Indonesian/English

Syntax Variants

English: The old black dog was running down the road.
Indonesian: Dog black that is old runs the street.

English: I see the black dog.
Indonesian: I see dog black that.

There is only one tense, the present. For example: Today I <u>cook</u> rice. Yesterday I <u>cook</u> rice.

When speaking, the singular form of the word is said two times. In order to show plural when writing, a small "2" is written:

Anak = child (singular)

Anak^2 = children (plural)

Possessives are indicated by an ending word form (nya). The translated possessive is:

English: The boy's sweater.
Indonesian: Sweater of the boy.

There is no form of "to be." I am happy = I happy.

Different Letter Blends and Sound Transpositions

The unvoiced "th" as in thick = ti. The voiced "th" as in the = da. The final unvoiced "th" = "t" or "f" (teet or teef). The letters S/Z are often confused (sipper/zipper), as are U/ju, F/V, C = ch. The "C" in Indonesian has a "ch" sound. For example, chair or children would be spelled phonetically "cair" and children with no "H." The letter "C" never has a "k" sound, always "ch."

Vowels

a = ah

e = ay

i = ee

o = oh

u = oo as in good

Alphabet sounds are the same as for Dutch with these exceptions:

q = koo

u = oo as in tooth

g = g as in gay

Indonesian Alphabet pronunciation

A = ah
B = bay
C = say
D = day
E = aye
F = ef
G = gay
H = hah
I = e
J = yea
K = ka
L = l
M = m
N = n
O = o
P = pay
Q = koo
R = err
S = s
T = te
U = oo as in tooth
V = vay
W = way
X = ix
Y = aie
Z = zet

Word Pair Comparisons

sipper – zipper
use – juice
thought – taught
teet – teef
lit – lid
thick – tick

head – hat
whear – wear
then – den
jeep – cheep
jew – view

Linguistic Interference with Italian/English

Syntax Variants

There is no j or h sound. J = ya as in year. The letter C has different sound patterns. As pronounced in **English:** C, followed by I, say chee; C, followed by A, say ka; C, followed by U, say koo; C, followed by E, say chay; C, followed by O, say ko. In **Italian:** C followed by I = chee; chi = key; che = kay. The letter S, when appearing singularly in a word, with vowels on each side, has the sound of z. Sci = sh, and sh = si (long I); ph = p; gh = hard g. The language is phonetic. Knife = k, neefa; know = k, nov; knee = k, nay; knew = k, nayeuv; white = vita; window = vindov; owner = ovner; cute = cootay. The initial "th" and the final t are difficult. Th, as in the = da; that = dat; this = dis; brother = brotayer; yard = eeard. Words with double consonants (ca*ll*ing) are pronounced as cal-ling. Gli (as in glider = the sound of lli, as in million). Gni = nye. The letter G, like the C has many different pronounciation rules: G, when followed by I = dsj; G, followed by A = ga (hard g, as in got); G, followed by E = dzja; G, followed by U = goo; G, followed by O = go (same as go in English); ghi = gee (hard G); ghe = gay.

The adjective comes after the noun — I see the dog black. The word *do* is not used in a sentence. *Vuoi del dolce?* = Do you want some cake? The word *will* is not used. Instead, a future form is used. *Andró a lavoraze.* = I will go to work. Gender, masculine or feminine, affects the final vowel. Masculine is usually O; feminine, A. The word *my* has four forms: masculine singular/plural, and feminine singular/plural. Adjectives and nouns must agree with gender and number.

Difficult Word Pairs

fad – fed	read – red
band – bend	leave – live
bad – bed	his – is
reed – rid	piece – peace
fool – full	

Vowel and Consonant Transpositions

A = always the short a sound as in father

E = always the long a sound as in gate

I = always the long e sound as in ease

O = always the long o sound as in potato

U = always the sound of oo as in school

Alphabet With Italian Pronunciation

A

B

C = che (long e sound)

D

E = long a sound

F = efa (long a)

G

H = aka

I = long e sound

L

M = ema (long a)

N = ena (long a)

O

P

Q = coo

R = erra (long a, "rolled r" as in Spanish with a tilde)

S = essa (long a)

T

U = oo

V

W = v

Y = long e

Z = zeta

Linguistic Interference with Japanese/English

Syntax Variants

English:	I see the black dog.
Japanese:	I the black dog see.
English:	The old black dog is running down the street.
Japanese:	The black old dog is down the street running.

Women speak differently than men — in that there are words and phrases that are considered feminine, as the phrase in English, "Oh, isn't that darling!" The masculine response might be, "That looks attractive!"

There is formal speech, reserved for the Emperor, boss, and people of great respect. There is a "polished" form for friends and everyday talk. The children and poorly educated people speak in "common" talk.

There are actually three methods of writing Japanese. In the primary grades in school, children first learn to write the primary alphabet, *Hiragana.* As the student advances, he or she begins to learn *Kanji,* which is used by better educated people. There are 800 characters for the Kanji alphabet, which originated in China in 600 A.D. Most written material such as newpapers, story books and magazines are written in Kanji, with a column beside the Kanji, saying the same thing, written in Hiragana. By writing in both methods, the poorly educated and young children can enjoy reading — as well as the better educated. Hiragana and Kanji are written in vertical columns. The line of writing is from top to bottom and the columns are read from right to left.

The third kind of writing is called *Katakana.* This form is usually written horizontally, left to right, and read from left to right. This form is used mostly for advertisements and for translating a foreign language into Japanese. It is also the usual method of writing used in Science and Math texts.

Simple Kanji originated with a picture. For example, a field was illustrated by a square that was divided into four equal sections. A man usually worked in the field. Hence, by combining the picture of field and man, which equals the power of work in the fied, the word *man* is printed. 男

Word Pair Comparisons

love – lave or rub	red – lead
van – ban	horse – hose
very – berry	born – bone
fifty – hifty	worm – warm
thousand – sousand	gum – gam

Vowel and Consonant Transposition

The following letters that are in the English alphabet do not appear in the Japanese alphabet: C, when read and pronounced by a Japanese-speaking person = "she," L = "elu" and is usually transposed to an R; F = "efoo," R = "aru" and is usually pronounced as L; V = "buwee" and is usually pronounced as b; Z = "dzet," th, and wh.

Victory is usually pronounced as bictory, very = berry, love = rub, thousand = sousand. The final th as in with = S = wis. The initial th as in think = surink. The initial th as in the = da or dza, there = dere. An I followed by R, as in bird = bad. There are 48 vowels in Japanese.

English Alphabet with Japanese Pronounciation

A	エ	H	エッチ	O	オ	V	ブイ
B	ビ	I	アイ	P	ピ	W	ダブリュウ
C	シー	J	ヂェイ	Q	キュ	X	エックス
D	ヂィ	K	ケイ	R	アール	Y	ワイ
E	イ	L	エル	S	エス	Z	ゼット
F	エフ	M	エム	T	テー		
G	ジー	N	エヌ	U	ユウ		

Words for Numerals in Japanese

1	一	11	十一	50	五十
2	二	12	十二	60	六十
3	三	13	十三	70	七十
4	四	14	十四	80	八十
5	五	15	十五	90	九十
6	六	16	十六	100	百
7	七	20	二十	101	百一
8	八	30	三十	110	百十
9	九	40	四十	200	二百
10	十				

Hiragana

ă	ē	ōō	ĕ	ō
A	I	U	E	O
Ka	Ki	Ku	Ke	Ko
Sa	Shi	Su	Se	So
Ta	Thi	Tsu	Te	To
Na	Ni	Nu	Ne	No
Ha	Hi	Hu	He	Ho
Ma	Mi	Mu	Me	Mo
Ya	Yi	Yu	Ye	Yo
Ra	Ri	Ru	Re	Ro
Wa	Wi	Wu	We	Wo
Un				

Pa	Pi	Pu	Pe	Po
Ga	Gi	Gu	Ge	Go
Za	Zi	Zu	Ze	Zo
Da	Di	Dsu	De	Do
Ba	Bi	Bu	Be	Bo

Katakana

ă	ē	ōō	ĕ	ō
A	I	U	E	O
Ka	Ki	Ku	Ke	Ko
Sa	Shi	Su	Se	So
Ta	Thi	Tsu	Te	To
Na	Ni	Nu	Ne	No
Ha	Hi	Hu	He	Ho
Ma	Mi	Mu	Me	Mo
Ya	Yi	Yu	Ye	Yo
Ra	Ri	Ru	Re	Ro
Wa	Wi	Wu	We	Wo
Un				

	ǎ		ē		o̅o̅		ě		o̅
パ	Pa	ピ	Pi	プ	Pu	ペ	Pe	ポ	Po
ガ	Ga	ギ	Gi	グ	Gu	ゲ	Ge	ゴ	Go
ザ	Za	ヂ	Zi	ズ	Zu	ゼ	Ze	ゾ	Zo
ダ	Da	ヂ	Di	ヅ	Dsu	デ	De	ド	Do
バ	Ba	ビ	Bi	ブ	Bu	ベ	Be	ボ	Bo

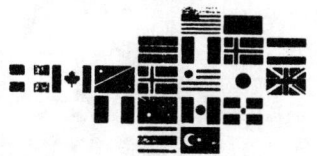

新報

The small print to the right of each column of large print is *Hiragana*.

KANJI
KATAKANA
HIRAGANA

交渉の妥結は目前に
核兵器の先制使用せず
カーター大統領が国連で演説

【ニューヨーク四日＝AP】カーター大統領は四日午前、国連総会で演説し、米ソ両国が戦略核兵器を制限する第二次SALT協定に合意するのは目前に見えていると言明した。大統領はまた、新SALT交渉合意の域を超えた将来にも触れ「米国はソ連が同様な手段をとるならば、核兵器を十％、二十％あるいは五十％までも削減する用意がある」と強調した。

大統領はまた、核爆発実験の全面禁止交渉の合意を訴え「米国は軍事、平和利用などいかなる理由にしろ、すべての核爆発実験を打ち切る時期にきている」と述べた。中東問題については大統領は次のように言明した。

われわれは中東諸国に外部から解決策を押しつける意図はない。しかしイスラエルおよびアラブ諸国の基本的権利と利益は受け入れられなければならない。イスラエルにとっては、これは国境が認められ安全ということを意味する。イスラエルの安全保障に対する米国のコミットメ…

よび同盟国が抑止力としての軍事力を持つにしても。世界の安全保障は永久に "恐怖のバランス" に依存することはできないと述べた。そして "勝ち負けのない" 核時代に、外交手段としての戦争はもはや許されず、米ソの責任は極めて大きいと指摘した。

こうした立場に立って、大統領は「私は米国を代表して米国が自衛の場合のほかは核兵器を使用しないことを宣言する。自衛の場合とは米国の領土あるいは同盟国のそれに対する核兵器あるいは通常兵器による実際の攻撃である」と述べた。

大統領はさらに、核軍拡および核拡散の脅威を強く訴えるとともに、米国は実際に攻撃を受けた際の自衛のほかは核兵器を使用しないとの立場を明らかにした。これは、いわゆる「核の先制使用」一の事実上の放棄につ…

ながるもので、米核戦略にとって大きな変化を意味する。大統領は現状のままでは今世紀末までには数十カ国が核兵器を保有する可能性があり、それに対する核兵器を使用したいという誘惑に抗しがたい状況がくると警告、米国述べた。

Linguistic Interference with Korean/English

Syntax Variants

English: S (subject) – V (verb) – O (object)
Korean: S (subject) – O (object) – V (verb)

English: I went to the school.
Korean: I the school to went.

English: I made my son a sailor.
Korean: I my son a sailor made.

Word Pair Comparisons

hold – fold	border – barter
white – fight	word – ward
jeep – zip	sought – thought
lice – rice	vigor – bigger
light – right	thank – dank

Vowel and Consonant Transpositions

A   A vowel followed by R, as in *arcade, Churchill, birth, water* = (the R is dropped) acade, Chuchhill, bith, watah.

B   The letter B is pronounced as a V. Boys = voices

D   Th = D, This = dis, thick = dick (usually initial dipthong, final S can change) smith = smis, thank = dank, smooth = smood

F   Becomes wh, h as in hold = fold, white = fight, full = fool, what = wat or fat

J   Is pronounced as a z. Jenis = dzenis, jink = zink, or jeep = zip

L   L = R, fry = fly, lice = rice, light = right, lake = rake

O   Vowel followed by R or A followed by R = bord = bart, word = ward, oo = U, full = fool.

S   S = Z, S = th, think = sink, thought = sought or dought, seem or seam = theme, smith = smis, is = iz, sh = S, brush = vrus.

Z   Z = S, gas = gaz, jazz = jass

Linguistic Interference with Laotian/English

Syntax Variants

Most sentences would be said with the same sentence structure as that found in English. For example, "I go to school," is proper in both English and Laotian. There are, however, three levels of speaking. These are determined by the age, rank, or other "station" in life. For instance, children use one level, out of respect, when they address their parents or grandparents, another when speaking with friends, and a very high form will be used when speaking to a doctor, professor, or civil leader. It is sort of a caste system of language use.

Laotian people, when learning English, frequently have problems with all the forms of "person" such as *I, we, you, them.* The helping verbs, *is, am, are, was, were,* cause problems also. They become confused as to when to use an, a, and the. This needs to be explained. Perhaps it is easiest to say, "Use *an* before a noun which has a vowel *sound,* or has a vowel as its first letter. Use *a,* or *the,* before other nouns."

Blends That Are Confusing

Th as in this = dis (da)

Th as in teeth = teet

R, when preceded by a vowel, is hard to say. For example: girl = gull.

T, when in the final position, is frequently dropped. For example: fast = fas.

Word Pairs

slip – sleep	jip – zip
ship – sheep	this – dis
fit – pit	teeth – teet
girl – gull	got – cot
had – has	fat – pat

Alphabet Problems

F = P

Q = F

G = K if hard, or C. For example: got = cot

J = Z

Comments

There are 21 main consonant sounds in Laotian which can be written with one of the 27 consonant symbols. The consonant symbols are divided into three groups according to the tone on which they are spoken.

1.   There are six *Akson Sung* (rising tone) consonant symbols:

2.   There are eight *Akson Kang* (low tone) consonant symbols:

3.   There are 13 *Akson Tam* (high tone) consonant symbols which correspond to the sounds of the Akson Sung consonants, both of which are spoken on a different level of tone:

Vowels

Single consonants		**Double consonants**	
	(poon) = line		(vung) = hope
	(gi:n) = eat		(mu) = pig
	(ro:t) = car		(kree) = teacher
	(bung) = hide		(pro:m) = carpet

Linguistic Interference with Blue Mong/English

Syntax Variants

English: I see the black dog.
Hmong: I see the black dog.

There are three tenses for the Mong language. However, only the present tense is used. For example, *I go* is used for the past, present, and future. This morning I go to the store. No use of past tense. Never use *was* or *were*. The morning is already gone, so no need for *went*. Plurals are made by adding a number and using the singular word form: boys = one boy, or two boy; several men = many man.

The forms of *to be* are different. For example, in English, *I am, you are*. In Hmong, *I am, you am*. The third person also used *am*. They *am*, it *am*. The word "is" is not used. For example, he sick; he fat; he old.

Direction of reading and writing is left to right. There are seven voice tones or language markings. The use of the following letters at the end of a word denotes this: M, S, G, D, V, J, B. *Maum, maus, maug, maud, mauv, mauj, maub*. The voice tones give meaning and expression to the word. For example, *maum* = sister, *maus* = to buy, *maug* = sale, *mauj* = have, *maub* = give.

Difficult Blends or Sound Transpositions

th
r
x
b/p
d/t
ch
sh
k/ng

Word Pair Comparisons

choose – shoes	think – thing
bed – bet	three – tree
pay – bay	thought – though
wear – were	wrist – rest
let – left	race – raise
dot – dog	letter – ledder
laugh – leaf	lift – left

Vowels

The vowels are always pronounced the same way:

A as in f<u>a</u>ther
E = a as in g<u>ay</u>
I = e as in f<u>ee</u>t
O = o as in <u>o</u>ff
U = o as in do
W = oo as in flu
OO = o as in phone
AU = as in out
UA = ōwa
IA = ēya
AI = i as in nice
AW = er as in fath<u>er</u>
EE = ing as in ri<u>ng</u>

Mong Alphabet and Pronunciations

A = ah
B = np = (ba)
C = jua
D = daw
E = a
F = fa (fah)
G = g
H = how
I = e
J = j
K = k<u>o</u> as in c<u>o</u>t
L = l
M = m
N = n
O = ou as in <u>o</u>ff
P = p as in s<u>p</u>ot
Q = (no English sound)
R = djau
S = s
T = t
U = oo
V = vā
W = er + w
x = zaw
y = yaw
z = zjaw

Linguistic Interference with Navajo/English

Syntax Variants

English:	I see the black dog.
Navajo:	Dog black I see.

English:	I am going to see mother tomorrow.
Navajo:	Tomorrow mother going I see.

Plural forms are confusing. For example: I will haul woods. He has sheeps. Tenses are confusing. For example: She *came* to school. = She *comes* to school. I *drive* my truck to the store. = I *drove* my truck to the store. Final consonants are frequently dropped. For example: don't = don, like = lie. A consonant occurring in the middle or end of a word is often dropped in pronounciation. For example: shiprock = shira. The ending "se" as in license, is often sounded as, licen*t*. Cease = seat. It can, however, sound as Z. For example: blouse = blouz. Confusing blends are: Initial th that is voiced. For example: the = da, this = dis. Initial th, unvoiced. For example: think = tink, thank = tank or dank. Final th, as in with = wif or wit, both = bot or bof, teeth = teef or teet. Ch and sh are often confused. For example: wash = watch, chip = ship. O before an R = ore.

Word Pairs

thank – tank	teeth – teet
think – dink	with – wif
mother – mudder	send – sand
farther – farder	bring – brin
both – bof	pick – big

Alphabet Problems

C is confused with K

D = t

G = gh

I = sometimes like a long e or short a

L = in final position with s = z. For example: girls = gurz

L = W when in initial position. For example: little = widdle

O = short a, sometimes

S = Z, sometimes. For example: sister = sizzo, mister = mizzer

T = P, sometimes. jet = jep

Z = S. Example: zipper = sipper, jazz = jass

Vowels in Navajo

There are four different sounds for each of the vowels, a, e, i, o, therefore creating 16 vowel sounds.

A, as in father. AA, as in gate (long a). Ą, nasoral = an. ĄĄ, long nasal ą.

E, as in met. EE, as in they. Ę, nasoral (long). ĘĘ, nasoral (longer).

I, as in it. II, sound of e as in need. Į, nasoral. ĮĮ, long i.

O, as in so. OO, as in school. Ǫ, nasoral. ǪǪ, nasoral (longer o).

Dipthongs

(ai) like the y in my.

(aii) similar to the ai, but with the last element long.

(aai) similar to ai, aii, but with the first part long.

(ao) like the English ow.

(aoo) a + long o.

(ei) ey of they.

(eii) same as ei, but the last part is long.

(oi) never like the oi of oil, but like oughy as in doughy, or as ewy of dewy.

(ooi) like oi, but the first part is long.

(ouu) o + long uu sound.

Linguistic Interference with Norwegian/English

Syntax Variants

English:	I see the black dog.
Norwegian:	I see the black dog.

English:	The old black dog is running down the road.
Norwegian:	The old black dog runs down road.

Word Pair Comparisons

chips – ships	word – verd
choose – shoes	with – wid
church – shurch	thick – tick
jello – yellow	think – tink

Vowel and Consonant Transpositions

There are five vowels: A = ah (pa), E = e (pet), I = e (feet), O = oo (school), and U = u (blue). G usually has a hard sound. George = Gay-org. J = y, jump = yump. O = oo as in school. Off = oof. Most of the time the letter R is "rolled." U = oo, up = oop. W = v, window = vindow. O = u, Close = cluse. Th as in this, the, that, them, those = T (tis, te, tat, tem, tuse). Th as in think, thick, three = tink, tick, tre. Th in the final position, as used in with, both, teeth, is pronounced as D or T. With = wid or wit, both = bot or bod, teeth = teet or teed. The initial Sh = the usual pronounciation as found in English (shoes). The initial ch = sh. Chips = ships, choose = shoes, church = shurch. The final ch usually is pronounced with no difficulty. Hu = ch, Hughes = choose, huge = chooj.

Alphabet Pronounciation in Norwegian

A = ăh	J = yōde	Q = kōo	Y = euh
B = bĕh	K = kō	R = ară	a = o as in vogue
C = sĕh	L = ĕl	S = ĕs	o = uh
D = dĕh	M = ĕm	T = tĕh	æ = a as in ad
E = ĕh	N = ĕn	U = ōo (blue)	
F = ĕf	O = ōo (school)	V = vĕh	
G = gĕh	P = pĕh	W = double vĕh	
H = ho		X = x	
I = ee			

Linguistic Interference with (Persian) Farsi/English

Syntax Variants

The noun is followed by an adjective, as in Spanish: For example: I see the dog black. Reading is done from right to left. Alphabet characters are different. There is no letter O. To make an O, the character for A plus the character for V are written. There is no Q, U, W, or X. To create, in English, the sounds for these missing letters, the appropriate sound combinations, in Persian, are substituted. When writing a word, such as *cat,* in Persian, the vowel always is elevated above the line of print. For example: T^{A}C. The word for he or she is the same. There is no gender.

Word Pair Comparisons

girl – curl	word – world
thick – think	sleep – slip
tree – three	it – eat
three – through	is – ease
what – white	her – hair

Vowel and Consonant Transpositions

There are only three vowels: A (short a sound), A (long a sound), and O (long o sound). The initial Th, as in three, is difficult = tree. W sounds are called V, window = vindow. The final D = T, did = dit. The final L preceded by an R, as in girl = gil. The initial consonant g sound can be pronounced as a c. Girl = curl. Dictation of spelling words and the alphabet are most difficult, as are double vowels or vowel dipthongs.

Persian Alphabet (Farsi) الفبای فارسی

English	Pronunciation		Letter	Nos.
A	Alef	الف	آ - ا	۱
B	Beaa	بِ	ب - بـ - ـبـ	۲
P	Peaa	پِـ	پ - پـ - ـپـ	۳
T	Teaa	تِـ	ت - ـت - ـتـ	۴
C-S	Seaa	ثِـ	ث - ـث - ـثـ	۵
J	Gim	جیم	ج - جـ	۶
CH	Cheaa	چ	چ - چـ	۷

English	Pronunciation	Letter		Nos.
H	Heaa	ح	ح - حـ	٨
KH	Kheaa	خ	خ - خـ	٩
D	Dall	دال	د - د	١٠
Z	Zall	زال	ذ - ذ	١١
R	Rea-Rae	ر	ر - ر	١٢
Z	Zea-Zae	ز	ز - ز	١٣
J (French)	Jae	ژ	ژ - ژ	١٤
C-S	Seen	سین	س - سـ - ـسـ - ـس	١٥
SH	Sheen	شین	ش - شـ - ـشـ - ـش	١٦
S	Sawd	صاد	ص - صـ - ـصـ	١٧
Z	Zawd	ضاد	ض - ضـ - ـضـ	١٨
T	Taw	طا	ط	١٩
Z	Zaw	ظا	ظ	٢٠
AA	Aine	عین	ع - عـ - ـعـ - ـع	٢١
GH	Ghine	غین	غ - غـ - ـغـ - ـغ	٢٢
F-PH	Fea-Fae	ف	ف - ـف	٢٣
GH	Ghaff	قاف	ق - ـق	٢٤
K	Kaff	کاف	ک - ـک	٢٥
G	Guff	گاف	گ - ـگ	٢٦
L	Lawm	لام	ل - ـل	٢٧
M	Mimm	میم	م - مـ - ـمـ	٢٨
N	Noon	نون	ن - نـ - ـنـ	٢٩
W,V,O,U	Vav	واو	و	٣٠
H	Heaa	هـ	ه - هـ - ـهـ - ـه	٣١
I-Y	Yea	ی	ی - یـ - ـیـ	٣٢

Linguistic Interference with Polish/English

In Polish there are no articles (a, an, the). Polish distinguishes the formal and informal ways of addressing people. Similarly to Spanish, the pronoun "ty" (you) is used only when addressing close friends, children, etc. "Pan" (masculine) or "pani" (feminine) is used when addressing casual friends, professional, or business acquaintances. They correspond to the term "usted" in Spanish. The verbs following "pan" or "pani" will then be used in the third person singular rather than in the second, which belongs exclusively to the casual "ty."

All nouns, adjectives, and verbs in Polish consist of a stem (or root) of the word and a grammatical ending that changes depending on the case in which it appears. All nouns, pronouns, and adjectives in Polish have cases and undergo *declension*. Their "dictionary" form is usually the nominative case. Sometimes not only the ending of a particular noun but also the stem itself changes, undergoing some "reshuffling." Therefore, one has to know the nominative case of a given word to be able to locate it in a dictionary. For example:

To jest pies. This is a <u>dog.</u> (nominative)

Mam psa. I have a <u>dog.</u> (accusative)

There are several different declensions in Polish, depending on the gender of nouns or adjectives, as well as their stem endings. Also, in Polish all adjectives have either masculine, feminine, or neuter gender, which has to agree with that of the noun they modify. Most feminine nouns end in "a," although there are some exceptions. Most masculine nouns end in a consonant.

The function of cases in Polish:

Nominative: indicates the subject of a sentence.

Genitive: indicates possession. In English replaced by the use of "of" or "s."

Dative: indicates indirect object. In English indicated by the use of "for" or "to."

Accusative: indicates direct object. *Mam psa.* I have a dog.

Instrumental: indicates by means of instruments, write with a pencil *(pisac ólowkiem).*

Locative: indicates placement, location, or position. Used after such prepositions such as "w" (in), "na" (on), "o" (about), "przy" (by, near).

Vocative: used when addressing someone directly: *Kasiu!* (Kathy!)

A Polish child may, therefore, have difficulty grasping the English syntax where the nouns, pronouns, and adjectives do not change their form or endings.

In Polish, the endings of verbs indicate which person they refer to:

I write: piszę

You write: piszesz

He, she, it writes: pisze

It is therefore not necessary to use pronouns in front of the verbs; their form is self-explanatory. Verbs are conjugated in all three basic tenses (past, present, and future). There are also some irregular verbs, whose conjunction does not follow any specific rules.

Simple yes-or-no type of questions are formed in Polish by adding the word "czy" at the beginning of a simple statement:

Mam psa. I have a dog.

Czy mam psa? Do I have a dog?

Alphabet

A – aah

Ą – nasal, does not exist in English

B – běh

C – tse

Ć – very soft ch

D – děh

E – ěh

Ę – nasal, similar to "vin" in French

F – eff

G – geah (as in goat)

H – hah

I – ēe

J – yot

K – kăh

Ł – ell

L – ew (as in water)

M – em

N – en

Ń – soft as in canyon

O – o (as in bought)

Ó – oo (as in poor)

P – pěh

Q – koo

R – err (vibrating)

S – ess

Ś – very soft sh

T – těh

U – oo (equivalent of o)

W – voo

X – ēeks

Y – egreque

Z – zet

Ż = Ƶ – jet (hard)

Ź – very soft jet

Consonant clusters

sz – sh

cz – ch

dz – tz (hard for English)

rz – z p as in beige

dź – soft as in juice, judge

dż – harder, similar to the above

ch – h – hah

Substitution of hard for soft consonants (sz for s) changes the meaning completely. Example:

proszę: please (hard sz)

prosię: piglet (soft s)

There is no sound in Polish resembling the English "th"; therefore children tend to replace it with either "s," "t," or "d."

Word Pairs:

hut – hat	think – sink
blend – bland	thank – sank
slit – sleet	thin – tin
very – vary	three – tree
green – grin	

Linguistic Interference with Portuguese/English

Syntax Variants

English:	I see the black dog.
Portuguese:	I see the dog black.

The adjective usually comes after the noun.

The second person pronouns *tu* and *vos* are used only in addressing intimate friends, children and then only in some regions. *Voce* is the more common form for "you." When speaking with an older person or one for whom you wish to show respect, *o senhor* and *a senhora* are often used.

Gender

Masculine, feminine, neuter. Gender is noted by the final letter or letters. English has no gender.

Possessive pronouns and adjectives must agree in gender and number with the nouns to which they refer:

Meus livros azuis. My blue books.

Meu livro azul. My blue book.

Articles must agree in gender and number also.

The date is placed before the name of the month. Ordinal numbers are not used for the date except *primeiro*. Neither the day of the week nor the month are capitalized: "Today is thursday, 21 july 1997."

Questions are formed by raising the voice at the end of a statement. The auxiliary verb "do" is not used.

Letters and Sounds

Each vowel is pronounced clearly and crisply.

A single consonant is pronounced with the following vowel.

The tilde (til) (~) over a vowel indicates a nasal sound: Joaõ.

Vowels

A as in ah, f<u>a</u>ther

E as in eh, b<u>e</u>st

I as in mach<u>i</u>ne

O as in <u>o</u>ff and r<u>o</u>se

U as in r<u>u</u>le

Consonants and Consonant Groups

Ch as in ma<u>ch</u>ine

H is never pronounced

Lh as in mi<u>lli</u>on

M and N tend to nasalize the vowel before them, the lips are not closed in pronouncing a final M

Nh as in o<u>ni</u>on

S between vowels as "Z" or as "S" in rose; initial "S" or "ss" as in lesson.

C before A, O, U, and before any other consonant is like C in cat or *carta* (letter)

C before E and I is like the C in center: *sincero* (sincere). Used only before a, o, or d is like c in facade: *moco* (young man).

G before E and I is like the S in measure: *gente* (people)

G otherwise is like G in go: *gato* (cat)

J is similar to G before E and I: *jantar* (to dine)

L is formed with the tongue forward, the tip near the upper teeth: *paleto* (jacket)

L (final) is quite soft: *mal* (evil)

Qu before A or O is like qu in quota: *quadro* (picture)

Qu before E or I is usually like K: *que?* (what?)

X has the following sounds: like z: *exame* (examination), like sh: *caixa* (box), like s in see: *maximo* (maximum), like x in wax: taxi (taxi)

Vowel Combinations

Ai – ai as in aisle

Au – ou as in out

Ei – ey as in they

Éi – similar sound with open e

Eu – ey as in they plus u of lute

Éu – similar but with open e

Ia – ya as in yard

Ié – ye as in yes

Ie – similar but with close e

Io – yo as in yoke

Iu – e plus u of lute

Oi – oy as in boy

Ói – similar but with open o

Ou – ou as in soul

Ua – wah, as ua in quadrangle

Ué – we as in wet

Ui – we (if the main stress is on u, however, like u of lute plus e)

Uo – wo as in woe, or as uo

Nasal Sounds

This nasal quality is especially strong in Brazil. In Continental Portuguese it may be slight or even absent.

M, n, and nh nasal sounds tend to nasalize the vowel preceding them. M, n followed by a consonant are not pronounced, nor in final position, merely nasalize the preceding vowel.

A and o are nasalized: *la* (wool), *manha* (morning).

Nasal vowel combinations: *mãe* (mother), *licões* (lessons), *mão* (hand), *põe* (he puts).

Punctuation

The dash is used in dialogues to indicate quotations: – *Como vai o senhor?*

Capitals are not used as frequently: *eu* (I).

Decimal points and commas in figures vary: *6.247 metros* (6,247 meters), *cr $4.800,50.*

Stress

Words ending in a, e, or o (or in one of these vowels and s, m, or ns) are stressed on the next to last syllable: *casa* (house). Words ending in any letter, in a nasal vowel or diphthong are stressed on the last syllable: *papel* (paper), *descansei* (I rested). Words not following the above rules have a written accent mark indicating the stressed syllable: *café* (coffee).

The Alphabet

A – a (ah)

B – bêh

C – cêh

D – dêh

E – êh

F – efe

G – jêh

H – ag ah

I – e

J – j jota

L – ele

M – eme

N – ene

O – ó

P – pêh

Q – kêh

R – erre

S – esse

T – têh

U – oo

V – vêh

X – xis (she's)

Z – zêh

Word Pairs

Portuguese-speaking students learning English tend to put a vowel on the end of every word ending in a consonant because most of their words end in vowels. Sometimes a tendency to put a w sound in front of words beginning with a closed vowel is noted.

ship – sheep	bat – bet
slip – sleep	pat – pet
chip – cheap	tin – teen
is – ease	reap – rip
will – we'll	feet – fit

Linguistic Interference with Russian/English

Syntax Variants

The teacher should take into consideration that there are no articles (a, an, the) in Russian, and the verb "to be" in all its forms of present tense is never used so students may have trouble in English.

English:	This is a dog.
Russian:	This – – dog.

English:	There is a dog.
Russian:	There – – dog.

In general, syntax is about the same.

English:	There is a black dog.
Russian:	There – – black dog.

Sequence of tenses in Russian is not as obligatory as in English. In some verb-tense combinations, it's not used at all.

English:	I knew you would come.
Russian:	I knew you will come.

All animals and other inanimate objects have neuter genders in English. In Russian all objects including inanimate ones are divided into three genders: masculine, feminine, and neuter. For instance, the word corresponding to *home* is masculine, *cottage* is feminine, and *building* is neutral. The student may use "she" and "he" and their derivatives in reference to inanimate objects: *He* [is a] stone (speaking about a stone), or *she* [is a] cat.

Forms of questioning may be difficult because in Russian it is not necessary to use certain word order. Thus, a question may be stated just by intonation of voice.

English:	Will he come?
Russian:	He will come?

It also may be helpful to know there are six different cases in Russian. This means words change their endings in every case, similar to Latin.

Confusing Letters and Sound Transpositions

C – V
G – D
E – as in <u>ye</u>llow
U – as in gr<u>ee</u>n
N – P

P – sort of R, but harder (rolled)

C – S, never like K (cat)

M – T

Y – as in m<u>oo</u>n, g<u>oo</u>se

X – H (as in <u>h</u>urt)

R – ch (as in <u>ch</u>air)

Sounds

The "r" sound is difficult. In Russian, it is completely different. It is either rolled or sort of a growl. Children may pronounce it almost as a "ӡ" sound (like confu<u>si</u>on) or like a hard Russian "r" (rolled). Teeth sounds do not exist is Russian. Students may pronounce the "th" sound like "f" or "t" or "s" or "z." The "w" sound does not exist, just "v."

In Russian all letters in any word are pronounced. There are no letter combinations. Students may pronounce the last "r" in such words, as in "letter," or may have other difficulties when reading.

Some vowels may be confusing:

b<u>a</u>d – b<u>e</u>d

c<u>o</u>rn – c<u>o</u>n

r<u>ea</u>d – r<u>i</u>d

Vowels

A – as in f<u>a</u>ther

E – as in y<u>e</u>llow

Ë – as in y<u>o</u>lk

U – as in gr<u>ee</u>n

O – as in c<u>o</u>rn or d<u>o</u>g

Y – as in moon

Y – as in lid

Y – as in b<u>a</u>d

Y – as in c<u>u</u>be

Y – as in yard, yarn

Word Pairs

three – free or tree	well – vell
think – sink	water – vater
that – zat	weather – vezer
teeth – teef or tees	both – boz

Russian Alphabet

Letter	Handwriting	English Equivalent of Pronunciation
А а	*Аа*	hall
Б б	*Бб*	b
В в	*Вв*	v
Г г	*Гг*	g, gun
Д д	*Дд*	d
Е е	*Ее*	yellow
Ё ё	*Ёё*	yolk, York
Ж ж	*Жж*	confusion
З з	*Зз*	z
И и	*Ии*	green
Й й	*Йй*	y, toy, joy, clay
К к	*Кк*	k
Л л	*Лл*	l
М м	*Мм*	m
Н н	*Нн*	n
О о	*Оо*	corn, dog
П п	*Пп*	p
Р р	*Рр*	r, (but harder)
С с	*Сс*	s
Т т	*Тт*	t
У у	*Уу*	moon
Ф ф	*Фф*	f
Х х	*Хх*	kh
Ц ц	*Цц*	ts, cats
Ч ч	*Чч*	ch, chair
Ш ш	*Шш*	sh, share
Щ щ	*Щщ*	shch, (or a soft sh, fashion)
ь	*ь*	soft sign, ((мягкий знак))
Ы ы	*Ыы*	like oy, boy (only not fully pronouncing the o)
ъ	*ъ*	hard sign, ((твёрдый знак))
Э э	*Ээ*	Ed, elephant
Ю ю	*Юю*	cube, cute
Я я	*Яя*	yawn, yard

Linguistic Interference with Samoan/English

Syntax Variants

In the Samoan language, the adjectives come after the nouns they describe.

English: The old black dog is running down the road.

Samoan: The dog old black is running down the road.

Samoan language is somewhat restrictive in political, social, and scientific phenomena that do not relate to their mode of life. There are four levels of speaking. One is for the common use. This is the elementary form. A more proper form is used for instruction purposes as in church or schools. The respectful form is reserved for guests and older people. The most difficult, and very abstract form is reserved for the use of the chief only. The real chief does not speak — instead, he has a "speaking chief" who states the message to the people or other officials while using the abstract and highly technical form.

Confusing Blends

Unvoiced th as in thick = ti =tick , think = tink, three = tree. Voiced th as in the = da = dhe, that = dat, those = dose. Th as used in the final position, as in with = f = wif, or sh = wish; both = bof or bosh. Initial ch as in chunk, may be said as junk. John = chon, chump = jump. The blend of *gh* (as in f) and as a silent blend is confusing, as is the *ph* blend. The Samoan speaker does not know when to interpret the blends with an f sound and when to omit the sound. Why can't fish be spelled *phish?* Words like *cone* and *done* and *goes* and *does* cause confusion. English is not consistent.

When using common daily language, many Samoans use the letter K for the letter T. This is done only in conversation, not in reading or writing: thing = ting or king. When reading words wtih the letter G, pronounciation is never like a J: garage = *ngarange* (sound as g in go).

Word Pair Comparisons

pick – bick	both – bof
pig – big	thing – think
bought – pot	zone – sone
still – steel	sip – zip
mess – mass	king – ging
last – lust	

Vowel and Consonant Transpositions

Most Samoans have difficulty with the long and short sounds of vowels. The long form is foreign to them. Minimal word pairs are frequently mispronounced: mess/mass, last/lust. The letters P and B, G and K, Z and S are often interchanged: pib = big, go = ko, zip = sip.

Alphabet Comparisons

In the Samoan alphabet, there are no heavy sounds such as a, b, d, g, j, q, or w. The letter G is pronounced *nga*. In the original Samoan language, the K, R, and H, were not written or used. These letters were added when the Bible was translated. Each vowel has one stable sound: A = ah, E = e as in pen, I = i as in tip, O = o as in no, U = u as in tune. A consonant is always followed by one or more vowels. The following is the Samoan alphabet: A, E, I, O, U, F, G, L, M, N, P, S, T, V, (K, R, H).

Linguistic Interference with Spanish/English

Syntax Variants

English:	I see the black dog.
Spanish:	I see the dog black. (In Spanish, the adjective comes after the noun.)

The pronoun *tu* and *usted* are used as follows: the regular second person pronoun is *tu,* but it is used only in addressing intimate friends, children. *Usted* is the pronoun of more formal conversation with business, professional, or casual acquaintances (*tu,* and *usted* = you). Object pronouns generally come before the verb (i.e., *Nos invitan a comer.* They invite us to dinner.). Possessive pronouns, like adjectives, must agree in gender and number with the nouns they refer to: *Mi libro* = My book. *Mis libros* = My books.

In Spanish the day and date are placed before the name of the month: "hoy es martes, 31 de diciembre de 1998." English: "Today is Thursday, December, 31, 1998." Note also, in Spanish the name of the day and the name of the month are not capitalized, as they are in English. Only when they are the first word of the sentence, are they capitalized. In addition, ordinal numbers are not used for the date in Spanish (except *primero*).

In Spanish questions, it is customary to place the inverted question mark at the beginning of the sentence and to put a regular one at the end. This is done for the mark of exclamation also.

In Spanish, the auxiliary verb *do* is not used: *¿Pronouncia usted las palabras?* (¿Pronounce you the words?).

In Spanish, an adjective must be gendered masculine or feminine, and the number and the article *(el, la)* must also agree with the noun it is modifying: *El barco es bonito.* (o = masculine) The ship is pretty. *La niña es bonita.* (a = feminine) The girl is pretty.

Word Pair Comparisons

ship – sheep	chip – cheap
year – ear	chop– shop
yellow – jello	is – ease
sleep – slip	share – chair
it – eat	her – hair

Vowel and Consonant Transpositions

B　the Spanish b is always softer than English.

C　has the sound of the English c in cook, but before E and I, it is pronounced like s as in see.

D　is formed between the tip of the tongue and the lower back of the upper front teeth. It is softer than in English, and between vowels, is often pronounced like the th in though.

G   when before A, E, I, O, U, is pronounced as in gate; if after, as in *pagina,* the g = h sound (pahina)

H   is soundless in Spanish. *Hermano* = ermano

J   is sounded as an h. *Caja* = caha

LL   is sounded as y as in year.

Ñ   is sounded as ny as in canyon.

R   is stronger and more distinct. When R begins a word, the tongue "trills" or "rolls" the letter R — but not as much as when two R's occur in the middle of a word.

PR   is "trilled" or "rolled" also.

S   has approximately the sound of s as in saw.

V   is sometimes sounded as a v and sometimes as b.

X   has the sound of x as in English, except when followed by a consonant, when it has the sound of s, as in *explicar* = esplicar.

Y   sound is usually e, as in feet, when used as a conjunction, or ya, when it appears in words such as Yolanda.

Alphabet Comparisons

A = ah	N = ene
B = bay	Ñ = en-yeh (see above)
C = say	O = o
D = day	P = pay
E = eh	Q = koo
F = efay	R = erray
G = hay	S = essay
H = ah-che	T = tay
I = e as in feet	U = oo as in too
J = hoe' tah	V = vay
K = ka	W = doble vay
L = ele	X = eckis
LL = (see above)	Y = e gree eg a (see above)
M = eme	Z = zeta

Linguistic Interference with Swedish/English

Syntax Variants

In Swedish there are some differences in the use and formation of plurals as well as differences in the use of "ing." The apostrophe is not used in Swedish.

English:	I see the black dog.
Swedish:	I see the black dog.
English:	The old black dog is running down the road.
Swedish:	The old black dog runs down the road.
English:	Let's go to the store.
Swedish:	Now go we to the store.

Sound Transpositions

v = w, w = v

very = wery, word = vord

j = y, y = u, as in used.

jewel = yule, j = h as in hide.

z = s

zoo = sue

ja = ch

Sometimes the voiced "th" as in "da" and the unvoiced "th" as in thin or teeth, "ta."

Word Pair Comparisons

yes – jes

jewel – yule

chest – jest

work – vork

zoo – sue

zip – sip

seal – zeal

just – yust

joke – yoke

thank – tank

gin – chin

Swedish Vowels

A – as in f<u>a</u>ther, c<u>ŭ</u>t
E – as in <u>e</u>levator, s<u>ĕ</u>t
I – as in s<u>ee</u>n, s<u>ĭ</u>t
O – as in p<u>oo</u>l, b<u>ŏ</u>ok
U – y<u>u</u>le, fl<u>ŭ</u>te
Å – r<u>a</u>w, c<u>ă</u>ught
Ä – f<u>a</u>re, h<u>ă</u>t
Ö – <u>e</u>arly, fl<u>ŭ</u>tter
Y – <u>u</u>sed, gr<u>ĭ</u>pped

Swedish Alphabet

A – as in f<u>a</u>ther
B – as in b<u>e</u>d
C – as in <u>s</u>eance
D – as in <u>d</u>entist
E – as in <u>e</u>levator
F – as in e<u>ff</u>ort
G – as in <u>g</u>ift
H – as in <u>h</u>aul
I – as in s<u>ee</u>m
J – as in <u>y</u>ule, hide
K – as in <u>c</u>ar
L – as in <u>l</u>ong
M – as in <u>m</u>other
N – as in <u>n</u>oise
O – as in b<u>oo</u>k
P – as in <u>p</u>ull
Q – as in <u>q</u>ueen
R – as in ai<u>r</u>
S – as in <u>s</u>tove
T – as in <u>t</u>ake
U – as in vie<u>w</u>
V – as in o<u>v</u>en
W – similar to V
X – as in e<u>x</u>cellent
Y – as in <u>u</u>sed
Z – as in settle
Å – as in r<u>a</u>w
Ä – as in h<u>a</u>t
Ö – as in <u>e</u>arly

Linguistic Interference with Thai/English

Syntax Variants

English:	I see the black dog.
Thai:	I see the dog black.

English:	The old black dog is running down the road.
Thai:	The dog old black is running down the road.

Plurals: In Thai, plurals are formed by designating the number of objects while using the singular form of the noun. For example: seven boys = boy seven, three women = woman three.

Possessive: I go to my sister's house = I go to the house of my sister. That is my sister's sweater = That is the sweater of my sister.

Tenses are the same as in English.

Word Endings: One of the most difficult problems when learning English is getting accustomed to pronouncing the basic word endings. In English we voice our endings, such as cake. In Thai, they are not voiced:

cake – cay

nine – nie

five – fie

went – wen

The use of "ing" is shown by a word form called *Kamlang,* which means "in the process of." For example: running = *kamlang wîng* (in the process of) run

There are no articles, instead classifiers are used. There are approximately 50 classifiers. For example: *khon* = persons. There are five levels or types of speech, similar to a caste system.

Difficult and Confusing Letters and Combinations

Another problem a Thai speaker may experience is a difficulty pronouncing combined consonants at the beginning of a word. For example: stop – satop (the t is a forced d) or sadop, space – sapace, school – sagool.

Final "l" when preceded by u or a = n. For example: beautiful – beautifoon, small – smorn.

Final unvoiced th = t, as in with = wit, both = bot.

Th = tr as in three or tree.

Final p = b as in stop = stob. Sometimes the final p is omitted. For example: stamp = stam. Other final consonants may also be omitted.

th – th, voiced: the = duh, unvoiced (aspirated): three = tree

V – w, voiced: walentine, unvoiced: heawy

ch – sh, voiced: chair, unvoiced (aspirated): shair

rl – r = l, l = r. These two letters sound the same to the Thai and are difficult to pronounce differently.

r,l – as endings, voiced: car, unvoiced (aspirated): caa; voiced: pail, unvoiced (aspirated): paero or paeow

t – our pronounced t often sounds as ch (their t is much clearer). For example: ten sounds like chen.

endings – multiple endings like stands, boxes, and adapts are very difficult to pronounce.

w – no difference in w and wh, window and wheel

z – may be too difficult at first, zoo = soo

Word Pair Comparisons

fire – fine, five	lie – light
hot – hard	rice – lice
six – sick	light – right
fry – fly	love – rub
three – tree	free – flee
good – goose	full – foon

There are five voice tones. The first is a normal tone and the other four get progressively higher in pitch like in music. Each new tone changes the word meaning.

Alphabet Comparisons

Thai has 44 alphabet characters. These characters can be combined to duplicate English sounds. There are 24 vowels in Thai, written before, after, or above the consonant. The direction of reading and writing is left to right.

Linguistic Interference with Tongan/English

Syntax Variants

English:	I see the black dog.
Tongan:	I see the dog black.

English:	The black dog is running down the street.
Tongan:	The running down dog black street.

There are 120 pronouns dealing with singular, dual (two), plural (three or more), inclusive (who is speaking and who is being spoken to), exclusive (deleting yourself or the person to whom you are speaking). The final letter of every Tongan word is a vowel. A vowel goes between each consonant. There are never two consonants together, but two vowels may appear together. They usually are the same.

Usually speakers will make mistakes with internal and final consonants rather than with the initial consonant. Also mispronounciations usually result in contrasting pairs.

decay = degay
garbage = karpache
garment = karment
do = two
down = town
dock = talk
rude = lude (no r sound)
route = lute
sit = cid

Confusion with ch, sh, and j: cheep, sheep, jeep, chop, shop, sham, jam, show, Joe, chew, shoe, jew, rich, lich, ridge, lidge.

Sound Transpositions

B and P	G and K	Z and S	Th and O
by = pie	grow = crow	those = dose	thy = thigh
ben = pen	gap = cap	loose = lose	either = ether
bond = pond	good = could		thing = ring
bound = pound	beg = bake		with = wif
bill = pill	wig = wick		both = bof
cab = cap	gum = come		the = ta
nab = nap	dog = dock		that = tat
stab = step	mag = mac		this = tis
big = pick	nag = nack		
	pig = pick		

The Tongan Alphabet

A, E, F, H, I, K, L, M, N, NG, O, P, S, T, U, V, '. " ' " = the glottal stop. With it, the throat is more closed and the sounds are more sharp or crisp. It is used only before vowels or between them; and at the beginning or middle of a word. It is never separated from or left alone on a line if it is necessary to separate a word at the end of the line of writing. There are no th blends. Th at the start of a word (the) = ta, that = tat, this = tis. With = wif, both = bof, teeth = teef. There is no R in Tongan. Rude = lude, route = lute.

Linguistic Interference with Vietnamese/English

Syntax Variants

The Vietnamese language is different than the other oriental languages. It uses the Roman alphabet, six voice tones, and is patterned closely after Portugese and Spanish in syntax and use of vowels. Syntax order is noun, adjective, the same as in Spanish. English is adjective, noun.

English: The black dog ran.
Vietnamese: The dog black ran.

There are no plural endings in Vietnamese. For example: two boys = one boy, two boy. The boy's sweater is new = The boy sweater is new. All words in Vietnamese are one syllable. This causes the student to read in a choppy manner because, to the student, each syllable of a word in English is a new word, and, therefore, he can pause, as we might, after each "word" as desired. For example: Elephant = El e phant, "I see the el e phant."

Word Pair Comparisons

feet – fit	top – stop
lock – rock	think – sink
cheap – sheep	watch – wash
fly – fry	sky – ski
bath – path	

Vowel and Consonant Transpositions

B = p, as in boy = poy

Ch = sh, cheap = sheep

D = j, dog = jog; D = Y, dog = eog (y = long e); D = Z, dog = zog

L = r, lock = rock

U = oo, university = ooniversity

Y = long e sound of i as in Spanish

W = h, win = heen, window = heendo

T = s, top = stop

FL = fr, fly = fry

Unvoiced th as in thank = tank or sank. Voiced th as in the = za, that = zat.

Section 3
Picture Word List of Things
(Nouns) from A to Z

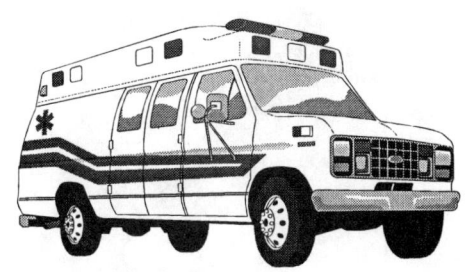

Ambulance = _____

Antlers = _____

Arm = _____

Alligator = _____

Apple = _____

Airplane = _____

Ax = _____

Angel = _____

Ant = _____

Anchor = _____

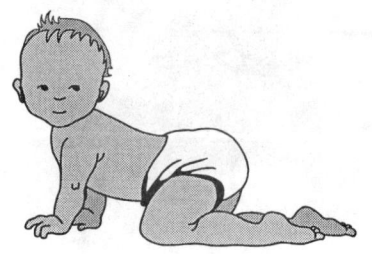

Baby = _____

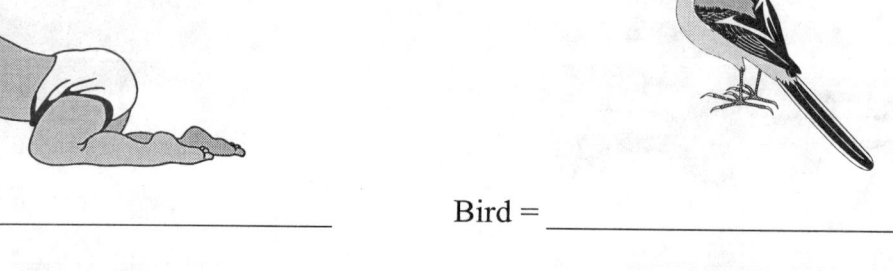

Bird = _____

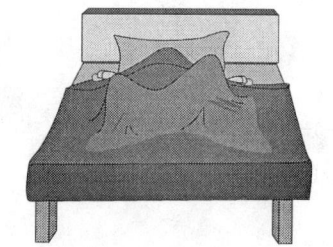

Bed = _____

Bear = _____

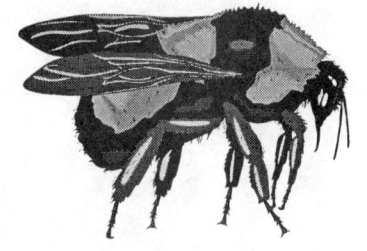

Bumblebee = _____

Boat = _____

Butterfly = _____

Bridge = _____

Ball = _____

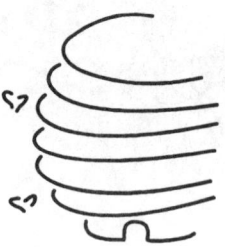

Beehive= _____

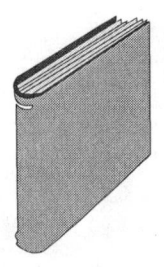

Book = _____

Beaver = _____

Boy = _____

Butcher = _____

Broom = _____

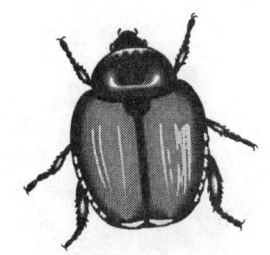

Beetle = _____

Bathrobe = _____

Bone = _____

Binoculars = _____

Barn = _____

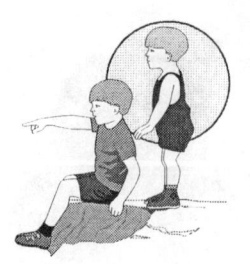

Boys = _____

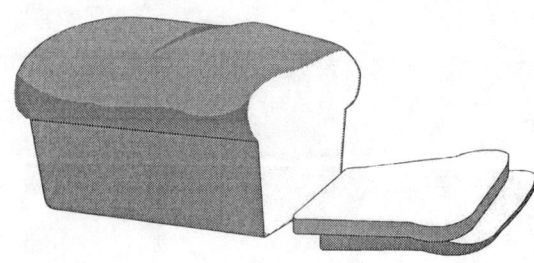

Bread = _____

Bus = _____

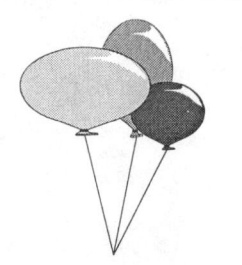

Balloons = _____

Bananas = _____

Bottle = _____

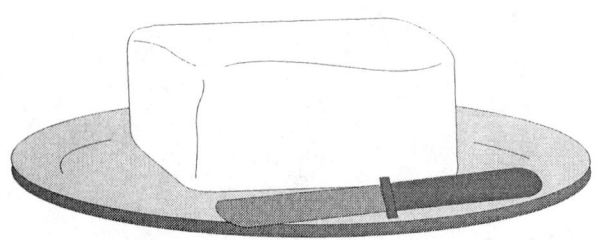

Butter = _____

Birdhouse = _____

Bat = _____

Bells = _____

Briefcase = _____

Boot = _____

Bicycle = _____

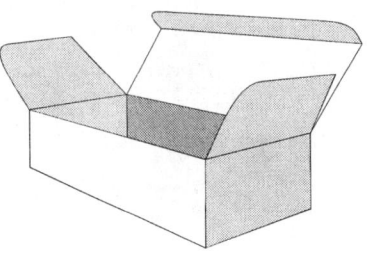

Box = _____

Bucket = _____

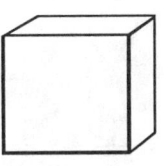

Block = _____

Badge = _____

Bathtub = _____

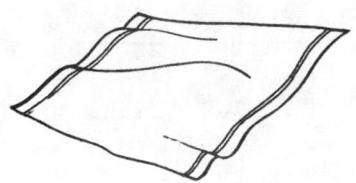

Blanket = _____

Brush = _____

Camera = _____

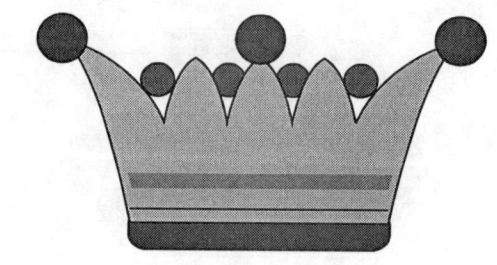

Crown = _____

Carrot = _____

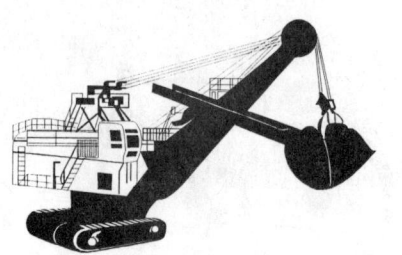

Crane = _____

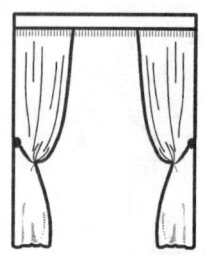

Curtains = _____

Calculator = _____

Cards = _____

Castle = _____

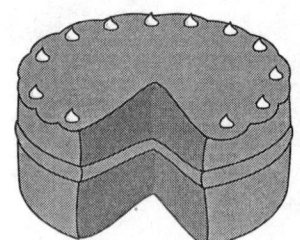

Cake = _____

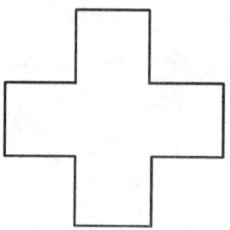

Cross = _____

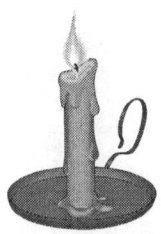

Candle = _____

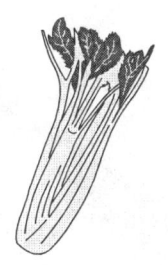

Celery = _____

Car = _____

Can = _____

Clock = _____

Cat = _____

Calf = _____

Chair = _____

Clams = _____

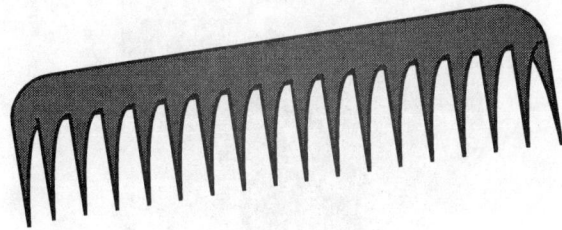

Comb = _____

Check mark = _____

Cup = _____

Camel = _____

Cupid = _____

Clothespin = _____

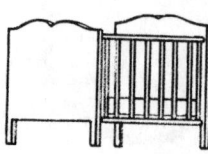

Crib = _____

Clown = _____

Church = _____

Cherries = _____

Chicken = _____

Dinosaur = _____

Door knob = _____

Dolphin = _____

Dog = _____

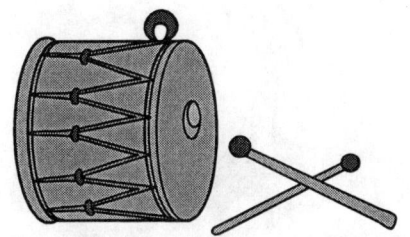

Drum = _____

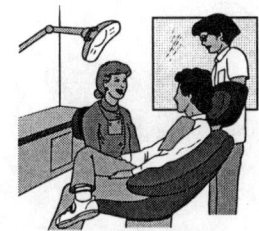

Dentist = _____

Doll = _____

Desk = _____

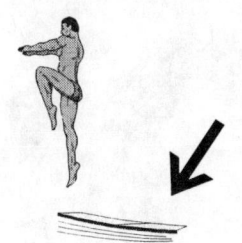

Diving board = _____

Dust pan = _____

Dice = _____

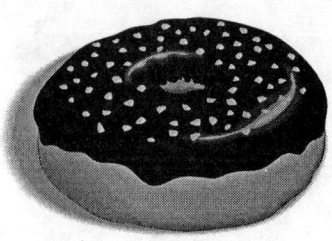

Doughnut = _____

Doors = _____

Deer = _____

Duck = _____

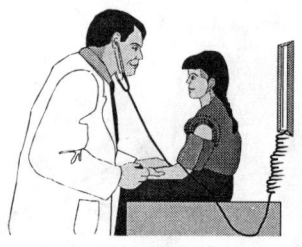

Doctor = _____

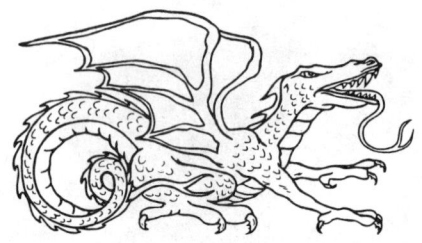

Dragon = _____

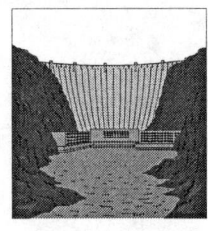

Dam = _____

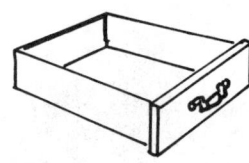

Drawer = _____

Donkey = _____

11

Eleven = _____

Eagle = _____

Envelope = _____

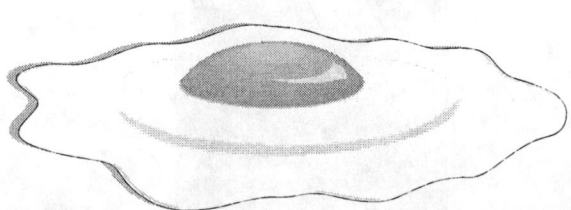

Egg = _____

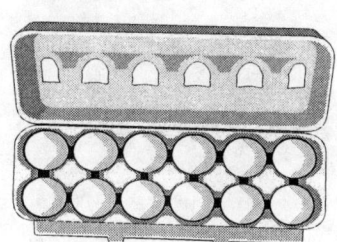

Eggs = _____

8

Eight = _____

Elevator = _____

Ear = _____

Elephant = _____

Elf = _____

Ferris wheel = _____

Fairy = _____

Flower = _____

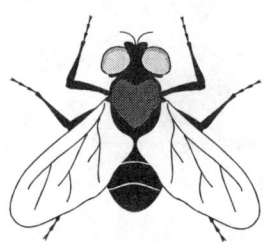

Fly = _____

Five = _____

Furniture = _____

Fireplace = _____

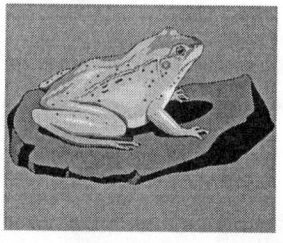

Frog = _____

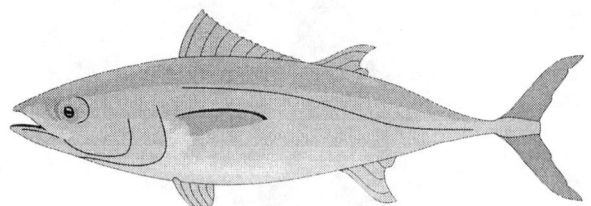

Fish = _____

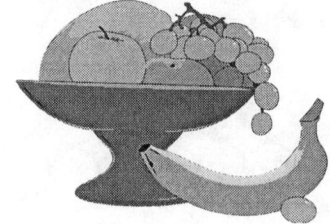

Fruit = _____

Flute = _____

File cabinet = _____

Flash light = _____

Fifteen = _____

Flag = _____

Fire = _____

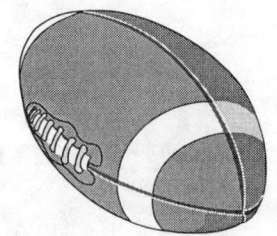

Football = _____

Fire engine = _____

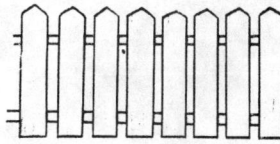

Fence = _____

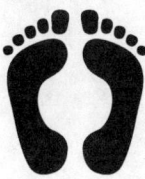

Feet = _____

50

Fifty = _____

Four = _____

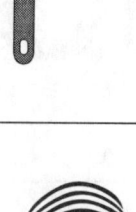

Fork = _____

Fox = _____

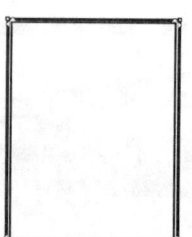

Fingerprint = _____

Fireworks = _____

Frame = _____

Frying pan = _____

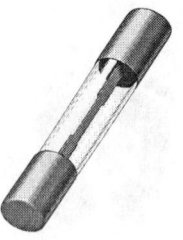

Fuse = _____

Film = _____

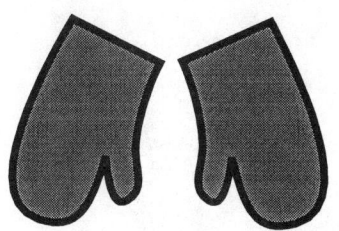

Gloves = _____

Girl = _____

Garbage = _____

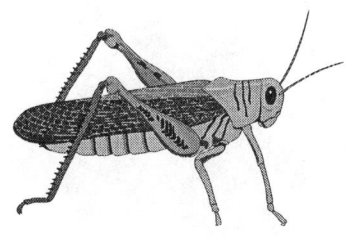

Grasshopper = _____

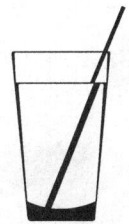

Glass = _____

Guitar = _____

Glasses = _____

Gun = _____

Gorilla = _____

Goose = _____

Glue = _____

Gum = _____

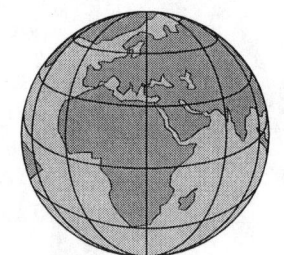

Globe = _____

Grapes = _____

Grapefruit = _____

Giraffe = _____

Ghost = _____

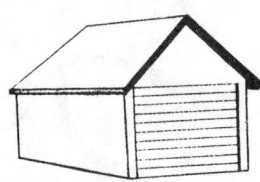

Garage = _____

Goat = _____

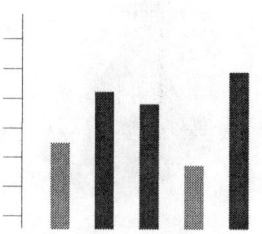

Graph = _____

Hippopotamus = _____

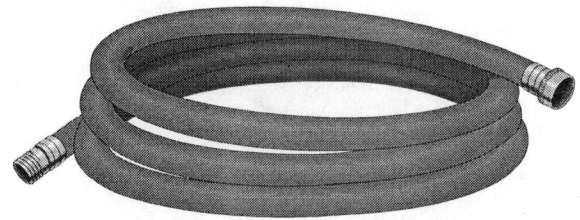

Hose = _____

Hat = _____

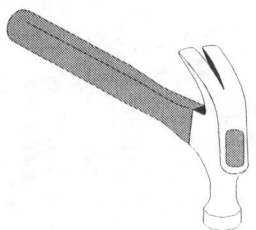

Hammer = _____

Hanger = _____

Handkerchief = _____

Honey = _____

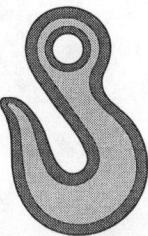

Hook = _____

Harp = _____

Hand = _____

Handcuffs = _____

Helicopter = _____

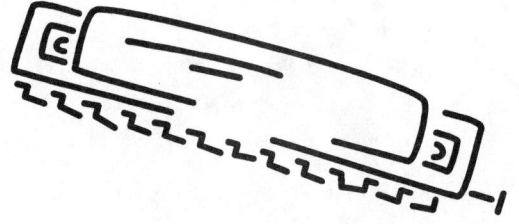

Harmonica = _____

Hamburger = _____

Heart = _____

House = _____

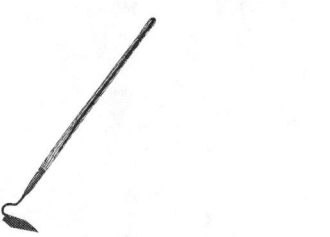

Hoe = _____

Horse = _____

Hoof = _____

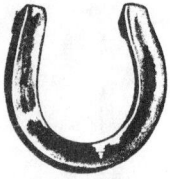

Horseshoe = _____

Ice skate = _____

Ironing board = _____

Ice cream = _____

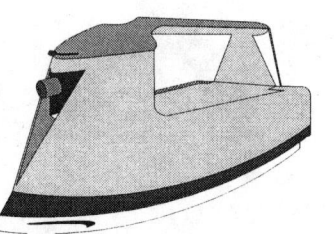

Iron = _____

Indian = _____

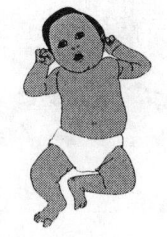

Infant = _____

Jacks = _____

Jar = _____

Judge = _____

Jack = _____

Jail = _____

Jug = _____

Jeep = _____

Jack-in-the-Box = _____

Jacket = _____

Jump rope = _____

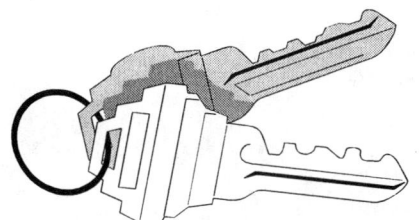

Keys = _____

Kitten = _____

Kangaroo = _____

Kite = _____

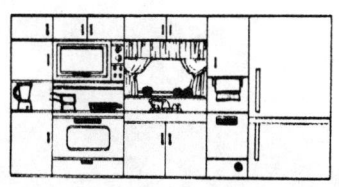

Kitchen = _____

King = _____

Knight = _____

Keyhole = _____

Knife = _____

Knot = _____

Lemons = _____

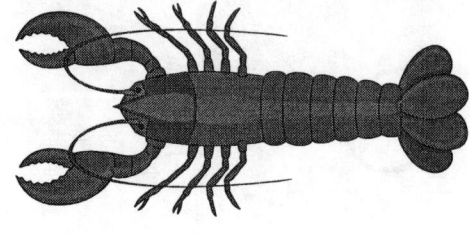

Lobster = _____

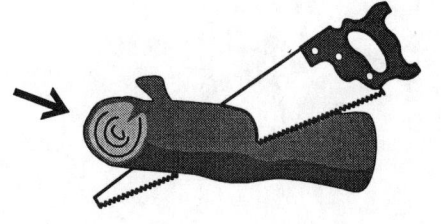

Log = _____

Lantern = _____

Lamb = _____

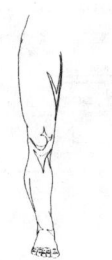

Leg = _____

Lawnmower = _____

Lady = _____

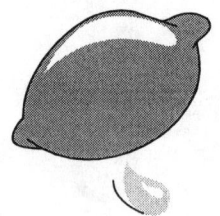

Lime = _____

Leopard = _____

Lighthouse = _____

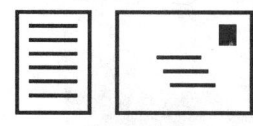

Letter = _____

Light switch = _____

Ladder = _____

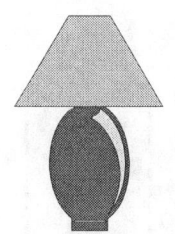

Lamp = _____

Leaf = _____

Lettuce = _____

Lion = _____

Lightning = _____

Lizard = _____

Mermaid = _____

Mailbox = _____

Marbles = _____

Microphone = _____

Moon = _____

Milk = _____

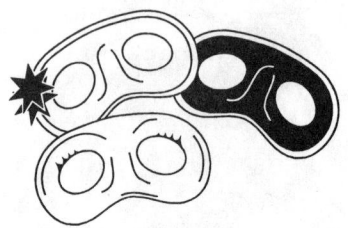

Masks = _____

Man = _____

Mouse = _____

Microscope = _____

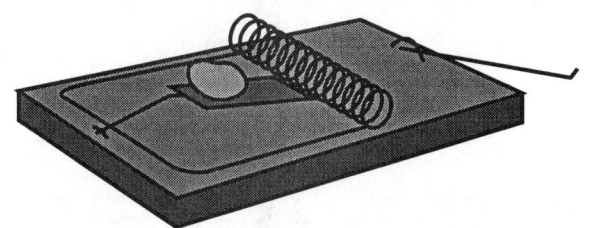

Mousetrap = _____

Map = _____

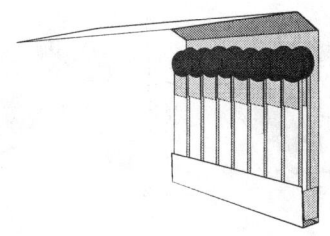

Matches = _____

Music = _____

Motorcycle = _____

Medal = _____

Mailman = _____

Mountain = _____

Merry-go-round = _____

Monkey = _____

Nose = _____

Nurse = _____

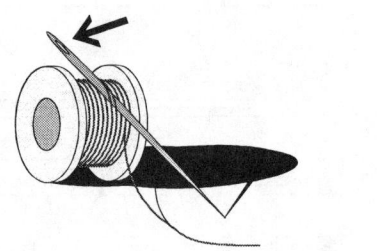

Needle = _____

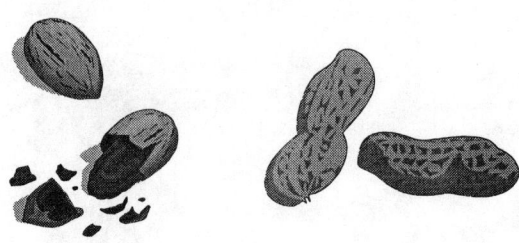

Nuts = _____

Note = _____

Nine = _____

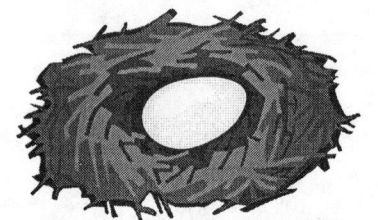

Nest = _____

Nail = _____

Organ = _____

Orange = _____

Octopus = _____

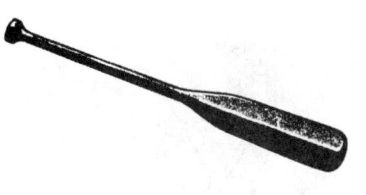

Oar = _____

Owl = _____

Ostrich = _____

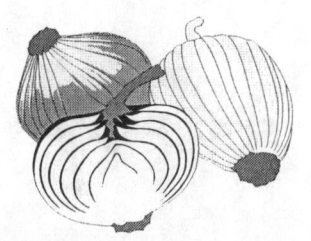

Onions = _____

One = _____

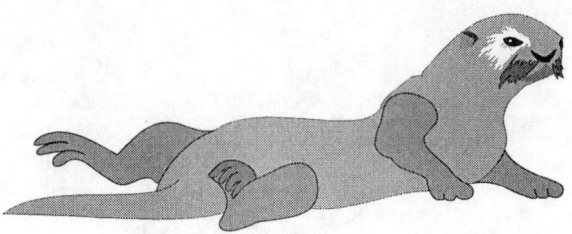

Otter = _____

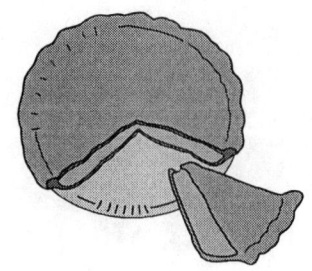

Pie = _____

Puppet = _____

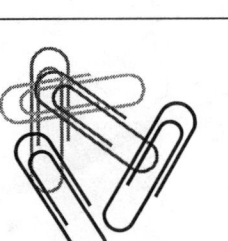

Paper clips = _____

Pen = _____

Penguin = _____

Pinecone = _____

Pear = _____

Piano = _____

Paper (Newspaper) = _____

Pumpkin = _____

Pirate = _____

Porcupine = _____

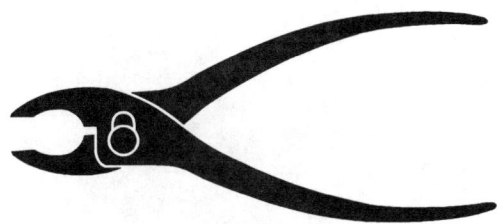

Pliers = _____

Popcorn = _____

Pitcher = _____

Paddlewheel = _____

Pig = _____

Pinwheel = _____

Parachute = _____

Projector = _____

Penny = _____

Pocketknife = _____

Pineapple = _____

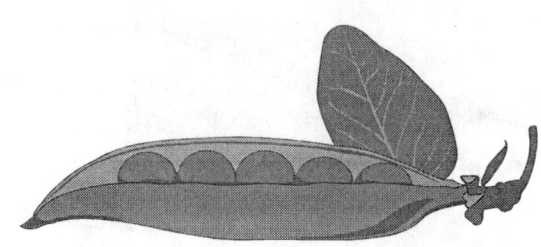

Peas = _____

Playpen = _____

Puzzle = _____

Presents = _____

Parrot = _____

Policeman = _____

Pencil = _____

Pajamas = _____

Piggy bank = _____

Purse = _____

Peach = _____

Potatoes = _____

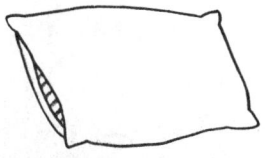

Pillow = _____

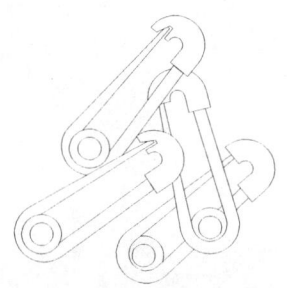

Pins = _____

Peacock = _____

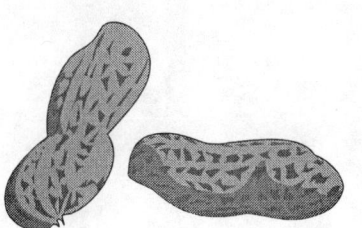

Peanuts = _____

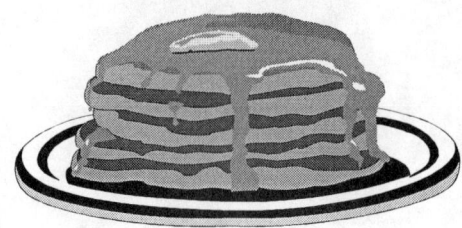

Pancakes = _____

Queen = _____

Quilt = _____

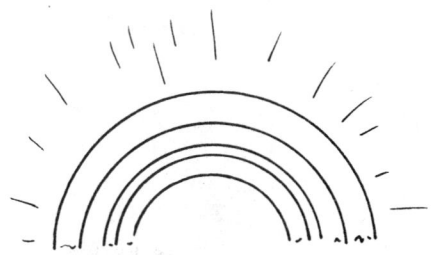

Rainbow = _____

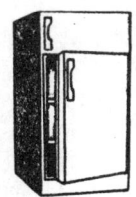

Refrigerator = _____

Rake = _____

Rope = _____

Razor = _____

Rolling pin = _____

Rattle = _____

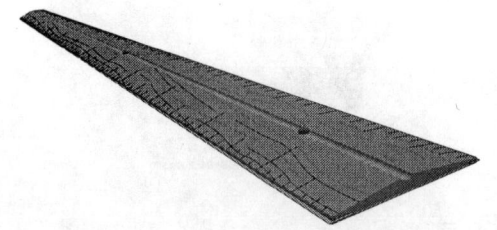

Ruler = _____

Ring = _____

Racoon = _____

Rabbit = _____

Rocking chair = _____

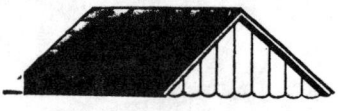

Roof = _____

Rocking horse = _____

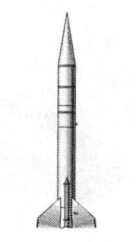

Rocket = _____

Rooster = _____

Radio = _____

Saddle = _____

Spoon = _____

Sandal = _____

Safe = _____

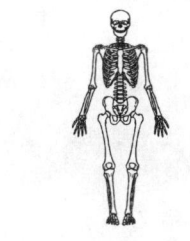

Skeleton = _____

Six = _____

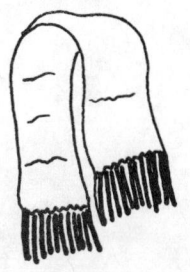

Scarf = _____

Skillet = _____

Sled = _____

Stamp = _____

Sun = _____

Spotlight = _____

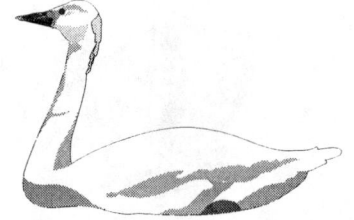

Swan = _____

Scissors = _____

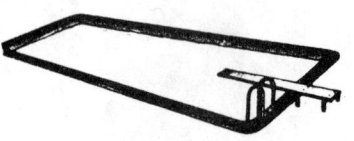

Swimming pool = _____

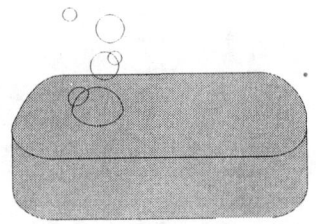

Soap = _____

Sailor = _____

Saw = _____

Scarecrow = _____

Snail = _____

Seal = _____

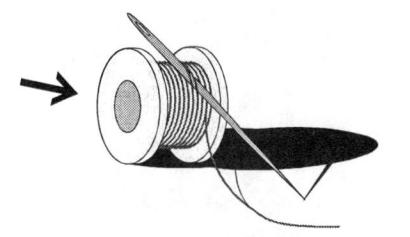

Spool = _____

Sink = _____

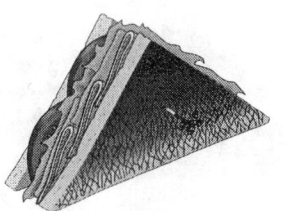

Sandwich = _____

Sweater = _____

Saltshaker = _____

Skis = _____

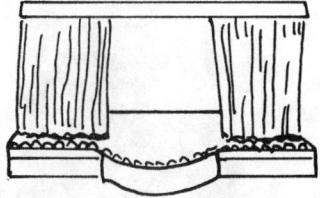

Stage = _____

Star = _____

Stapler = _____

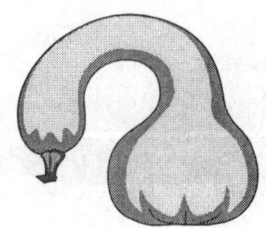

Squash = _____

Snake = _____

Stationwagon car = _____

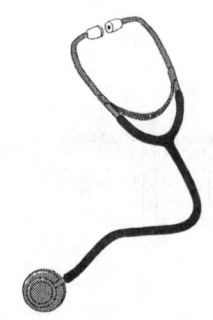

Stethoscope = _____

Slingshot = _____

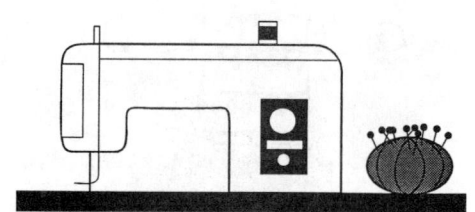

Sewing machine = _____

Stagecoach = _____

Slide = _____

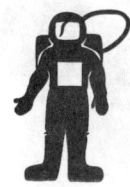

Spacesuit = _____

Sleigh = _____

Squirrel = _____

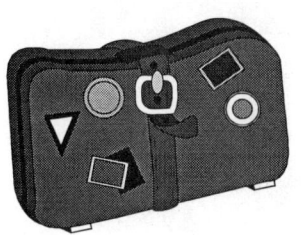

Suitcase = _____

Snowshoe = _____

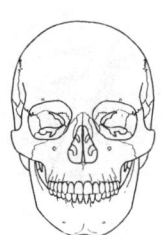

Skull = _____

Soup = _____

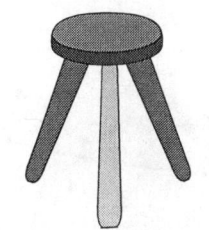

Stool = _____

Statue = _____

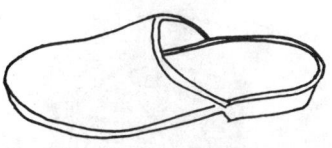

Slipper = _____

Soldier = _____

Spider = _____

Scale = _____

Socks = _____

Sawhorse = _____

Skunk = _____

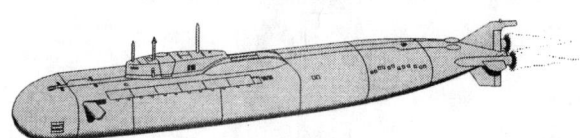

Submarine = _____

Seven = _____

Stove = _____

Spinning wheel = _____

Soda = _____

Snowman = _____

Strainer = _____

Santa = _____

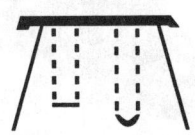

Swings = _____

Sleeve = _____

Sugar cubes = _____

Shovel = _____

Shirt = _____

Shepherd = _____

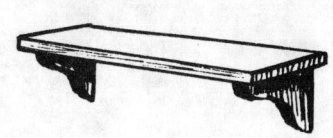

Shelf = _____

Shark = _____

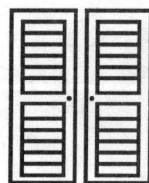

Shutters = _____

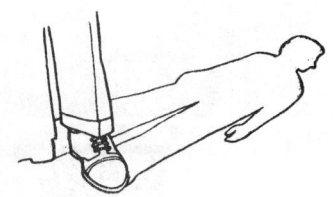

Shadow = _____

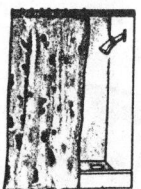

Shower = _____

Shoe = _____

Shell = _____

Ship = _____

Sheep = _____

Shrimp = _____

Strawberries = _____

Spaghetti = _____

Truck = _____

Twenty = _____

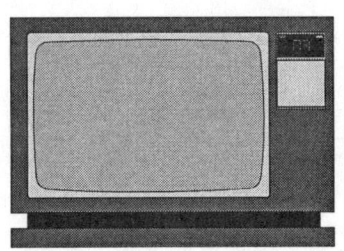

Television = _____

Tent = _____

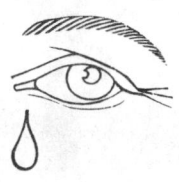

Tear = _____

Top = _____

Tennis racquet = _____

Tire = _____

Tiger = _____

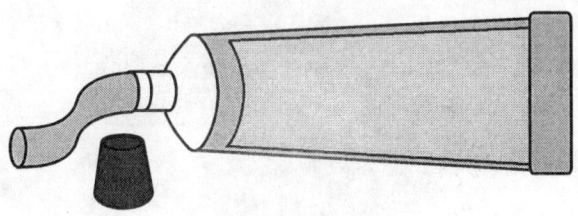

Toothpaste = _____

Tickets = _____

Toothbrush = _____

Telephone booth = _____

Typewriter = _____

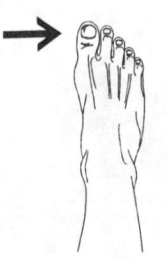

Toe = _____

Tie = _____

Turtle = _____

Table = _____

Two = _____

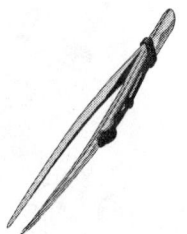

Tweezers = _____

Tornado = _____

Tractor = _____

Ten = _____

Tea kettle = _____

Treasure chest = _____

Tank = _____

Turkey = _____

Tree = _____

Tuba = _____

Tape measure = _____

Twelve = _____

Tricycle = _____

Thirteen = _____

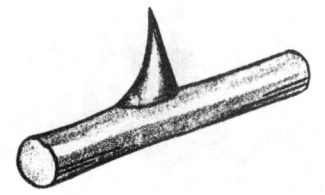

Thorn = _____

Three = _____

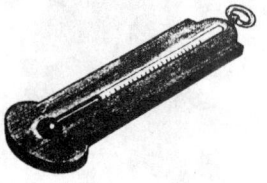

Thermometer = _____

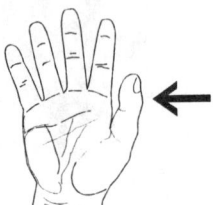

Thumb = _____

Thermos = _____

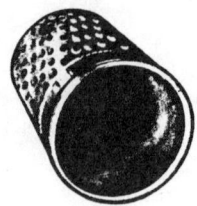

Thimble = _____

Theater = _____

Telephone = _____

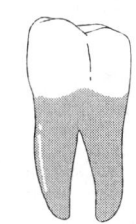

Tooth = _____

Taxi = _____

Toilet = _____

Tomato = _____

Teddy bear = _____

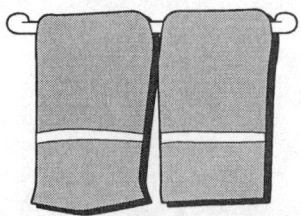

Towels = _____

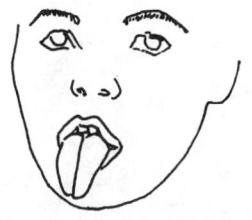

Tongue = _____

Tube (innertube) = _____

Triangle = _____

Vest = _____

Veil = _____

Valentine = _____

Vegetables = _____

Volcano = _____

Vase = _____

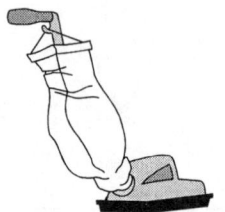

Vacuum cleaner = _____

Violin = _____

Wagon = _____

Washing machine = _____

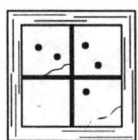

Window = _____

Wallet = _____

Windmill = _____

Wand = _____

Well = _____

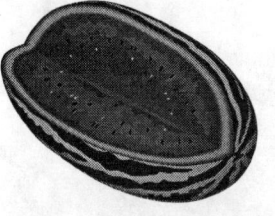

Watermelon = _____

Worm = _____

Wolf = _____

Washtub = _____

Walrus = _____

Whistle = _____

Wheel = _____

Wheat = _____

Wheelbarrow = _____

Whip = _____

Whisk broom = _____

Whale = _____

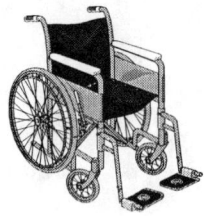

Wheelchair = _____

Xylophone = _____

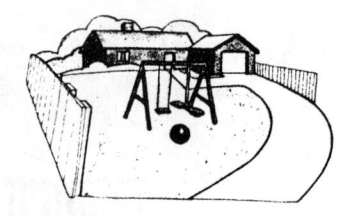

Yawn = _____

Yard = _____

Yarn = _____

Yo-yo = _____

Zebra =

Zero = _____

Zip code = _____

Zipper = _____

Zoo = _____

Section 4
Picture Word List of Opposites

Full = _____   Empty = _____

Open = _____   Closed = _____

Day = _____   Night = _____

Push = _____   Pull = _____

Off = _____   On = _____

Awake = _____   Asleep = _____

Cold = _____   Hot = _____

Thin = _____   Fat = _____

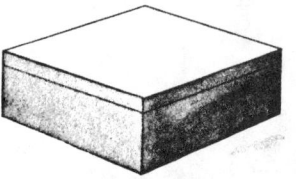

Little = _____   Big = _____

Hill = _____   Valley = _____

Up = _____

Down = _____

Young = _____

Old = _____

Under = _____

On = _____

Over = _____

Over = _____

In (inside) = _____

In (inside) = _____

Out = _____   In = _____

Whole = _____   Broken = _____

Short = _____   Long = _____

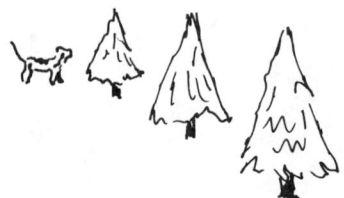   

Far = _____   Close = _____

Small = _____   Big = _____

Section 5
Picture Word List of Actions

Surprise = _____

Angry = _____

Happy = _____

Sad = _____

Blow bubbles = _____

Run = _____

Chase = _____

Jump = _____

Fight = _____

Lick (Taste) = _____

Planting = _____

Sledding = _____

Sawing = _____

Skating = _____

Buying = _____

Knocking = _____

Making a snowman = _____

Melting = _____

Licking = _____

Feeding = _____

Pulling = _____

Loving = _____

Smelling = _____

Eating = _____

Hanging = _____

Throwing = _____

Blowing bubbles = _____

Digging = _____

Talking = _____

Catching = _____

Kicking = _____

Bouncing a ball = _____

Diving = _____

Batting a ball = _____

Raking leaves = _____

Picking = _____

Painting = _____

Zipping coat = _____

Buttoning coat = _____

Brushing teeth = _____

Washing face = _____

Combing hair = _____

Brushing hair = _____

Tying shoe = _____

Dressing = _____

Section 6
Picture Word List of Colors, Numbers, and Shapes

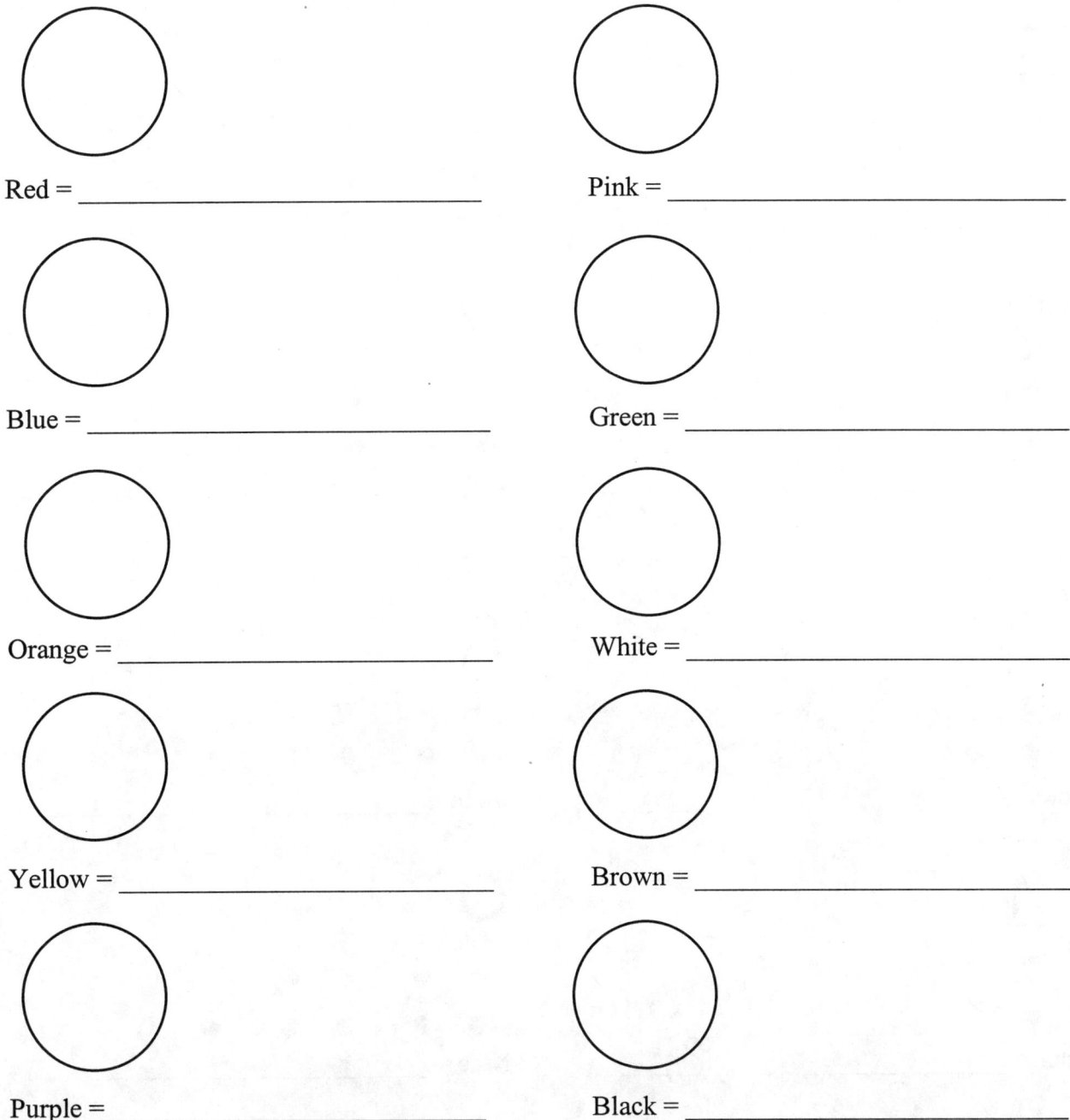

Red = _____

Pink = _____

Blue = _____

Green = _____

Orange = _____

White = _____

Yellow = _____

Brown = _____

Purple = _____

Black = _____

Note to teacher: Color in the appropriate circle with the corresponding color named below it.

1
•

One = _____

2
•
•

Two = _____

3
•
• •

Three = _____

4
• •
• •

Four = _____

5
• •
• • •

Five = _____

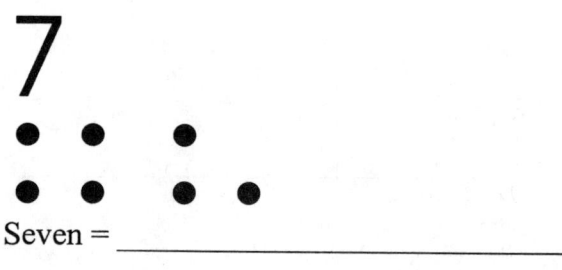

Six = _____

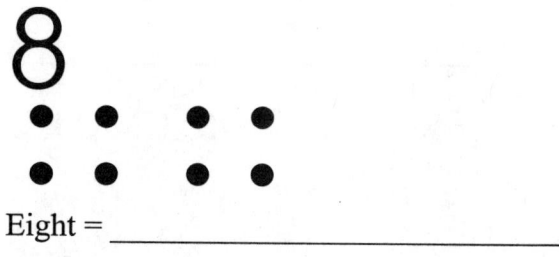

Seven = _____

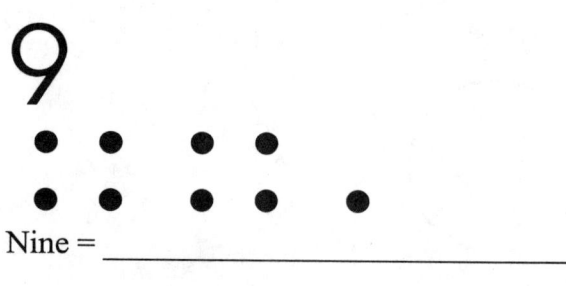

Eight = _____

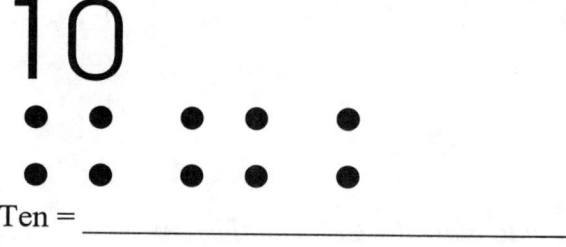

Nine = _____

10

• • • • •
• • • • •

Ten = _____

Eleven = _____

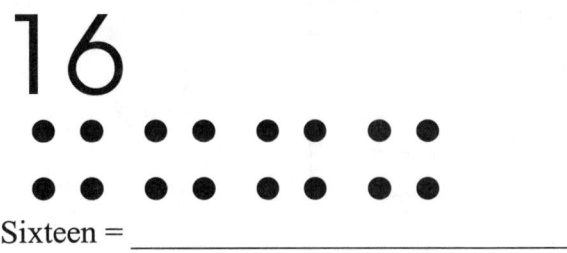

Sixteen = _____

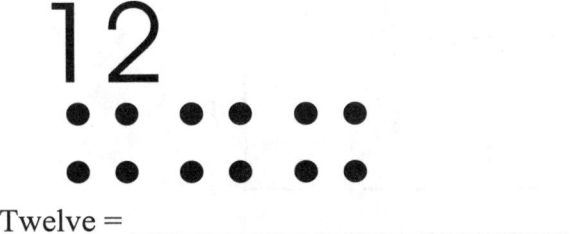

Twelve = _____

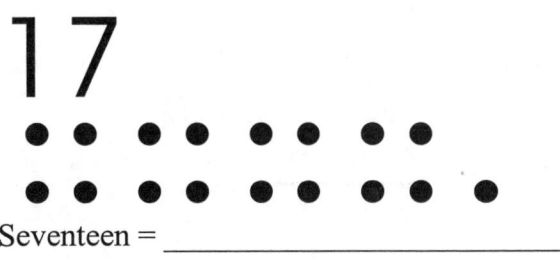

Seventeen = _____

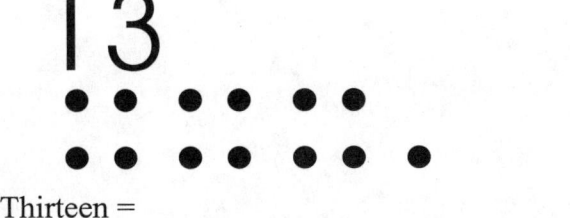

Thirteen = _____

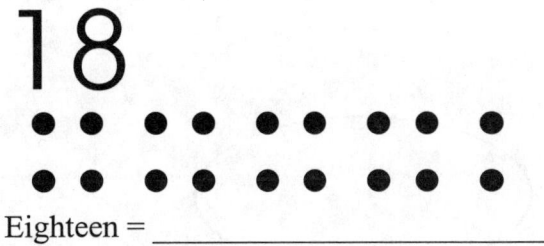

Eighteen = _____

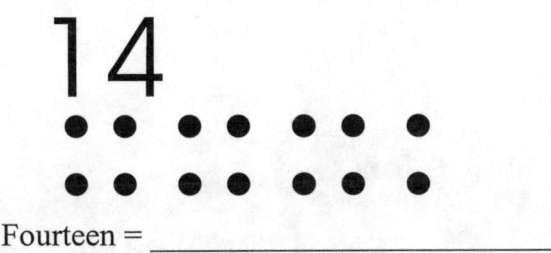

Fourteen = _____

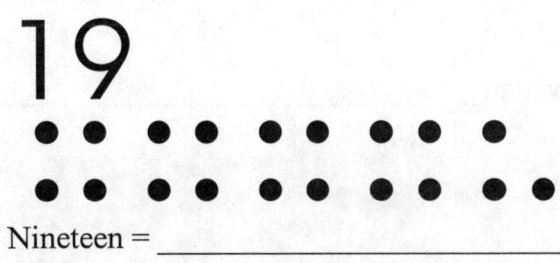

Nineteen = _____

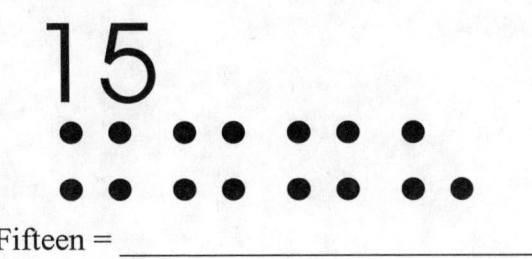

Fifteen = _____

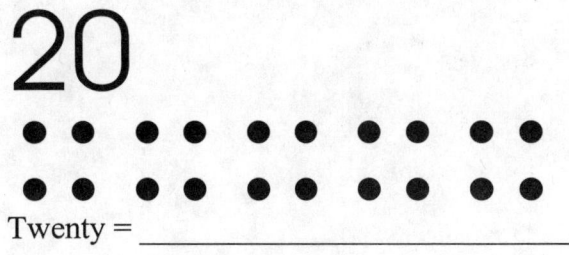

Twenty = _____

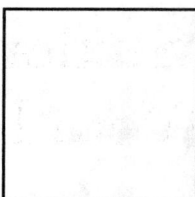

Square = _____

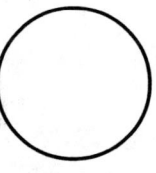

Circle = _____

Triangle = _____

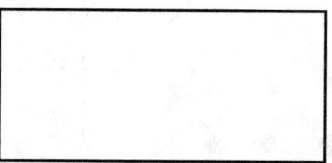

Rectangle = _____

Oval = _____

Section 7
The Dolch Basic Word List

This section includes the Dolch Basic Word List* translated into in the following languages:

English	German	Navajo
Arabic	Greek	Norwegian
Bengali	Hebrew	Persian (Farsi)
Cambodian	Hindi	Polish
Chinese	White Hmong	Portuguese
Croatian	Hungarian	Russian
Czech	Indonesian	Samoan
Danish	Italian	Spanish
Dutch	Japanese	Swedish
Filipino (Tagalog)	Korean	Thai
Finnish	Laotian	Tongan
French	Blue Mong	Vietnamese

*Reprinted by permission of the publisher from Edward W. Dolch, *220 Basic Sight Word List,* Garrard Publishing Company.

Dolch Basic Word List – English

Pre-primer

1. a _____
2. and _____
3. big _____
4. blue _____
5. can _____
6. come _____
7. down _____
8. for _____
9. funny _____
10. get _____
11. go _____
12. green _____
13. have _____
14. help _____
15. here _____
16. I _____
17. in _____
18. is _____
19. it _____
20. jump _____
21. little _____
22. look _____
23. make _____
24. me _____
25. my _____

26. not _____
27. play _____
28. red _____
29. ride _____
30. run _____
31. said _____
32. saw _____
33. see _____
34. the _____
35. this _____
36. to _____
37. up _____
38. want _____
39. we _____
40. with _____
41. work _____
42. you _____

Primer

1. all _____
2. am _____
3. are _____
4. at _____
5. away _____
6. black _____
7. but _____
8. came _____
9. did _____
10. do _____
11. eat _____
12. fast _____
13. find _____
14. good _____
15. he _____
16. laugh _____
17. like _____
18. new _____
19. no _____
20. now _____
21. on _____
22. one _____
23. out _____
24. please _____
25. put _____

26. ran _____
27. say _____
28. she _____
29. so _____
30. some _____
31. stop _____
32. thank _____
33. that _____
34. then _____
35. they _____
36. three _____
37. too _____
38. two _____
39. was _____
40. went _____
41. what _____
42. where _____
43. white _____
44. will _____
45. yellow _____
46. yes _____
47. your _____

First

1. about _____
2. after _____
3. again _____
4. an _____
5. around _____
6. as _____
7. ask _____
8. ate _____
9. be _____
10. before _____
11. brown _____
12. by _____
13. call _____
14. cold _____
15. could _____
16. can't _____
17. every _____
18. far _____
19. first _____
20. five _____

21. fly _____
22. found _____
23. four _____
24. from _____
25. gave _____
26. give _____
27. going _____
28. had _____
29. has _____
30. her _____
31. him _____
32. his _____
33. how _____
34. if _____
35. into _____
36. just _____
37. know _____
38. let _____
39. long _____
40. made _____

41. many _____
42. may _____
43. much _____
44. must _____
45. never _____
46. of _____
47. old _____
48. once _____
49. open _____
50. or _____
51. our _____
52. over _____
53. pretty _____
54. round _____
55. show _____
56. sing _____
57. sleep _____
58. soon _____
59. take _____

60. them _____
61. there _____
62. think _____
63. us _____
64. very _____
65. walk _____
66. were _____
67. when _____
68. who _____
69. why _____
70. wish _____

Second

1. always _____	21. hold _____	41. small _____
2. any _____	22. hot _____	42. start _____
3. because _____	23. hurt _____	43. tell _____
4. been _____	24. its _____	44. ten _____
5. best _____	25. keep _____	45. their _____
6. better _____	26. kind _____	46. these _____
7. both _____	27. light _____	47. those _____
8. bring _____	28. live _____	48. today _____
9. buy _____	29. myself _____	49. together _____
10. carry _____	30. off _____	50. try _____
11. clean _____	31. only _____	51. under _____
12. cut _____	32. own _____	52. upon _____
13. does _____	33. pick _____	53. use _____
14. done _____	34. pull _____	54. warm _____
15. drink _____	35. read _____	55. wash _____
16. fall _____	36. right _____	56. well _____
17. full _____	37. seven _____	57. which _____
18. goes _____	38. shall _____	58. would _____
19. got _____	39. sit _____	59. write _____
20. grow _____	40. six _____	60. draw _____
		61. eight _____

Dolch Basic Word List – Arabic

PRE-PRIMER

1. a — ✓
2. and — د
3. big — كبير
4. blue — ازرق
5. can — يقدر
6. come — جاء
7. down — تحت
8. for — لدن
9. funny — مضحك
10. get — حصل
11. go — اذهب
12. green — اخضر
13. have — له
14. help — ساعد
15. here — هنا
16. I — انا
17. in — في
18. is — يكون
19. it — شي
20. jump — يقفز
21. little — صغير
22. look — انظر
23. make — اعمل
24. me — انا
25. my — لي
26. not — لا
27. play — العب
28. red — احمر
29. ride — اركب
30. run — اركض
31. said — قال
32. saw — رأى
33. see — ينظر
34. the — ال..
35. this — هذا
36. to — الى
37. up — فوق
38. want — يحتاج
39. we — نحن
40. with — مع
41. work — شغل
42. you — انت

PRIMER

1. all — لكل
2. am — يكون
3. are — يكون
4. at — عند
5. away — بعيد
6. black — اسود
7. but — لكنه
8. came — اتى/جاء
9. did — عمل
10. do — يعمل
11. eat — يأكل
12. fast — سريع
13. find — يجد
14. good — جيد
15. he — هو

16. laugh — اضحى
17. like — مثل
18. new — جديد
19. no — لا
20. now — الان
21. on — على
22. one — واحد
23. out — خارج
24. please — من فضلك
25. put — ضع
26. ran — ركض
27. say — قل
28. she — هي
29. so — كذا
30. some — بعض
31. stop — قف
32. thank — اشكر
33. that — ذلك
34. then — عند ذلك
35. they — هم/هن
36. three — ثلاثة
37. too — ايضا
38. two — اثنان
39. was — كان
40. went — ذهب
41. what — ماذا
42. where — اين
43. white — ابيض

FIRST

44. will — ارادة/سوف
45. yellow — اصفر
46. yes — نعم
47. your — لك

1. about — نحو
2. after — بعد
3. again — ايضا
4. an — ✓
5. around — حول
6. as — مثل
7. ask — اسأل
8. ate — أكل
9. be — يكون
10. before — قبل
11. brown — بني
12. by — بجانب
13. call — ينادي
14. cold — بارد
15. could — يقدر
16. can't — غير قادر
17. every — كل
18. far — بعيد
19. first — اول
20. five — خمسة
21. fly — يطير
22. found — يجد
23. four — اربعة

24. from من	53. pretty جميلة	11. clean نظيف	40. six ستة
25. gave اعطى	54. round دائري	12. cut اقطع	41. small صغير
26. give يعطي	55. show يظهر	13. does يعمل	42. start ابدأ
27. going يذهب	56. sing غنى	14. done معمول	43. tell قل
28. had عنده	57. sleep نام	15. drink يشرب	44. ten عشرة
29. has له	58. soon حالاً/سريعاً	16. fall وقع	45. their لهم
30. her هي/لها	59. take خذ	17. full ملآن	46. these هؤلاء
31. him هو	60. them هم	18. goes يذهب	47. those هؤلاء
32. his له	61. there هناك	19. got استلم	48. today اليوم
33. how كيف	62. think فكر	20. grow نمى	49. together معاً
34. if اذا	63. us نحن	21. hold استلم	50. try حاول
35. into في/في داخل	64. very جداً	22. hot حار/ساخن	51. under تحت
36. just عادل	65. walk مشى	23. hurt مؤلم	52. upon فوقه
37. know يعرف	66. were كانوا	24. its لها	53. use استعمل
38. let اسمح	67. when عندما	25. keep احتفظ	54. warm دافئ
39. long طويل	68. who من	26. kind نوع	55. wash اغسل
40. made عمل	69. why لماذا	27. light نور	56. well بخير
41. many كثير	70. wish يتمنى	28. live يكن/يعيش	57. which الذي
42. may هل ممكن	**SECOND**	29. myself نفسي	58. would يقدر
43. much كثير	1. always دائماً	30. off اقفل	59. write اكتب
44. must يجب	2. any احد	31. only فقط	60. draw ارسم
45. never ابداً/لا	3. because لأن	32. own يحتفظ	61. eight ثمانية
46. of من	4. been كان	33. pick اجمع	
47. old قديم	5. best الاحسن	34. pull شد	
48. once مرة	6. better احسن	35. read اقرأ	**PRE-PRIMER**
49. open افتح	7. both كلاهما/كلاً	36. right صحيح	29. ride يركب
50. or او	8. bring احضر	37. seven سبعة	
51. our لنا	9. buy اشترى	38. shall سوف	**PRIMER**
52. over فوقه	10. carry احمل	39. sit اجلس	15. he هو

Dolch Basic Word List – Bengali

PRE-PRIMER

1. a আমি
2. and এবং
3. big বড়
4. blue নিল
5. can পারা
6. come আসা
7. down নিচে
8. for জন্য, ইচ্ছা
9. funny মজার
10. get পাওয়া
11. go যাওয়া
12. green সবুজ
13. have আছে, থাকা
14. help সাহায্য
15. here এখানে
16. I আমি
17. in ভিতরে
18. is হয়
19. it ইহা
20. jump লাফ
21. little ছোট
22. look দেখা
23. make তৈরি করা
24. me আমি
25. my আমার
26. not না
27. play খেলা
28. red লাল
29. ride চড়া

30. run ছোটা
31. said বলা
32. saw দেখিয়াছিল
33. see দেখা
34. the ইহা, ইহারা
35. this ইহা
36. to প্রতি
37. up উপরে
38. want চাওয়া
39. we আমরা
40. with সঙ্গে
41. work কাজ
42. you তুমি, আপনি

PRIMER

1. all সব
2. am আমি
3. are হয়
4. at তে, তাতে
5. away দূরে
6. black কালো
7. but কিন্তু
8. came আসিয়াছিল
9. did করা
10. do করা
11. eat খাওয়া
12. fast দ্রুত
13. find খোঁজা
14. good ভাল
15. he সে

16. laugh হাসা
17. like পছন্দ
18. new নতুন
19. no না
20. now এখন
21. on উপরে
22. one এক
23. out বাহিরে
24. please অনুগ্রহ
25. put রাখা
26. ran ছোটা
27. say বলা
28. she সে (মেয়ে)
29. so তাই, এতে
30. some কিছু
31. stop থামা
32. thank ধন্যবাদ
33. that উহা
34. then তারপর
35. they তাহারা
36. three তিন
37. too বেশি
38. two দুই
39. was ছিল
40. went গিয়াছিল
41. what কি
42. where কোথায়
43. white সাদা

44. will করিবে?
45. yellow হলুদ
46. yes হাঁ
47. your তোমার

FIRST

1. about সম্বন্ধে
2. after পরে
3. again আবার
4. an একটি
5. around চারিদিকে
6. as যেমন
7. ask জিজ্ঞাসা করা
8. ate খাইয়াছিল
9. be হওয়া
10. before পূর্বে
11. brown বাদামি
12. by দ্বারা
13. call ডাকা
14. cold ঠান্ডা
15. could পারিত
16. can't পারে না
17. every প্রত্যেক
18. far দূরে
19. first প্রথম
20. five পাঁচ
21. fly উড়া
22. found পাওয়া
23. four চার

24. from _____
25. gave _____
26. give _____
27. going _____
28. had _____
29. has _____
30. her _____
31. him _____
32. his _____
33. how _____
34. if _____
35. into _____
36. just _____
37. know _____
38. let _____
39. long _____
40. made _____
41. many _____
42. may _____
43. much _____
44. must _____
45. never _____
46. of _____
47. old _____
48. once _____
49. open _____
50. or _____
51. our _____
52. over _____

53. pretty _____
54. round _____
55. show _____
56. sing _____
57. sleep _____
58. Soon _____
59. take _____
60. them _____
61. there _____
62. think _____
63. us _____
64. very _____
65. walk _____
66. were _____
67. when _____
68. who _____
69. why _____
70. wish _____

SECOND

1. always _____
2. any _____
3. because _____
4. been _____
5. best _____
6. better _____
7. both _____
8. bring _____
9. buy _____
10. carry _____

11. clean _____
12. cut _____
13. does _____
14. done _____
15. drink _____
16. fall _____
17. full _____
18. goes _____
19. got _____
20. grow _____
21. hold _____
22. hot _____
23. hurt _____
24. its _____
25. keep _____
26. kind _____
27. light _____
28. live _____
29. myself _____
30. off _____
31. only _____
32. own _____
33. pick _____
34. pull _____
35. read _____
36. right _____
37. seven _____
38. shall _____
39. sit _____

40. six _____
41. small _____
42. start _____
43. tell _____
44. ten _____
45. their _____
46. these _____
47. those _____
48. today _____
49. together _____
50. try _____
51. under _____
52. upon _____
53. use _____
54. warm _____
55. wash _____
56. well _____
57. which _____
58. would _____
59. write _____
60. draw _____
61. eight _____

Dolch Basic Word List – Cambodian

Pre-primer

1. a _____ ម្យួ
2. and និង
3. big ធំ
4. blue ពណ៌ខៀវ
5. can អាច
6. come មក
7. down ក្រោម
8. for ដើម្បី
9. funny គួរឱ្យសើច
10. get ទទួល
11. go ទៅ
12. green ខៀវ
13. have មាន , ពុន
14. help ជួយ
15. here ទីនេះ
16. I ខ្ញុំ
17. in ក្នុង
18. is គឺ , ជា
19. it វា
20. jump លោត , ផ្លោះ
21. little បន្តិចបន្តួច
22. look មើល
23. make ធ្វើ
24. me ខ្ញុំ
25. my របស់ខ្ញុំ
26. not មិន , គ្មាន
27. play លេង
28. red ក្រហម
29. ride ជិះ

30. run រត់
31. said ពុននិយាយ
32. saw ពុនឃើញ
33. see ឃើញ
34. the បញ្ហាក់របស់មិន បំរោះ
35. this នេះ
36. to ក្រោះ
37. up លើ
38. want ចង់
39. we យើង
40. with ជាមួយ
41. work ធ្វើការ
42. you ឯង , លោក

PRIMER

1. all ទាំងអស់
2. am គឺ , ជា
3. are គឺ , ជា
4. at ឯ
5. away ឆ្ងាយ
6. black ពណ៌ខ្មៅ
7. but ប៉ុន្ដែ
8. came ពុនមក
9. did ពុនធ្វើ
10. do ធ្វើ
11. eat ស៊ី , ញ៉ាំ
12. fast រហ័ស
13. find រកឃើញ
14. good ល្អ , ស្អាត
15. he គាត់ , វា

16. laugh សើច
17. like ចូលចិត្ត
18. new ថ្មី
19. no ទេ , គ្មាន
20. now ឥឡូវ
21. on លើ
22. one មួយ , ចំនួនមួយ
23. out ក្រៅ
24. please សូម , និករាយ
25. put ដាក់ , ទុក
26. ran ពុនរត់
27. say និយាយ
28. she នាង , គាត់
29. so ដូចនេះ , អ៊ីចឹង
30. some ខ្លះ
31. stop ឈប់
32. thank អរគុណ
33. that នោះ
34. then បន្ទាប់
35. they ពួកគេ
36. three ចំនួន បី
37. too ផងដែរ
38. two ចំនួន ពីរ
39. was គឺ ពីមុន
40. went ពុនទៅ
41. what អ្វី
42. where ទីកន្លែង
43. white ពណ៌ ស

44. will នឹង , បំណង
45. yellow ពណ៌លឿង
46. yes ពុទ
47. your របស់លោក , អ្នក

FIRST

1. about អំពី , ប្រហែល
2. after ក្រោយ
3. again ទៀត , ថ្មីដល
4. an មួយ
5. around ជុំវិញ , ទៅវិញ ទៅមក
6. as ដូច , សើ
7. ask សូរ , ស៊ើរ
8. ate ពុនស៊ី , ពុនញ៉ាំ
9. be គឺ , ជា
10. before មុន , ពីមុន
11. brown ពណ៌ត្នោត
12. by ដោយ , ក៏ក្ប
13. call ហៅ
14. cold ត្រជាក់ , រងារ
15. could អាចពីមុន
16. can't មិនអាច
17. every គ្រប់ទាំងអស់
18. far ចម្ងាយឆ្ងាយ
19. first ទីមួយ
20. five ចំនួនប្រាំ
21. fly ហោះ៖ហើរ
22. found ពុនរកឃើញ
23. four ចំនួនបួន

#			#			#			#		
24.	from	ពី, មកពី	53.	pretty	ល្អ, ស្អាត	11.	clean	សំអាត	40.	six	ចំនួនប្រាំមួយ
25.	gave	បានឲ្យ	54.	round	មូល	12.	cut	កាត់	41.	small	តូច
26.	give	ឲ្យ	55.	show	បង្ហាញ	13.	does	វាធ្វើរធ្វើ	42.	start	ផ្ដើម
27.	going	នឹង, កំពុង	56.	sing	ច្រៀង	14.	done	បានធ្វើ, ធ្វើរួច	43.	tell	ប្រាប់
28.	had	មានកាលពីមុន	57.	sleep	ដេក, គេង	15.	drink	ផឹក	44.	ten	ម្ភ័ននដប់
29.	has	វាធ្វើរមាន	58.	soon	ឆាប់	16.	fall	ធ្លាក់ចុះ	45.	their	របស់ពួកគេ
30.	her	របស់នាង	59.	take	យក	17.	full	ពេញ	46.	these	ទាំងអស់នេះ
31.	him	ខ្លួនគាត់	60.	them	ខ្លួនគេទាំងអស់	18.	goes	វាធ្វើរទៅ	47.	those	ទាំងអស់នោះ
32.	his	របស់គាត់	61.	there	ទីនោះ	19.	got	បានទទួល	48.	today	ថ្ងៃនេះ
33.	how	យ៉ាងម៉េច	62.	think	គិត	20.	grow	ដុះដាល, វាលដាល	49.	together	រួមគ្នា, ជាមួយគ្នា
34.	if	ប្រសិនបើ	63.	us	ខ្លួនយើង	21.	hold	ទប់, កាន់	50.	try	សាក, ភ្លក្ស
35.	into	ទៅក្នុង	64.	very	យ៉ាងខ្លាំង	22.	hot	ក្ដៅ	51.	under	ក្រោម, ពីក្រោម
36.	just	ប៉ុណ្ណោះ	65.	walk	ដើរ	23.	hurt	ឈឺចាប់	52.	upon	ពីលើ, ពីក្រោយពី
37.	know	ដឹង	66.	were	គឺ, ជា, នៅពី្	24.	its	របស់វា	53.	use	ប្រើប្រាស់
38.	let	អនុញ្ញាតិ	67.	when	កាលណា, ពេល	25.	keep	រក្សា	54.	warm	ក្ដៅ, ក្ដៅរលម
39.	long	វែង	68.	who	នរណា, ដែល	26.	kind	ប្រភេទ	55.	wash	ដុសលាង
40.	made	បានធ្វើ	69.	why	ហេតុអ្វី	27.	light	ភ្លើង, ស្រាល	56.	well	ល្អប្រសើ
41.	many	ច្រើន	70.	wish	ប្រាថ្នា, ប៉ង	28.	live	រស់នៅ	57.	which	ដែល "របស់"
42.	may	អាច, មានសិទ្ធិ		SECOND		29.	myself	ខ្លួនខ្ញុំផ្ទាល់	58.	would	មានបំណងនឹង, ប្រហែល នឹង
43.	much	ច្រើនមិនអាចរាប់	1.	always	ជានិច្ច	30.	off	ពេញពី	59.	write	សរសេរ
44.	must	ត្រូវតែ	2.	any	ខ្លះ, មិនបំរពោះ	31.	only	ប៉ុណ្ណោះ	60.	draw	គូរ, ពត, ដក
45.	never	មិនធ្លាប់	3.	because	ពីព្រោះ	32.	own	ផ្ទាល់ខ្លួន	61.	eight	ប្រាំបី
46.	of	នៃ	4.	been	គឺ, ជា	33.	pick	រើស, ច្រើសរើស			
47.	old	ចាស់, ជរា	5.	best	ប្រសិត, អស្ចារ្យ	34.	pull	ទាញ			
48.	once	ម្ដង, ជាបន្លាស់	6.	better	ប្រសើរជាង	35.	read	អាន, មើល			
49.	open	បើក	7.	both	ទាំងខ្ទរ	36.	right	ស្ដាំ, ត្រូវ			
50.	or	ឬ	8.	bring	យកមក	37.	seven	ប្រាំពីរ			
51.	our	របស់យើង	9.	buy	ទិញ	38.	shall	នឹង			
52.	over	លើស, ពីលើ	10.	carry	ជញ្ជូន	39.	sit	អង្គុយ			

សរណ្ដា ២

Dolch Basic Word List – Chinese

PRE-PRIMER

1. a	一個	29. ride	騎,乘	14. good	好	42. where	那兒
2. and	和	30. run	跑	15. he	他	43. white	白色
3. big	大	31. said	說	16. laugh	笑	44. will	將
4. blue	藍色	32. saw	看	17. like	喜歡	45. yellow	黃色
5. can	能,會	33. see	看	18. new	新	46. yes	是
6. come	來	34. the	這,那	19. no	不,沒有	47. your	你的
7. down	下	35. this	這個	20. now	現在	FIRST	
8. for	為了	36. to	到	21. on	上,在…上	1. about	大約
9. funny	好玩,好笑	37. up	上	22. one	一	2. after	在…之後
10. get	得	38. want	要	23. out	外	3. again	再
11. go	去	39. we	我們	24. please	請	4. an	一個
12. green	綠色	40. with	和;共同	25. put	放	5. around	四面地,圍繞
13. have	有	41. work	工作,做	26. ran	跑	6. as	像,如
14. help	幫助	42. you	你	27. say	說	7. ask	問
15. here	這兒	PRIMER		28. she	她	8. ate	吃
16. I	我	1. all	全,所有	29. so	所以,這麼	9. be	是,為
17. in	裏,在…內	2. am	是	30. some	一些	10. before	在…之前
18. is	是	3. are	是	31. stop	停止	11. brown	咖啡色
19. it	它	4. at	在…地方	32. thank	謝謝	12. by	在…側,在…旁
20. jump	跳	5. away	走開	33. that	那個	13. call	叫,呼
21. little	小	6. black	黑色	34. then	然後	14. cold	冷
22. look	看	7. but	但是	35. they	他們	15. could	能
23. make	做	8. came	來了	36. three	三	16. can't	不能
24. me	我	9. did	做	37. too	太…,亦	17. every	每,各
25. my	我的	10. do	做	38. two	二	18. far	遠
26. not	不,不是	11. eat	吃	39. was	是	19. first	第一
27. play	遊玩,玩,劇	12. fast	快	40. went	去	20. five	五
28. red	紅色	13. find	找	41. what	什麼	21. fly	飛

22. found 找	52. over 在…之上	11. clean 乾淨	41. small 小
23. four 四	53. Pretty 漂亮	12. cut 切	42. start 開始
24. from 從	54. round 圓	13. does 做	43. tell 告訴
25. gave 給	55. show 顯示,劇	14. done 做	44. ten 十
26. give 給	56. sing 唱	15. drink 喝	45. their 他們的
27. going 去,走	57. sleep 睡	16. fall 倒	46. these 這些
28. had 有	58. soon 快	17. full 全,飽	47. those 那些
29. has 有	59. take 帶	18. goes 走,去	48. today 今天
30. her 她的	60. them 他們	19. got 得到	49. together 一起
31. him 他	61. there 那兒	20. grow 長	50. try 試
32. his 他的	62. think 想	21. hold 握,持	51. under 在…之下
33. how 如何	63. us 我們	22. hot 熱	52. upon 在…之上
34. if 如果	64. very 很	23. hurt 傷	53. use 用
35. into 到,進入	65. walk 走	24. its 它的	54. warm 溫暖
36. just 就,僅	66. were 是	25. keep 維持	55. wash 洗
37. know 知道	67. when 何時	26. kind 種類,仁慈	56. well 好
38. let 讓	68. who 誰	27. light 光,輕	57. which 那個
39. long 長	69. why 為什麼	28. live 活	58. would 會
40. made 做	70. wish 希望	29. myself 我自己	59. write 寫
41. many 許多	SECOND	30. off 離	60. draw 畫
42. may 可能	1. always 總是	31. only 僅,只有	61. eight 八
43. much 多	2. any 任何	32. own 擁有	
44. must 必須	3. because 因為	33. pick 挑	
45. never 從不	4. been 是	34. pull 拉	
46. of 屬於…	5. best 最好	35. read 讀	
47. old 老	6. better 好些	36. right 右,對	
48. once 一次	7. both 兩者	37. seven 七	
49. open 打開	8. bring 帶	38. shall 將	
50. or 或	9. buy 買	39. sit 坐	
51. our 我們的	10. carry 提	40. six 六	

Dolch Basic Word List – Croatian

Pre-primer

1. a __no article__
2. and __i__
3. big __veliko__
4. blue __plavo__
5. can __moći__
6. come __doći__
7. down __dolje__
8. for __za__
9. funny __smiješno__
10. get __dobiti__
11. go __ići__
12. green __zeleno__
13. have __imati__
14. help __pomoći__
15. here __ovdje__
16. I __ja__
17. in __u__
18. is __je__
19. it __to__
20. jump __skočiti__
21. little __maleno__
22. look __gledati__
23. make __napraviti__
24. please __molim__
25. my __moje__

26. not __ne__
27. play __igrati (se)__
28. red __crveno__
29. ride __voziti (se)__
30. run __trčati__
31. said __rekao (je)__
32. saw __vidio (je)__
33. see __vidjeti__
34. the __no article__
35. this __to__
36. to __prema__
37. up __gore__
38. want __htjeti__
39. we __mi__
40. with __sa__
41. work __raditi__
42. you __ti (vi, like *du* and *sie* in German)__

Primer

1. all __sve__
2. am __sam__
3. are __smo__
4. at __kod__
5. away __daleko__
6. black __drno__
7. but __ali__
8. came __došao (je)__
9. did __učinio (je)__
10. do __učiniti (je)__
11. eat __jesti__
12. fast __brzo__
13. find __naći__
14. good __dobro__
15. he __on__
16. laugh __smijati (se)__
17. like __voljeti__
18. new __novo__
19. no __ne__
20. now __sada__
21. on __na__
22. one __jedan__
23. out __van__
24. please __molim__
25. put __staviti__

26. ran __trčati__
27. say __reći__
28. she __ona__
29. so __tako__
30. some __nešto__
31. stop __stati__
32. thank __zanvaliti (se)__
33. that __to__
34. then __onda__
35. they __oni__
36. three __tri__
37. too __isto__
38. two __dva__
39. was __bio (je)__
40. went __išao (je)__
41. what __što (šta)__
42. where __gdje__
43. white __bejelo__
44. will __će__
45. yellow __žuto__
46. yes __da__
47. your __tvoj__

First

1. about ____o____
2. after __iza, poslje__
3. again ____opet____
4. an ___no article___
5. around ____oko____
6. as ____kao____
7. ask ____pitati____
8. ate ____jeo (je)____
9. be ____biti____
10. before ____prije____
11. brown ____smede____
12. by ____kod____
13. call ____zvati____
14. cold ____hladno____
15. could ___mogao (je)___
16. can't ____ne može____
17. every ____svaki____
18. far ____daleko____
19. first ____prvi____
20. five ____pet____

21. fly ____letjeti____
22. found ___našao (je)___
23. four ____četiri____
24. from ____od____
25. gave ____dao (je)____
26. give ____dati____
27. going ____idući____
28. had ____imao (je)____
29. has ____ima____
30. her ____njezino____
31. him ____njega____
32. his ____njegovo____
33. how ____kako____
34. if ____ako____
35. into ____u____
36. just ____baš____
37. know ____znati____
38. let ____dati____
39. long ____dugo____
40. made __napravio (je)__

41. many ____mnogo____
42. may ____može____
43. much ____puno____
44. must ____morati____
45. never ____nikad____
46. of ____od____
47. old ____star____
48. once ____jednom____
49. open ____otvoreno____
50. or ____ili____
51. our ____naš____
52. over ____preko____
53. pretty ____lijepo____
54. round ____okruglo____
55. show ____pokazati____
56. sing ____pjevati____
57. sleep ____spavati____
58. soon ____skoro____
59. take ____uzeti____

60. them ____njih____
61. there ____tamo____
62. think ____misliti____
63. us ____nas____
64. very ____jako____
65. walk ____ići____
66. were ____gdje____
67. when ____kad____
68. who ____tko____
69. why ____zašto____
70. wish ____željeti____

Second

1. always __uvijek__	21. hold __držati__	41. small __malo__
2. any __svaki__	22. hot __vruce__	42. start __početi__
3. because __jer__	23. hurt __boliti__	43. tell __recí__
4. been __bio__	24. its __njegovo__	44. ten __deset__
5. best __najbolje__	25. keep __čuvati__	45. their __njihovo__
6. better __bolje__	26. kind __dobar__	46. these __ovo__
7. both __oboje__	27. light __svijetlo__	47. those __ono__
8. bring __donijeti__	28. live __živjeti__	48. today __danas__
9. buy __kupiti__	29. myself __ja (sam)__	49. together __zajedno__
10. carry __nositi__	30. off _____	50. try __probati__
11. clean __čisto__	31. only __samo__	51. under __ispod__
12. cut __rezati__	32. own __imati__	52. upon __na (to)__
13. does _____	33. pick __dići__	53. use __upotrijebiti__
14. done __napravljeno__	34. pull __vući__	54. warm __toplo__
15. drink __piti__	35. read __čitati__	55. wash __prati__
16. fall __pasti__	36. right __desno__	56. well __dobro__
17. full __pun__	37. seven __sedam__	57. which __koje__
18. goes __ide__	38. shall __ću__	58. would __bi__
19. got __ima__	39. sit __sjediti__	59. write __pisati__
20. grow __rasti__	40. six __šest__	60. draw __crtati__
		61. eight __osam__

Dolch Basic Word List – Czech

Pre-primer

1. a neurč. člen (jeden)
2. and _____ a _____
3. big _____ veliký _____
4. blue _____ modrý _____
5. can mohu, dovedu
6. come přicházím
7. down dolu, dole
8. for _____ pro _____
9. funny _____ legrační _____
10. get _____ dostávám _____
11. go _____ jdu _____
12. green _____ zelený _____
13. have _____ mám _____
14. help pomáhám, pomoc
15. here _____ zde _____
16. I _____ já _____
17. in _____ v _____
18. is _____ je _____
19. it _____ to _____
20. jump _____ skáčui _____
21. little _____ malý _____
22. look _____ dívám se _____
23. make dělám, vyrábím
24. please _____ prosím _____
25. my _____ můj _____

26. not ne- (zápor. castice)
27. play hraji, hraji si
28. red _____ červený _____
29. ride _____ jedu _____
30. run _____ běžim _____
31. said _____ řekl jsem _____
32. saw _____ viděl jsem _____
33. see _____ vidím _____
34. the urč. člen (ten)
35. this _____ toto _____
36. to k (předl s 3.pádem)
37. up _____ nahoru _____
38. want _____ chci _____
39. we _____ my _____
40. with _____ s _____
41. work _____ pracuji _____
42. you _____ ty, vy _____

Primer

1. all všichni, všechno
2. am _____ jsem _____
3. are jsme, jste, jsou
4. at _____ při, u, ve _____
5. away _____ pryč _____
6. black _____ černý _____
7. but _____ ale _____
8. came _____ přišel jsem _____
9. did _____ dělal jsem _____
10. do _____ dělám _____
11. eat _____ jim _____
12. fast rychlý, rychle
13. find _____ nacházím _____
14. good _____ dobrý _____
15. he _____ on _____
16. laugh _____ směji se _____
17. like mám rád, jako
18. new _____ nový _____
19. no _____ ne, žádný _____
20. now _____ nyní _____
21. on _____ na _____
22. one _____ jeden _____
23. out _____ ven _____
24. please _____ prosím _____
25. put _____ pokládám _____

26. ran _____ běžel jsem _____
27. say _____ říkám _____
28. she _____ ona _____
29. so _____ tak _____
30. some _____ trochu _____
31. stop zastavuji, zastávka
32. thank _____ děkuji _____
33. that _____ tamten, že _____
34. then _____ než _____
35. they _____ oni _____
36. three _____ tři _____
37. too _____ také, přiliš _____
38. two _____ dva _____
39. was byl, byla, bylo
40. went _____ šel jsem _____
41. what _____ co _____
42. where _____ kde, kam _____
43. white _____ bílý _____
44. will _____ budu, chci _____
45. yellow _____ žlutý _____
46. yes _____ ano _____
47. your _____ tvj, váš _____

First

1. about kolem, okolo, asi
2. after _____po_____
3. again __opět__
4. an neurč. člen (jeden)
5. around dokola, okolo
6. as _____jak_____
7. ask ____ptám se____
8. ate ____jedl jsem____
9. be _____býti_____
10. before před (časově)
11. brown __hnědý__
12. by _____u, vedle_____
13. call ____volám____
14. cold studený, nachlazení
15. could __mohl bych__
16. can't __nemohu__
17. every __každy__
18. far __daleký, daleko__
19. first __první__
20. five _____pět_____

21. fly __letím, moucha__
22. found __našel jsem__
23. four __čtyři__
24. from ____od____
25. gave ____dal jsem____
26. give ____dávám____
27. going __právě jdu__
28. had __měl jsem__
29. has _____má_____
30. her __její, ji, ni u__
31. him __jemu, mu__
32. his ____jeho____
33. how ____jak____
34. if _____jestliže_____
35. into ____dovnitř____
36. just jenom, právě, přesně
37. know ____vím____
38. let _____nechat_____
39. long ____dlouhý____
40. made udělal jsem, vyrobil

41. many ____mnoho____
42. may ____smím____
43. much ____hodně____
44. must ____musím____
45. never ____nikdy____
46. of (předl s 2. pádem)
47. old ____starý____
48. once ____jednou____
49. open otevírám, otevřený
50. or _____nebo_____
51. our _____náš_____
52. over _____přes_____
53. pretty pěkný, dosti
54. round ____kulatý____
55. show ukazuji představení
56. sing ____zpívám____
57. sleep ____spím____
58. soon ____brzy____
59. take _____beru_____

60. them jim, nich, jim
61. there ____tam____
62. think __myslím__
63. us ____náš, nám____
64. very velmi, skutečný
       prodázím se,
65. walk __procházka__
       byli jsme/jste,
66. were ____byli____
67. when kdy, když
68. who ____kdo____
69. why ____proč____
70. wish přeji si, přánií

Second

1. always __vždy__
2. any __jakýkoliv__
3. because __protože__
4. been __slovesa "býti"__ minulý tvar
5. best __nejlepší__
6. better __lepší, raději__
7. both __oba__
8. bring __přináším__
9. buy __kupuji__
10. carry __nesu__
11. clean __čistím, čistý__
12. cut __sekám, střih__
13. does __dělá__
14. done __uděláno__
15. drink __piji, nápoj__
16. fall __padám, pád, podzim__
17. full __plný__
18. goes __jde__
19. got __dostal jsem__
20. grow __rostu, pěstuji__

21. hold __držím__
22. hot __horký__
23. hurt __zranit__
24. its __jeho__
25. keep __zůstávám, nechávám__
26. kind __druh, milý__
27. light __světlo, světlý__
28. live __žiji__
29. myself __já sám__
30. off __pryč__
31. only __jenom pouze, jedíný__
32. own __vlastní__
33. pick __zvedám, sbírám__
34. pull __vytahuji__
35. read __čtu, četl jsem__
36. right __pravý, správný__
37. seven __sedm__
38. shall __budu__
39. sit __sedím__
40. six __šest__

41. small __malý__
42. start __začínám, začátek__
43. tell __říkám__
44. ten __deset__
45. their __jejich__
46. these __tyto, tato__
47. those __tamty, tamta__
48. today __dnes__
49. together __dohromady, spolu__
50. try __pokouším se, snazím se__
51. under __pod__
52. upon __na__
53. use __uživám__
54. warm __teplý__
55. wash __umývám__
56. well __dobře__
57. which __který, jenž__
58. would __bych, byste, by__
59. write __piši__
60. draw __kreslím, táhnu__
61. eight __osm__

Dolch Basic Word List – Danish

Pre-primer

1. a ___EN___	26. not ___IKKE___
2. and ___OG___	27. play ___LEGE___
3. big ___STOR___	28. red ___RØD___
4. blue ___BLAA___	29. ride ___RIDE___
5. can ___KAN___	30. run ___LØBE___
6. come ___KOMME___	31. said ___SAGDE___
7. down ___NED___	32. saw ___SAA___
8. for ___FOR___	33. see ___SE___
9. funny ___MORSOM___	34. the ___DET___
10. get ___TAGE___	35. this ___DETTE___
11. go ___GAA___	36. to ___TIL___
12. green ___GRØN___	37. up ___OP___
13. have ___HAR___	38. want ___ØNSKE___
14. help ___HJELP___	39. we ___OS___
15. here ___HER___	40. with ___MED___
16. I ___JEG___	41. work ___ARBEJDE___
17. in ___I___	42. you ___DE or DU___
18. is ___ER___	
19. it ___DET___	
20. jump ___SPRING___	
21. little ___LILLE___	
22. look ___SE___	
23. make ___LAVE___	
24. me ___JEG___	
25. my ___MIN___	

Primer

1. all ___ALLE___	26. ran ___LØB___
2. am ___ER___	27. say ___SIGE___
3. are ___ER___	28. she ___HUN___
4. at ___PAA or VED___	29. so ___SAA___
5. away ___VÆKÆ___	30. some ___NOGLE___
6. black ___SORT___	31. stop ___STOP___
7. but ___MEN___	32. thank ___TAK___
8. came ___KOM___	33. that ___DET___
9. did ___GJORDE___	34. then ___SAA___
10. do ___GØRE___	35. they ___DE___
11. eat ___SPISE___	36. three ___TRE___
12. fast ___HURTIGT___	37. too ___TIL___
13. find ___FINDE___	38. two ___TO___
14. good ___GOD___	39. was ___VAR___
15. he ___HAN___	40. went ___GIK___
16. laugh ___LE___	41. what ___HVAD___
17. like ___LIDE___	42. where ___HVOR___
18. new ___NY___	43. white ___HVIDT___
19. no ___NEJ___	44. will ___VIL___
20. now ___NU___	45. yellow ___GUL___
21. on ___PAA___	46. yes ___JA___
22. one ___EN___	47. your ___DIN-DERES___
23. out ___UD___	
24. please ___VÆR SAA VENLIG___	
25. put ___LÆG___	

First

1. about <u>CIRCA NÆSTEN</u>
2. after <u>EFTER</u>
3. again <u>IGEN</u>
4. an <u>ET or EN</u>
5. around <u>RUNDTOM</u>
6. as <u>SOM</u>
7. ask <u>SPØRGE</u>
8. ate <u>SPISTE</u>
9. be <u>BLIVE/VÆRE</u>
10. before <u>FØR</u>
11. brown <u>BRUN</u>
12. by <u>VED</u>
13. call <u>KALDE</u>
14. cold <u>KOLD</u>
15. could <u>KUND</u>
16. can't <u>KAN IKKE</u>
17. every <u>ALLE</u>
18. far <u>FJERNT</u>
19. first <u>FØRST</u>
20. five <u>FEM</u>

21. fly <u>FLYVE</u>
22. found <u>FINDE</u>
23. four <u>FIRE</u>
24. from <u>FRA</u>
25. gave <u>GAV</u>
26. give <u>GIVE</u>
27. going <u>GAAR</u>
28. had <u>HAVDE</u>
29. has <u>HAR</u>
30. her <u>HENDE</u>
31. him <u>HAM</u>
32. his <u>HANS</u>
  HVORLEDES'
33. how <u>HVORDAN</u>
34. if <u>HVIS</u>
35. into <u>INDI</u>
  BARE
36. just <u>RETFÆROIG</u>
37. know <u>VED</u>
38. let <u>LAD</u>
39. long <u>LANG</u>
40. made <u>LAVET-GJORT</u>

41. many <u>MANGE</u>
42. may <u>MAA</u>
43. much <u>MEGET</u>
44. must <u>SKAL</u>
45. never <u>ALDRIG</u>
46. of <u>AF</u>
47. old <u>GAMMEL</u>
48. once <u>ENGANG</u>
49. open <u>AABEN</u>
50. or <u>ELLER</u>
51. our <u>VORES</u>
52. over <u>OVER</u>
53. pretty <u>PÆN</u>
54. round <u>RUND</u>
55. show <u>FORESTILLING</u>
56. sing <u>SYNGE</u>
57. sleep <u>SOVE</u>
58. soon <u>SNART</u>
59. take <u>TAGE</u>

60. them <u>DEM</u>
61. there <u>DER</u>
62. think <u>TÆNKE</u>
63. us <u>OS</u>
64. very <u>MEGET</u>
65. walk <u>GAA</u>
66. were <u>VAR</u>
67. when <u>HVORNAAR</u>
68. who <u>HVEM</u>
69. why <u>HVORFOR</u>
70. wish <u>ONSKE</u>

Second

1. always ALTID
2. any NOGLE
3. because FORDI
4. been VÆRET
5. best BEDSTE
6. better BEDRE
7. both BEGGE
8. bring BRINGE
9. buy KØBE
10. carry BÆRE
11. clean REN
12. cut SNIT
13. does GØR
14. done GJORDT
15. drink TAAR
16. fall FALDE
17. full FULD
18. goes GAAR
19. got HAR-FIK
20. grow VOKSE

21. hold HOLDE
22. hot VARM
23. hurt GØRONDT
24. its DETS DENS
25. keep BEHOLDE
26. kind SLAGS
27. light LYS
28. live LEVENDE
29. myself MIGSELV
30. off AF
31. only KUN
32. own EGEN
33. pick PLUKKE
34. pull TRÆKKE
35. read LÆSE
36. right RIGTIGT
37. seven SYV
38. shall SKAL
39. sit SIDDE
40. six SEKS

41. small LILLE
42. start BEGYNDE
43. tell FORTÆLLE
44. ten TI
45. their DERES
46. these DIS'S'E
47. those DE
48. today I DAG
49. together TILSAMMEN
50. try PRØVE
51. under UNDER
52. upon PAA
53. use BRUGE
54. warm VARM
55. wash VADSKE
56. well GODT
57. which HVILKEN
58. would VILDE
59. write SKRIVE
60. draw TEGNE
61. eight OTTE

Dolch Basic Word List – Dutch

Pre-primer

1. a __een__
2. and __en__
3. big __groot__
4. blue __blauw__
5. can __kan/kunnen__
6. come __kom/komen__
7. down __beneden__
8. for __voor__
9. funny __grappig/leuk__
10. get __krijg/krÿgen__
11. go __gaan__
12. green __groen__
13. have __heb/hebben__
14. help __help/helpen__
15. here __hier__
16. I __ik/ikself__
17. in __in__
18. is __is__
19. it __het__
20. jump __spring/springen__
21. little __klein__
22. look __kijk/kÿken__
23. make __maak/maken__
24. me __ik__
25. my __mijn__

26. not __niet__
27. play __spelen__
28. red __rood__
29. ride __rijden/rit__
30. run __ren/rennen__
31. said __zei/zeiden__
32. saw __zag/zagen__
33. see __zie/zien__
34. the __de__
35. this __dit__
36. to __naar__
37. up __op__
38. want __wil/willen__
39. we __wij__
40. with __met__
41. work __werk/werken__
42. you __jij__

Primer

1. all __alles__
2. am __ben__
3. are __zijn__
4. at __bij__
5. away __weg__
6. black __zwart__
7. but __maar__
8. came __kwam__
9. did __gedaan__
10. do __doen__
11. eat __eet/eten__
12. fast __vlug__
13. find __vind/vinden__
14. good __goed__
15. he __hij__
16. laugh __lach/lachen__
17. like __gelijk, houden van__
18. new __nieuw__
19. no __nee__
20. now __nu__
21. on __aan__
22. one __een__
23. out __uit__
24. please __alstublieft__
25. put __zet/zetten__

26. ran __gerend__
27. say __zeg/zeggen__
28. she __zij__
29. so __zo__
30. some __iets/enige__
31. stop __stop/stoppen__
32. thank __dank/danken__
33. that __dat__
34. then __dan__
35. they __zij (plural)__
36. three __drie__
37. too __ook__
38. two __twee__
39. was __was__
40. went __ging/gingen__
41. what __wat__
42. where __waar__
43. white __wit__
44. will __wil/willen__
45. yellow __geel__
46. yes __ja__
47. your __jouw__

First

1. about ___bijna___
2. after ___na___
3. again ___nogmaals___
4. an ___een___
5. around ___rond___
6. as ___als___
7. ask ___vraag/vragen___
8. ate ___at/aten___
9. be ___zijn___
10. before ___voor___
11. brown ___bruin___
12. by ___bij___
13. call ___roep/roepen___
14. cold ___koud___
15. could ___kan/kunnen___
16. can't ___kan nict___
17. every ___ieder___
18. far ___ver___
19. first ___eerst___
20. five ___vijf___

21. fly ___vlieg/vliegen___
22. found ___vond/vonden___
23. four ___vier___
24. from ___van___
25. gave ___gaf/gaven___
26. give ___geef/geven___
27. going ___ga/gaan___
28. had ___had/hadden___
29. has ___heeft___
30. her ___haar___
31. him ___hem___
32. his ___zijn___
33. how ___hoe___
34. if ___als___
35. into ___in___
36. just ___juist___
37. know ___weet/weten___
38. let ___laat/laten___
39. long ___lang___
40. made ___gemaakt___

41. many ___veel/velen___
42. may ___mag/mogen___
43. much ___veel___
44. must ___moet/moeten___
45. never ___nooit___
46. of ___van___
47. old ___oud___
48. once ___eens___
49. open ___open___
50. or ___of___
51. our ___ons___
52. over ___over___
53. pretty ___mooi___
54. round ___rond___
55. show ___laten zien/vertonen___
56. sing ___zing/zingen___
57. sleep ___slaap/slapen___
58. soon ___gauw___
59. take ___neem/nemen___

60. them ___hun___
61. there ___daar___
62. think ___denk/denken___
63. us ___ons___
64. very ___zeer___
65. walk ___loop/lopen___
66. were ___waren___
67. when ___wanneer___
68. who ___wie___
69. why ___waarom___
70. wish ___wens/wensen___

Second

1. always __altijd__
2. any __eenige__
3. because __omdat__
4. been __geweest__
5. best __best__
6. better __beter__
7. both __beide__
8. bring __breng/brengen__
9. buy __koop/kopen__
10. carry __draag/dragen__
11. clean __schoon__
12. cut __snijden__
13. does __doet__
14. done __gedaan__
15. drink __drink/drinken__
16. fall __val/vallen__
17. full __vol__
18. goes __gaat__
19. got __kreeg__
20. grow __groei/groeien__

21. hold __houden__
22. hot __heet__
23. hurt __pijin doen/zeer doen__
24. its __het__
25. keep __houd/bewaar houden/bewaren__
26. kind __aardig/vriendelÿk__
27. light __licht__
28. live __leef/leven__
29. myself __mÿzelf__
30. off __af__
31. only __alleen__
32. own __eigen__
33. pick __plukken__
34. pull __trek/trekken__
35. read __lees/lezen__
36. right __recht__
37. seven __zeven__
38. shall __zal/zullen__
39. sit __zit/zitten__
40. six __zes__

41. small __smal/klein__
42. start __begin/beginnen__
43. tell __vertellen__
44. ten __tien__
45. their __hun__
46. these __deze__
47. those __deze__
48. today __vandaag__
49. together __samen__
50. try __probeer/proberen__
51. under __onder__
52. upon __op__
53. use __gebruik/gebruiken__
54. warm __warm__
55. wash __was__
56. well __gezond/wel__
57. which __welk__
58. would __zou/zouden__
59. write __schryf/schrÿven__
60. draw __teken/tekenen__
61. eight __acht__

Dolch Basic Word List – Filipino (Tagalog)

Pre-primer

1. a ___ibang___
2. and ___at___
3. big ___malaki___
4. blue ___asul/bughaw___
5. can ___maaari___
6. come ___halika___
7. down ___ibaba___
8. for ___para___
9. funny ___nakakatawa___
10. get ___kunin___
11. go ___pumunta___
12. green ___berde___
13. have ___may/mayroon___
14. help ___tulong___
15. here ___dito/dine___
16. I ___ako___
17. in ___sa/sa loob___
18. is ___ay___
19. it ___iyon___
20. jump ___tumalon___
21. little ___maliit___
22. look ___fingnan___
23. make ___gawin___
24. me ___akin___
25. my ___akin___

26. not ___hindi___
27. play ___larô___
28. red ___pulá___
29. ride ___sumakay___
30. run ___tumakbó___
31. said ___sinabi___
32. saw ___nakita___
33. see ___makita/tignan___
34. the ___ang___
35. this ___ito___
36. to ___sa___
37. up ___sa itaas___
38. want ___gusto___
39. we ___kami/tayo___
40. with ___sa/namin___
41. work ___trabaho___
42. you ___ikaw___

Primer

1. all ___lahát___
2. am ___ay___
3. are ___ay___
4. at ___at___
5. away ___malayo___
6. black ___itim___
7. but ___pero/ngunit___
8. came ___dumating___
9. did ___ginawa___
10. do ___gawín___
11. eat ___kumain___
12. fast ___mabilis___
13. find ___hanapin___
14. good ___mabuti___
15. he ___siya___
16. laugh ___tumawa___
17. like ___gusto___
18. new ___bágo___
19. no ___hindî___
20. now ___ngayón___
21. on ___sa/ibábaw___
22. one ___isa___
23. out ___sa/labás___
24. please ___paki___
25. put ___ilagay___

26. ran ___tumakbo___
27. say ___sabi/sinabi___
28. she ___siya___
29. so ___gayon___
30. some ___ilán___
31. stop ___hintô___
32. thank ___salamat___
33. that ___iyan/iyon___
34. then ___pagkatapos/noón___
35. they ___sila___
36. three ___tatlo___
37. too ___din/rin___
38. two ___dalawa___
39. was ___ay___
40. went ___umalís___
41. what ___ano___
42. where ___saan___
43. white ___putî___
44. will ___gustuhin___
45. yellow ___dilaw___
46. yes ___oo___
47. your ___iyo___

First

1. about __tungkól sa__	21. fly __lumipad__	41. many __marami__	60. them __sila__
2. after __pagkatápos__	22. found natagpuan/nakita	42. may __sana__	61. there __doon__
3. again __mulî__	23. four __apat__	43. much __morami__	62. think __mag-isip__
4. an __isang__	24. from __mulâ/buhat__	44. must __dapat__	63. us __kami/tayo__
5. around __sa paligid__	25. gave __binigay__	45. never kailan man hindî	64. very __napaka__
6. as __bilang__	26. give __mag bigay__	46. of __ng/ni__	65. walk __lumakad__
7. ask __itanóng__	27. going __aalis/pag-alis__	47. old __matanda__	66. were __ay__
8. ate __kumáin__	28. had __nagkaroon/ay__	48. once minsan/isang/beses	67. when __kailan__
9. be __ay/maging__	29. has __ay/mayroon__	49. open __bukas/buksan__	68. who __sino__
10. before __bago/dati__	30. her __kaniya__	50. or __o__	69. why __bakit__
11. brown kulay/tsokolate	31. him __kaniya__	51. our __amin/atin__	70. wish pangarap/sana
12. by __sa/sa tabi__	32. his __kaniya__	52. over __sa ibabaw__	
13. call __tawag/tawagin__	33. how __paano__	53. pretty __kaakit-akit marikit__	
14. cold __malamíg__	34. if __kung__	54. round __mabilog__	
15. could __maaarí__	35. into __sa/sa loob__	55. show __palabas/ipakita__	
16. can't hindi maaarí	36. just __lamang/tapat__	56. sing __kanta__	
17. every __bawat__	37. know __alam__	57. sleep __tulog__	
18. far __malayó__	38. let __bayaan__	58. soon __malapit na__	
19. first __una__	39. long __mahaba__	59. take __kunin__	
20. five __lima__	40. made __ginawá/gawá__		

Second

1. always ___lagí___
2. any ___alinman___
3. because ___dahil/kasi___
4. been ___ay___
5. best ___pinaka-mabuti___
6. better ___mas mabuti___
7. both ___pareho___
8. bring ___magdala/dalhin___
9. buy ___bili___
10. carry ___bitbitin___
11. clean ___linisin/malinis___
12. cut ___putol/magputol___
13. does ___gumagawâ___
14. done ___nagawa___
15. drink ___uminom/inumin___
16. fall ___taglagas/malaglag___
17. full ___punó___
18. goes ___lumakad/umalis___
19. got ___nakuha___
20. grow ___tumubó___

21. hold ___hawakan___
22. hot ___mainit___
23. hurt ___masakit___
24. its ___Kaniya/nitó/ niya niyan___
25. keep ___itago___
26. kind ___urî/mabait___
27. light ___sindihan/ilaw___
28. live ___buhay/mabuhay___
29. myself ___aking/sarili___
30. off ___mulâ rito/ mulâ ngayon___
31. only ___lamang___
32. own ___sarili___
33. pick ___pulutin___
34. pull ___hilahin___
35. read ___mag basa/basahin___
36. right ___tamá___
37. seven ___pitó___
38. shall ___ay___
39. sit ___maupo/umupo___
40. six ___anim___

41. small ___maliit___
42. start ___magsimula/simulá___
43. tell ___sabihin___
44. ten ___sampû___
45. their ___kanila___
46. these ___ito___
47. those ___iyón___
48. today ___ngayon___
49. together ___magkasama/ sama-sama___
50. try ___subukan/subukin___
51. under ___sa ilalim___
52. upon ___sa/sa ibabaw ng___
53. use ___gamitin___
54. warm ___malagihay___
55. wash ___maghugas___
56. well ___mabuti___
57. which ___alin___
58. would ___ay___
59. write ___sumulat/isulat___
60. draw ___gumuhit/bumunot___
61. eight ___walo___

Dolch Basic Word List – Finnish

Pre-primer

1. a ___-___	26. not ___ei___
2. and ___ja___	27. play ___leikkiä___
3. big ___iso, suuri___	28. red ___punainen___
4. blue ___sininen___	29. ride ___ratsastaa, ajaa___
5. can ___voida___	30. run ___juosta___
6. come ___tulla___	31. said ___sanoi___
7. down ___alas, alhaalla___	32. saw ___näki___
8. for ___-, varten___	33. see ___nähdä___
9. funny ___hassunkurinen___	34. the ___-___
10. get ___saada___	35. this ___tämä___
11. go ___mennä___	36. to ___-, (ending: -lle)___
12. green ___vihreä___	37. up ___ylös, ylhäällä___
13. have ___minulla on___	38. want ___tahtoa, haluta___
14. help ___auttaa, apu___	39. we ___me___
15. here ___tässä, täällä___	40. with ___mukana, kanssa, kera___
16. I ___minä___	41. work ___työ, tehdä työtä___
17. in ___-, sisässä, sisällä___	42. you ___sinä, te___
18. is ___on___	
19. it ___se___	
20. jump ___hypätä___	
21. little ___pieni___	
22. look ___katsoa___	
23. make ___tehdä___	
24. please ___ole hyvä___	
25. my ___minun___	

Primer

1. all ___kaikki___	26. ran ___juoksi___
2. am ___olen___	27. say ___sanoa___
3. are ___olet, olemme, olette, ovat___	28. she ___hän___
4. at ___-, luona___	29. so ___niin___
5. away ___pois, poissa___	30. some ___jotakin, hiukan___
6. black ___musta___	31. stop ___pysähtyä___
7. but ___mutta, vaan___	32. thank ___kiittää, kiitos___
8. came ___tuli___	33. that ___että, tuo, joka___
9. did ___teki___	34. then ___sitten___
10. do ___tehdä___	35. they ___he___
11. eat ___syödä___	36. three ___kolme___
12. fast ___nopea, nopeasti___	37. too ___liian, myös___
13. find ___löytää___	38. two ___kaksi___
14. good ___hyvä___	39. was ___oli___
15. he ___hän___	40. went ___meni___
16. laugh ___naurra___	41. what ___mikä___
17. like ___pitää___	42. where ___missä___
18. new ___uusi___	43. white ___valkoinen___
19. no ___ei___	44. will ___-___
20. now ___nyt___	45. yellow ___keltainen___
21. on ___-, päällä___	46. yes ___kyllä___
22. one ___yksi___	47. your ___sinun; teidän___
23. out ___ulos, ulkona___	
24. please ___ole hyvä___	
25. put ___panna___	

First

1. about ___-___
2. after ___jälkeen___
3. again ___jälleen, taas___
4. an ___-___
5. around ___ympäri___
6. as ___kuin, kuten___
7. ask ___kysyä, pyytää___
8. ate ___söi___
9. be ___olla___
10. before ___ennen___
11. brown ___ruskea___
12. by ___-___
13. call ___soittaa, kutsua___
14. cold ___kylmä___
15. could ___voi, voisi___
16. can't ___ei voi___
17. every ___jokainen___
18. far ___kauas, kaukana___
19. first ___ensimmäinen___
20. five ___viisi___

21. fly ___lentää___
22. found ___löysi___
23. four ___neljä___
24. from ___-___
25. gave ___antoi___
26. give ___antaa___
27. going ___menossa___
28. had ___minulla oli___
29. has ___hänellä on___
30. her ___hänen___
31. him ___hänelle, häntä___
32. his ___hänen___
33. how ___kuinka, miten___
34. if ___jos___
35. into ___-___
36. just ___juuri___
37. know ___tietää, tuntea___
38. let ___antaa, sallia___
39. long ___pitkä___
40. made ___teki___

41. many ___moni, monta___
42. may ___voi, saa___
43. much ___paljon___
44. must ___täytyy___
45. never ___ei koskaan___
46. of ___-___
47. old ___vanha___
48. once ___kerran___
49. open ___avata, avoin___
50. or ___tai, eli___
51. our ___meidän___
52. over ___-, yli___
53. pretty ___kaunis, soma___
54. round ___pyöreä___
55. show ___näyttää___
56. sing ___laulaa___
57. sleep ___nukkua___
58. soon ___pian___
59. take ___ottaa___

60. them ___heille, heitä___
61. there ___siellä, sinne___
62. think ___ajatella, luulla___
63. us ___meille, meitä___
64. very ___hyvin___
65. walk ___kävellä___
66. were ___olit, olimme olitte, olivat,___
67. when ___kun, koska?___
68. who ___kuka, ketkä___
69. why ___miksi___
70. wish ___toivoa, toivottaa___

Second

1. always ___aina___
2. any ___yhtään___
3. because ___koska___
4. been ___ollut___
5. best ___paras___
6. better ___parempi___
7. both ___molemmat___
8. bring ___tuoda___
9. buy ___ostaa___
10. carry ___kantaa___
11. clean ___puhdas___
12. cut ___leikata___
13. does ___tekee___
14. done ___tehnyt___
15. drink ___juoda___
16. fall ___pudota___
17. full ___täysi___
18. goes ___menee___
19. got ___sai___
20. grow ___kasvaa___

21. hold ___pitää___
22. hot ___kuuma___
23. hurt ___satuttaa, koskea___
24. its ___sen___
25. keep ___pitää___
26. kind ___ystävällinen___
27. light ___valoisa, kevyt, valo, valaista___
28. live ___elää___
29. myself ___itse___
30. off ___-___
31. only ___vain, ainoa___
32. own ___oma___
33. pick ___poimia, valita___
34. pull ___vetää___
35. read ___lukea___
36. right ___oikea, oikein___
37. seven ___seitsemän___
38. shall ___-___
39. sit ___istua___
40. six ___kuusi___

41. small ___pieni___
42. start ___alkaa___
43. tell ___kertoa, käskeä___
44. ten ___kymmenen___
45. their ___heidän___
46. these ___nämä___
47. those ___nuo___
48. today ___tänään___
49. together ___yhdessä___
50. try ___yrittää___
51. under ___alla, alle___
52. upon ___päällä___
53. use ___käyttää___
54. warm ___lämpöinen___
55. wash ___pestä___
56. well ___hyvin___
57. which ___mikä, joka___
58. would ___tahtoisi___
59. write ___kirjoittaa___
60. draw ___piirtää___
61. eight ___kahdeksan___

Dolch Basic Word List – French

Pre-primer

1. a ___un, une___
2. and ___et___
3. big ___gros___
4. blue ___bleu___
5. can ___pouvoir___
6. come ___venir___
7. down ___en bas___
8. for ___pour___
9. funny ___amusant___
10. get ___obtenir___
11. go ___aller___
12. green ___vert___
13. have ___avoir___
14. help ___aider___
15. here ___ici___
16. I ___Je___
17. in ___dans___
18. is ___est___
19. it ___il, elle___
20. jump ___sauter___
21. little ___petit___
22. look ___regarder___
23. make ___faire___
24. me ___moi___
25. my ___ma, mon___

26. not ___pas___
27. play ___jouer___
28. red ___rouge___
29. ride ___conduire___
30. run ___courir___
31. said ___dit___
32. saw ___vu___
33. see ___voir___
34. the ___le, la, les___
35. this ___ce___
36. to ___à___
37. up ___en haut___
38. want ___vouloir___
39. we ___nous___
40. with ___avec___
41. work ___travailler___
42. you ___vous, tu___

Primer

1. all ___tout, tous___
2. am ___suis___
3. are ___sommes___
4. at ___à___
5. away ___loin___
6. black ___noir___
7. but ___mais___
8. came ___venu___
9. did ___fait___
10. do ___faire___
11. eat ___manger___
12. fast ___vite___
13. find ___trouver___
14. good ___bon___
15. he ___il___
16. laugh ___rire___
17. like ___aimer___
18. new ___nouveau___
19. no ___non___
20. now ___maintenant___
21. on ___sur___
22. one ___un___
23. out ___denors___
24. please ___s'il vous plaît___
25. put ___mettre___

26. ran ___couru___
27. say ___dire___
28. she ___elle___
29. so ___ainsi___
30. some ___quelques___
31. stop ___arrêter___
32. thank ___merci___
33. that ___ce___
34. then ___alors___
35. they ___ils, elles___
36. three ___trois___
37. too ___aussi___
38. two ___deux___
39. was ___étais___
40. went ___parti___
41. what ___qui, que___
42. where ___où___
43. white ___blanc___
44. will ___vouloir___
45. yellow ___jaune___
46. yes ___oui___
47. your ___votre___

First

1. about __à peu près__
2. after __après__
3. again __encore__
4. an __un, une__
5. around __autour__
6. as __comme__
7. ask __demander__
8. ate __mangé__
9. be __être__
10. before __avant__
11. brown __marron__
12. by __par__
13. call __appeler__
14. cold __froid__
15. could __pourriez__
16. can't __ne pas pouvoir__
17. every __chaque__
18. far __loin__
19. first __premier__
20. five __cinq__

21. fly __voler__
22. found __trouver__
23. four __quatre__
24. from __de__
25. gave __donné__
26. give __donner__
27. going __il part__
28. had __eu__
29. has __a__
30. her __sa, son__
31. him __lui__
32. his __sa, son__
33. how __comment__
34. if __si__
35. into __dans__
36. just __juste__
37. know __savoir, connaître__
38. let __laisser__
39. long __long__
40. made __fait__

41. many __plusieurs__
42. may __pouvoir__
43. much __beaucoup__
44. must __devoir__
45. never __jamais__
46. of __de__
47. old __vieux__
48. once __une fois__
49. open __ouvrir__
50. or __ou__
51. our __notre__
52. over __par-dessus__
53. pretty __joli__
54. round __rond__
55. show __montrer__
56. sing __chanter__
57. sleep __dormir__
58. soon __bientôt__
59. take __prendre__

60. them __eux, elles__
61. there __là__
62. think __penser__
63. us __à nous__
64. very __trés__
65. walk __marcher__
66. were __étiez__
67. when __quand__
68. who __qui__
69. why __pourquoi__
70. wish __souhaiter__

Second

1. always __toujours__
2. any __quelque__
3. because __parce que__
4. been __été__
5. best __le mieux__
6. better __meilleur__
7. both __tous les deux__
8. bring __apporter__
9. buy __acheter__
10. carry __transporter__
11. clean __nettoyer__
12. cut __couper__
13. does __faire__
14. done __fait__
15. drink __boire__
16. fall __tomber__
17. full __plein__
18. goes __aller__
19. got __obtenu__
20. grow __pousser__

21. hold __tenir__
22. hot __chaud__
23. hurt __faire mal__
24. its __sa, son, ses__
25. keep __garder__
26. kind __gentil__
27. light __lumière__
28. live __habiter__
29. myself __moi-même__
30. off __au loin__
31. only __seulement__
32. own __posséder__
33. pick __cueillir__
34. pull __tirer__
35. read __lire__
36. right __droit__
37. seven __sept__
38. shall __devoir__
39. sit __s'asseoir__
40. six __six__

41. small __petit__
42. start __commencer__
43. tell __dire__
44. ten __dix__
45. their __leur, leurs__
46. these __ces__
47. those __ces__
48. today __aujord'hui__
49. together __ensemble__
50. try __essayer__
51. under __dessous__
52. upon __sur__
53. use __utiliser__
54. warm __tiède__
55. wash __laver__
56. well __bien__
57. which __lequel__
58. would __voudriez__
59. write __écrire__
60. draw __dessiner__
61. eight __huit__

Dolch Basic Word List – German

Pre-primer

1. a ____ein____

2. and ____und____

3. big ____gross____

4. blue ____blau____

5. can ____kann, können____

6. come ____kommen____

7. down ____herunter____

8. for ____für____

9. funny ____komisch____

10. get ____holen, bekommen____

11. go ____gehen____

12. green ____grün____

13. have ____haben____

14. help ____helfen____

15. here ____hier____

16. I ____ich____

17. in ____in____

18. is ____ist____

19. it ____es____

20. jump ____springen____

21. little ____klein____

22. look ____sehen____

23. make ____machen____

24. me ____mich____

25. my ____mein____

26. not ____nicht____

27. play ____spielen____

28. red ____rot____

29. ride ____reiten, fahren____

30. run ____rennen____

31. said ____sagte____

32. saw ____sah____

33. see ____sehen____

34. the ____der, die, das____

35. this ____dieses____

36. to ____zu____

37. up ____auf____

38. want ____wünschen____

39. we ____wir____

40. with ____mit____

41. work ____arbeiten____

42. you ____du____

Primer

1. all ____alle____

2. am ____bin____

3. are ____sind, seid____

4. at ____bei____

5. away ____fort____

6. black ____schwarz____

7. but ____aber____

8. came ____kam____

9. did ____tat____

10. do ____tun____

11. eat ____essen____

12. fast ____schnell____

13. find ____finden____

14. good ____gut____

15. he ____er____

16. laugh ____lachen____

17. like ____wie____

18. new ____neu____

19. no ____nein____

20. now ____jetzt____

21. on ____auf____

22. one ____eins____

23. out ____aus____

24. please ____bitte____

25. put ____setzen, stellen, legen____

26. ran ____lief____

27. say ____sagen____

28. she ____sie____

29. so ____so____

30. some ____einige____

31. stop ____halten____

32. thank ____danke____

33. that ____das____

34. then ____dann____

35. they ____sie____

36. three ____drei____

37. too ____auch____

38. two ____zwei____

39. was ____war____

40. went ____ging____

41. what ____was____

42. where ____wo____

43. white ____weiss____

44. will ____will____

45. yellow ____gelb____

46. yes ____ja____

47. your ____dein____

First

1. about ___etwa___
2. after ___nach___
3. again ___wieder___
4. an ___ein___
5. around ___herum___
6. as ___wie___
7. ask ___fragen___
8. ate ___ass___
9. be ___sein___
10. before ___vor___
11. brown ___braun___
12. by ___durch, bei___
13. call ___rufen___
14. cold ___kalt___
15. could ___konnte___
16. can't ___kann nicht___
17. every ___jede(r) (s)___
18. far ___weit___
19. first ___zuerst___
20. five ___funf___

21. fly ___fliegen___
22. found ___fand___
23. four ___vier___
24. from ___von___
25. gave ___gab___
26. give ___geben___
27. going ___gehen___
28. had ___hatte___
29. has ___hat___
30. her ___ihr___
31. him ___ihm___
32. his ___sein___
33. how ___wie___
34. if ___falls, wenn, ob___
35. into ___in___
36. just ___gerade___
37. know ___wissen, verstehen___
38. let ___lassen___
39. long ___lange___
40. made ___machte___

41. many ___viele___
42. may ___dürfen___
43. much ___viel___
44. must ___muss, müssen___
45. never ___nie___
46. of ___von, vom___
47. old ___alt___
48. once ___einmal___
49. open ___offen___
50. or ___oder___
51. our ___unser___
52. over ___vorüber, darüber___
53. pretty ___hübsch___
54. round ___rund___
55. show ___zeigen___
56. sing ___singen___
57. sleep ___schlafen___
58. soon ___bald___
59. take ___nehmen___

60. them ___sie, ihnen___
61. there ___dort___
62. think ___denken___
63. us ___uns___
64. very ___sehr___
65. walk ___gehen___
66. were ___waren___
67. when ___wann___
68. who ___wer___
69. why ___warum___
70. wish ___wünschen___

Second

1. always ___immer___
2. any ___irgend___
3. because ___weil___
4. been ___gewesen___
5. best ___am besten___
6. better ___besser___
7. both ___beide___
8. bring ___bringen___
9. buy ___kaufen___
10. carry ___tragen___
11. clean ___saubern, sauber___
12. cut ___schneiden___
13. does ___tut___
14. done ___getan___
15. drink ___trinken___
16. fall ___fallen___
17. full ___voll___
18. goes ___geht___
19. got ___bekam___
20. grow ___wachsen___

21. hold ___halten___
22. hot ___heiss___
23. hurt ___wehtun___
24. its ___sein___
25. keep ___behalten___
26. kind ___gütig, sorte___
27. light ___licht, leicht, hell___
28. live ___leben___
29. myself ___ich selbst, mir selber___
30. off ___ab, davon___
31. only ___nur___
32. own ___eigen___
33. pick ___aussuchen___
34. pull ___ziehen___
35. read ___lesen___
36. right ___richtig, rechts___
37. seven ___sieben___
38. shall ___werden, sollen___
39. sit ___sitzen___
40. six ___sechs___

41. small ___klein___
42. start ___anfangen___
43. tell ___sagen, erzählen___
44. ten ___zehn___
45. their ___ihr___
46. these ___diese___
47. those ___jene___
48. today ___heute___
49. together ___zusammen___
50. try ___versuchen___
51. under ___unter___
52. upon ___auf___
53. use ___benutzen___
54. warm ___warm___
55. wash ___waschen___
56. well ___gut___
57. which ___welches___
58. would ___würde___
59. write ___schreiben___
60. draw ___ziehen, zeichnen___
61. eight ___acht___

Dolch Basic Word List -- Greek

Pre-primer

1. a   ἕυα, μία
2. and   καί
3. big   μεγάλο
4. blue   γαλαυό
5. can   μπορῶ
6. come   ἔρχομαι
7. down   κάτω
8. for   γιά
9. funny   ἀστεῖο
10. get   παίρνω
11. go   πηαίνω
12. green   πράσινο
13. have   ἔχω
14. help   βοηθῶ
15. here   ἐδῶ
16. I   Ἐγώ
17. in   μέοα
18. is   εἶναι
19. it   αὐτό
20. jump   πηδῶ
21. little   μικρό
22. look   κοιτάζω
23. make   φτιάχνω
24. me   ἐμέ
25. my   μου

26. not   δέν
27. play   παίζω
28. red   κόκκινο
29. ride   πηγαραίνω με τό αὐτοκίνητο
30. run   τρέχω
31. said   εἶπα
32. saw   εἶδα
33. see   βλέπω
34. the   ὁ, ἡ, τό
35. this   αὐτό
36. to   εἰς τό
37. up   ἐπάνω
38. want   θέλω
39. we   ἐμεῖς
40. with   μέ
41. work   δουλεύω
42. you   ἐσύ

Primer

1. all   ὅλοι
2. am   εἶμαι
3. are   εἶναι
4. at   στό
5. away   πέρα
6. black   μαῦρο
7. but   ἀλλά
8. came   ἦλθα
9. did   ἔκανα
10. do   κάνω
11. eat   τρώγω
12. fast   γρήγορα
13. find   εὑρίσκω
14. good   καλό
15. he   αὐτός
16. laugh   γελῶ
17. like   μοῦ ἀρέσει
18. new   καινούριο
19. no   ὄχι
20. now   τώρα
21. on   πάνω
22. one   ἕνα
23. out   ἔξω
24. please   παρακαλῶ
25. put   βάνω

26. ran   ἔτρεξα
27. say   λέγω
28. she   αὐτή
29. so   ἐπομένως
30. some   μερικά
31. stop   σταματῶ
32. thank   εὐχάριστῶ
33. that   ἐκεῖνο
34. then   τότε
35. they   αὐτοί
36. three   τρία
37. too   ἐπίσης
38. two   δύο
39. was   ἦταν
40. went   ἐπῆγα
41. what   τί
42. where   ποῦ
43. white   ἄσπρο
44. will   θά
45. yellow   κίτρινο
46. yes   μάλιστα ναί
47. your   σου

First

1. about περίπου
2. after μετά
3. again πάλι
4. an ἕναα
5. around γύρω
6. as καθώς
7. ask ἐρωτῶ
8. ate ἔφαγαα
9. be νά εἶνααι
10. before πρίν
11. brown καστανό
12. by δίπλα
13. call καλῶ
14. cold κρύο
15. could μποροῦσα
16. can't δέν μπορῶ
17. every κάθε
18. far μακρυά
19. first πρῶτο
20. five πέντε

21. fly πετῶ
22. found βρῆκα
23. four τέσσερα
24. from ἀαπό
25. gave ἔδωσα
26. give δίνω
27. going πηλαίνω
28. had εἶχάα
29. has ἔχει
30. her ἀαυτήν
31. him ἀαυτόν
32. his του
33. how πῶς
34. if ἐάν
35. into μέσα
36. just ἀαπλῶς
37. know ξέρω
38. let ἀαφήνω
39. long μακρύ
40. made ἔφτιαξα

41. many πολλά
42. may μπορῶ
43. much πολύ
44. must πρέπει
45. never ποτέ
46. of τοῦ, τῆς
47. old παλαιό
48. once μιά φορά
49. open ἀανοίγω
50. or ἤ
51. our μάάς
52. over ἀαπό πάνω
53. pretty ὄμορφο
54. round στρογγυλό
55. show δείχνω
56. sing τράάγουδῶ
57. sleep κοιμᾶμαι
58. soon σύντομάά
59. take παίρνω

60. them ἀαυτούς
61. there ἐκεῖ
62. think νομίζω
63. us ἐμᾶς
64. very παρά
65. walk περπατῶ
66. were ἦσαν
67. when πότε
68. who ποιός
69. why γιατί
70. wish εὔχομαι

Second

1. always __πάντοτε__
2. any __ὁπωσδήποτε__
3. because __ἐπειδή__
4. been __θά ἦτο__
5. best __κάλλιστο__
6. better __καλύτερο__
7. both __καί τό δύο__
8. bring __φέρω__
9. buy __ἀαγοράζω__
10. carry __μεταφέρω__
11. clean __καθαρίζω__
12. cut __κόβω__
13. does __κάνει__
14. done __καμομένο__
15. drink __πίνω__
16. fall __πέφτω__
17. full __γεμάτο__
18. goes __πηγααίνει__
19. got __ἐπῆρα__
20. grow __μεγααλώνω__

21. hold __κρατῶ__
22. hot __ζεστό__
23. hurt __πονῶ__
24. its __ἀαυτοῦ__
25. keep __φυλλάγω__
26. kind __εἶδος__
27. light __φῶς__
28. live __ζῶ__
29. myself __ἐγώ ὁ ἴδιος__
30. off __ἀαπό__
31. only __μόνον__
32. own __δ ι κό μου__
33. pick __διαλέγω__
34. pull __τραβῶ__
35. read __διαβάζω__
36. right __δεξιό,σωστό__
37. seven __ἑπτά__
38. shall __θά__
39. sit __κάθομαι__
40. six __ἔξη__

41. small __μικρό__
42. start __ἀαρχίζω__
43. tell __λέγω__
44. ten __δέκα__
45. their __τους__
46. these __ἀαυτά__
47. those __ἐκεῖναα__
48. today __σήμερα__
49. together __μάάζύ__
50. try __προσπάάθῶ__
51. under __ἀαπό κάτω__
52. upon __ἐπάνω__
53. use __χρησιμοποιῶ__
54. warm __ζεσρό__
55. wash __πλένω__
56. well __κάλα, πηγάδι__
57. which __ποιό__
58. would __θά__
59. write __γράφω__
60. draw __ζωγράάφίζω__
61. eight __ὀκτώ__

Dolch Basic Word List – Hebrew

PRE-PRIMER

1. a _____
2. and ___ ־ו
3. big ___ גדול
4. blue ___ כחול
5. can ___ יכול
6. come ___ בא
7. down ___ למטה
8. for ___ ־ל , עבור
9. funny ___ מצחיק
10. get ___ מקבל
11. go ___ הולך
12. green ___ ירוק
13. have ___ יש ־ל
14. help ___ עזר
15. here ___ כאן
16. I ___ אני
17. in ___ ב־
18. is _____
19. it ___ הוא , היא
20. jump ___ קופץ
21. little ___ קטן , קטנה
22. look ___ מביט
23. make ___ עושה
24. me ___ אותי , לי
25. my ___ שלי
26. not ___ לא
27. play ___ משחק
28. red ___ אדום
29. ride ___ רוכב , נוסע

30. run ___ רץ
31. said ___ אמר
32. saw ___ ראה
33. see ___ רואה
34. the ___ ה־
35. this ___ זה , זאת
36. to ___ ־ל , אל
37. up ___ למעלה
38. want ___ רוצה
39. we ___ אנחנו
40. with ___ עם
41. work ___ עבודה
42. you ___ אתה , אתם

PRIMER

1. all ___ הכל , כל
2. am _____
3. are _____
4. at ___ ב־ , אצל
5. away ___ הרחק
6. black ___ שחור
7. but ___ אבל
8. came ___ בא
9. did ___ עשה
10. do ___ עושה
11. eat ___ אוכל
12. fast ___ מהר
13. find ___ מוצא
14. good ___ טוב
15. he ___ הוא

16. laugh ___ צוחק
17. like ___ אוהב
18. new ___ חדש
19. no ___ לא
20. now ___ עכשיו
21. on ___ על
22. one ___ אחד
23. out ___ החוצה
24. please ___ בבקשה
25. put ___ שם
26. ran ___ רץ
27. say ___ אומר
28. she ___ היא
29. so ___ כך
30. some ___ אחדים , קצת
31. stop ___ עצור
32. thank ___ תודה
33. that ___ ההוא , הוא
34. then ___ אז
35. they ___ הם
36. three ___ שלוש
37. too ___ גם
38. two ___ שניים
39. was ___ היה
40. went ___ הלך
41. what ___ מה
42. where ___ איפה
43. white ___ לבן

44. will _____
45. yellow ___ צהוב
46. yes ___ כן
47. your ___ שלך

FIRST

1. about ___ בערך
2. after ___ אחרי
3. again ___ שוב
4. an _____
5. around ___ מסביב
6. as ___ כמו
7. ask ___ שואל
8. ate ___ אכל
9. be ___ להיות
10. before ___ לפני
11. brown ___ חום
12. by ___ על יד
13. call ___ קורא , משחק , טלפון
14. cold ___ קר
15. could ___ יכול
16. can't ___ לא יכול
17. every ___ כל
18. far ___ רחוק
19. first ___ ראשון
20. five ___ חמש
21. fly ___ עף
22. found ___ מצא
23. four ___ ארבע

24. from ___	53. pretty ___	11. clean ___	40. six ___
25. gave ___	54. round ___	12. cut ___	41. small ___
26. give ___	55. show ___	13. does ___	42. start ___
27. going ___	56. sing ___	14. done ___	43. tell ___
28. had ___	57. sleep ___	15. drink ___	44. ten ___
29. has ___	58. soon ___	16. fall ___	45. their ___
30. her ___	59. take ___	17. full ___	46. these ___
31. him ___	60. them ___	18. goes ___	47. those ___
32. his ___	61. there ___	19. got ___	48. today ___
33. how ___	62. think ___	20. grow ___	49. together ___
34. if ___	63. us ___	21. hold ___	50. try ___
35. into ___	64. very ___	22. hot ___	51. under ___
36. just ___	65. walk ___	23. hurt ___	52. upon ___
37. know ___	66. were ___	24. its ___	53. use ___
38. let ___	67. when ___	25. keep ___	54. warm ___
39. long ___	68. who ___	26. kind ___	55. wash ___
40. made ___	69. why ___	27. light ___	56. well ___
41. many ___	70. wish ___	28. live ___	57. which ___
42. may ___	SECOND	29. myself ___	58. would ___
43. much ___	1. always ___	30. off ___	59. write ___
44. must ___	2. any ___	31. only ___	60. draw ___
45. never ___	3. because ___	32. own ___	61. eight ___
46. of ___	4. been ___	33. pick ___	
47. old ___	5. best ___	34. pull ___	
48. once ___	6. better ___	35. read ___	
49. open ___	7. both ___	36. right ___	
50. or ___	8. bring ___	37. seven ___	
51. our ___	9. buy ___	38. shall ___	
52. over ___	10. carry ___	39. sit ___	

Dolch Basic Word List – Hindi

PRE-PRIMER

1. a — एक (one)
2. and — और
3. big — बड़ा
4. blue — नीला
5. can — सकना
6. come — आईये
7. down — नीचे
8. for — के लिये
9. funny — अजीब
10. get — लिधाना
11. go — जाओ
12. green — हरा
13. have — पास है
14. help — मदद
15. here — यहाँ
16. I — मै
17. in — अन्दर
18. is —
19. it — यह
20. jump — कूदना
21. little — थोड़ा
22. look — देखो
23. make — बनाना
24. me — मै
25. my — मेरा
26. not — नहीं
27. play — खेलना
28. red — लाल
29. ride — चढ़ना

30. run — दौड़ना
31. said — कहा
32. saw — देखा
33. see — देखो
34. the — एक
35. this — यह
36. to — को
37. up — ऊपर
38. want — चाहिये
39. we — हम
40. with — साथ में
41. work — काम
42. you — तुम, आप

PRIMER

1. all — सब
2. am —
3. are —
4. at — पर
5. away — दूर
6. black — काला
7. but — पर
8. came — आया
9. did — किया
10. do — करो
11. eat — खाओ
12. fast — तेज़
13. find — पता करना
14. good — अच्छा
15. he — वह

16. laugh — हंसना
17. like — पसन्द
18. new — नया
19. no — ना
20. now — अभी
21. on — पर
22. one — एक
23. out — बाहर
24. please — कृपा
25. put — डालो
26. ran — दौड़ा
27. say — कहो
28. she — वह
29. so — तो
30. some — कुछ
31. stop — रुको
32. thank — मेहरबानी, शुक्रीया
33. that — वह
34. then — फिर
35. they — वे
36. three — तीन
37. too —
38. two — दो
39. was — था
40. went — गया
41. what — क्या
42. where — कहाँ
43. white — सफेद

44. will —
45. yellow — पीला
46. yes — हाँ
47. your — तुम्हारा

FIRST

1. about —
2. after — मेरे बाद
3. again — फिर
4. an —
5. around — चारो तरफ
6. as —
7. ask — पूछो
8. ate — खाया
9. be —
10. before — पहले
11. brown — भूरा
12. by — से
13. call — बुलाओ
14. cold — ठंडा
15. could — कर सकना
16. can't — नहीं कर सकना
17. every — सब
18. far — दूर
19. first — पहला
20. five — पांच
21. fly — उड़ना
22. found — मिला
23. four — चार

24. from — से
25. gave — दिया
26. give — दिया
27. going — जाना
28. had — था
29. has — है
30. her — उसका
31. him — उसको
32. his — उसका
33. how — कैसे
34. if — अगर
35. into — अन्दर
36. just — सिर्फ
37. know — मालूम
38. let — जाने दो
39. long — बड़ा
40. made — बनाया
41. many — बहुत
42. may — शायद
43. much — ज्यादा
44. must — ज़रूर
45. never — कभी नही
46. of — का
47. old — पुराना
48. once — एक बार
49. open — खोलो
50. or — या
51. our — हमारे
52. over — ऊपर

53. pretty — अच्छा
54. round — गोल
55. show — दिखाओ
56. sing — गाना
57. sleep — सोना
58. Soon — बहुत जल्दी
59. take — लो
60. them — उनको
61. there — उधर
62. think — सोचो
63. us — हम
64. very — बहुत
65. walk — चलना
66. were — वे
67. when — कब
68. who — कौन
69. why — क्यूँ
70. wish — काश

SECOND

1. always — हमेशा
2. any — कोई भी
3. because — इसलिये
4. been —
5. best — सबसे अच्छा
6. better — उससे अच्छा
7. both — दोनो
8. bring — लिआओ
9. buy — खरीदना
10. carry — पकड़ो

11. clean — साफ
12. cut — काटना
13. does — करना
14. done — किया
15. drink — पीना
16. fall — गिरा
17. full — भरा हुआ
18. goes — जाना
19. got — मिला
20. grow — बढ़ना
21. hold — पकड़ना
22. hot — गर्म
23. hurt — ज़ख्म
24. its — यह
25. keep — रखना
26. kind — दयाल
27. light — बिजली
28. live — रहना
29. myself — मुझे
30. off — उतरना
31. only — सिर्फ
32. own — मेरा
33. pick — चुनना
34. pull — खींचना
35. read — पढ़ना
36. right — ठीक
37. seven — सात
38. shall —
39. sit — बैठो

40. six — छः
41. small — छोटा
42. start — शुरू करना
43. tell — कहो
44. ten — दस
45. their — उनके
46. these — यह
47. those — वह
48. today — आज
49. together — दोनो मिलकर
50. try — कोशिश
51. under — अन्दर
52. upon — ऊपर
53. use — इस्तमाल
54. warm — कुनकुना
55. wash — धोना
56. well — बेहतर
57. which — कौनसा
58. would —
59. write — लिखो
60. draw — खींचो
61. eight — आठ

Dolch Basic Word List -- White Hmong

Pre-primer

1. a ib (siv tau rau xws li) (ib tug miv) etc.
2. and thiab
3. big loj
4. blue xiav (siv xiav)
5. can muaj cuab kav
6. come los, tuaj
7. down nqis hav
8. for rau, yog
9. funny lom zem
10. get muab
11. go mus
12. green ntsuab (siv ntsuab)
13. have muaj
14. help pab, cawm
15. here qhov nov, ntawm nov
16. I kuv
17. in hauv (nyob hauv)
18. is yog
19. it nws
20. jump caws qia
21. little me ntsis, me
22. look xyuas, saib
23. make ua, tsim
24. please mog, yuad
25. my kuv li

26. not tsi
27. play ua si
28. red liab (siv liab)
29. ride caij (caij nees)
30. run khiav
31. said hais (tag los lawm) pom, (tag los) kaw,
32. saw xyuas, ntsia
33. see xyuas, pom, ntsia
34. the
35. this qhov nov
36. to txog
37. up saum, (nyob siab)
38. want xav tau
39. we peb
40. with nrog, uake, sib xws
41. work ua hauj lwm, num
42. you koj

Primer

txhia tsav, tag huv
1. all tib, si
2. am yog (siv rau kuv) yog (koj yog,
3. are nej yog)
4. at qhov ntawd
5. away tawm mus, txav deb
6. black dub (siv dub)
7. but tiam sis los, tuaj
8. came (tag los)
9. did ua (tag los lawm)
10. do ua
11. eat noj
12. fast ceev, nrawm, sai
13. find pom, ntsib
14. good zoo
15. he nws (txiv neej)
16. laugh luag
17. like nyiam, ib yam, sibluag
18. new tshiab
19. no tsi, (tsi tau)
20. now tam sim no
21. on saum
22. one ib
23. out tawm, rho, nraum
24. please mog, yuad
25. put ntsaws rau

26. ran qhiav (tag los)
27. say hais
28. she nws (poj niam) ib yam
29. so (ib yam li)
30. some me ntsis
31. stop nres
32. thank ua tsaug
33. that tom, ntawd
34. then tom qab ntawd
35. they lawv
36. three peb
37. too ib yam, sib npaug
38. two ob
39. was yog (tag los)
40. went mus (tag los)
41. what dab tsi
42. where qhov twg
43. white dawb
44. will yuav (tom ntej)
45. yellow daj
46. yes wj, yog, awj
47. your koj li

First

1. about <u>kwv yees</u> (*ntshig txog*)
2. after <u>tom qab ntawd</u>
3. again <u>dua thiab</u>
4. an <u>ib qhov (siv rau tsav xwb)</u>
5. around <u>ncig</u>
6. as <u>xws li</u>
7. ask <u>nug, thom</u>
8. ate <u>noj (tag los)</u>
9. be <u>yog</u>
10. before <u>ua ntej</u>
11. brown _____
12. by <u>nrog, uake, dhau</u>
13. call <u>hu</u>
14. cold <u>no</u>
15. could <u>muaj cuab kav</u>
16. can't <u>tsi muaj cuab kav</u>
17. every <u>txhia txhia (tsav)</u>
18. far <u>deb deb</u>
19. first _____
20. five <u>tsib</u>

21. fly <u>ya</u>
22. found <u>ntsib, pom, tau</u>
23. four <u>plaub</u>
24. from <u>los, tuaj, ncaim</u>
25. gave <u>muab (tag los)</u>
26. give <u>muab</u>
27. going <u>mus (tab tom)</u>
28. had <u>muaj (tag los)</u>
29. has <u>muaj (nws muaj)</u>
30. her <u>nws (poj niam)</u>
31. him <u>nws (txiv neej)</u>
32. his <u>nws li (txiv neej)</u>
33. how <u>yuav ua li cas</u>
34. if <u>yog tias</u>
35. into <u>huav, ncaj nraim mus</u>
36. just <u>nyuam qhuav</u>
37. know <u>paub</u>
38. let <u>kom</u>
39. long <u>ntev, qeeb</u>
40. made <u>ua (tag los)</u>

41. many <u>ntau ntau</u>
42. may <u>tej zaum</u>
43. much <u>ntau (siv rau tsav suav tsitau)</u>
44. must <u>yuav tsum</u>
45. never <u>tsi txeev</u>
46. of <u>yog, uas yog</u>
47. old <u>lau</u>
48. once <u>ib zaug</u>
49. open <u>qhib</u>
50. or <u>los yog</u>
51. our <u>peb li</u>
52. over <u>dhau lawm, hla</u>
53. pretty <u>zoo, zoo nkauj</u>
54. round <u>ncig</u>
55. show <u>qhia, yam</u>
56. sing <u>hu nkauj</u>
57. sleep <u>tsaug zog</u>
58. soon <u>tsi ntev, ti ti (tsi ntev saum ntej no)</u>
59. take <u>muab, nqa</u>

60. them <u>lawv</u>
61. there <u>tom</u>
62. think <u>xav</u>
63. us <u>peb</u>
64. very <u>ntau</u>
65. walk <u>muskev</u>
66. were <u>yog (tag los)</u>
67. when <u>thaum twg</u>
68. who <u>leej twg</u>
69. why <u>vim li ca</u>
70. wish <u>xav tau</u>

Second

1. always <u>tib yam, sib laug</u>	21. hold <u>tuav, coj, nqa npaj, txheem</u>	41. small <u>me</u>
2. any <u>tej tsav</u>	22. hot <u>kuv, ceev</u>	42. start <u>chiv, pib, cuab</u>
3. because <u>rau qhov</u>	23. hurt <u>mob</u>	43. tell <u>qhia</u>
4. been <u>yog (tag los)</u>	24. its <u>nws li</u>	44. ten <u>kaum</u>
5. best <u>zoo kawg</u>	25. keep <u>ceev cia, khaws cia, tuav cia</u>	45. their <u>lawv li</u>
6. better <u>zoo dua</u>	26. kind <u>tsav</u>	46. these <u>tsav no</u>
7. both <u>ob tug, obtsav, nkawm</u>	27. light <u>teeb, pom kev</u>	47. those <u>tsav ntawd</u>
8. bring <u>coj, nqa</u>	28. live <u>nyob</u>	48. today <u>hnub no</u>
9. buy <u>yuav</u>	29. myself <u>kuv tus kheej</u>	49. together <u>uake</u>
10. carry <u>nqa, puag, tuav</u>	30. off <u>tag, tawm</u>	50. try <u>sim, xyaum</u>
11. clean <u>so, txhuam, cheb</u>	31. only <u>xwb</u>	51. under <u>hauv qab</u>
12. cut <u>txiav, ntov</u>	32. own <u>tuo kheej tus tswv kheej</u>	52. upon <u>saum, pem</u>
13. does <u>ua</u>	33. pick <u>de, lov</u>	53. use <u>siv</u>
14. done <u>tiav, tag lawm</u>	34. pull <u>ngus, rub</u>	54. warm <u>sov</u>
15. drink <u>hau</u>	35. read <u>twm, nyeem</u>	55. wash <u>ntxuav</u>
16. fall <u>vau, poob, ntog</u>	36. right <u>raug, sab xis yog</u>	56. well <u>zoo, yog</u>
17. full <u>puv, pov</u>	37. seven <u>xya</u>	57. which <u>xws li</u>
18. goes <u>mus, twb</u>	38. shall <u>yuav</u>	58. would <u>yuav</u>
19. got <u>tau lawm, twb muab lawm</u>	39. sit <u>zaum, nyob</u>	59. write <u>sau (sau ntawv)</u>
20. grow <u>loj hlob</u>	40. six <u>rau</u>	60. draw <u>zo duab</u>
		61. eight <u>yim</u>

Dolch Basic Word List -- Hungarian

Pre-primer

1. a _____egy_____
2. and _____és_____
3. big _____nagy_____
4. blue _____kék_____
5. can _____tud_____
6. come _____jön_____
7. down _____le_____
8. for _____miatt_____
9. funny _____vicces_____
10. get _____kap_____
11. go _____megy_____
12. green _____zöld_____
13. have _vknek, vmijevan_
14. help _____segít_____
15. here _____itt_____
16. I _____én_____
17. in _____be_____
18. is _____van_____
19. it _____az, azt_____
20. jump _____ugrik_____
21. little _____kevés_____
22. look _____néz_____
23. make _____csinál_____
24. me _____engem_____
25. my _____enyém_____

26. not _____nem_____
27. play _____játszik_____
28. red _____piros_____
29. ride _____lovagol_____
30. run _____szalad_____
31. said _____mondta_____
32. saw _____látta_____
33. see _____lát_____
34. the _____a_____
35. this _____ez_____
36. to _____-hoz, -hez_____
37. up _____föl_____
38. want _____akar_____
39. we _____mi_____
40. with _____-val, -vel_____
41. work _____dolgozik_____
42. you _____te, ti_____

Primer

1. all _____mind_____
2. am _____vagyok_____
3. are _____vagy_____
4. at _____-nál, -nél_____
5. away _____távolban_____
6. black _____fekete_____
7. but _____de_____
8. came _____jött_____
9. did _____tett_____
10. do _____tesz_____
11. eat _____eszik_____
12. fast _____gyors_____
13. find _____talál_____
14. good _____jó_____
15. he _____ö_____
16. laugh _____nevet_____
17. like _____szeret_____
18. new _____új_____
19. no _____nem, ne_____
20. now _____most_____
21. on _____rajta_____
22. one _____egy_____
23. out _____ki, kinn_____
24. please _____kérem_____
25. put _____tesz_____

26. ran _____futott_____
27. say _____mond_____
28. she _____ö_____
29. so _____úgy_____
30. some _____néhány_____
31. stop _____megáll_____
32. thank _____köszönöm_____
33. that _____az_____
34. then _____akkor_____
35. they _____ök_____
36. three _____három_____
37. too _____is, szintén_____
38. two _____kettö_____
39. was _____volt_____
40. went _____ment_____
41. what _____mi, mit_____
42. where _____hol_____
43. white _____fehér_____
44. will _____fog_____
45. yellow _____sárga_____
46. yes _____igen_____
47. your _____tied_____

First

1. about ___körül___
2. after ___után___
3. again ___újra___
4. an ___egy___
5. around ___körbe___
6. as ___mint___
7. ask ___kérdez___
8. ate ___evett___
9. be ___lenni___
10. before ___elött___
11. brown ___barna___
12. by ___mellett___
13. call ___hiv___
14. cold ___hideg___
15. could ___tudott___
16. can't ___nem tud___
17. every ___minden___
18. far ___messze___
19. first ___elsö___
20. five ___öt___

21. fly ___repül___
22. found ___talált___
23. four ___négy___
24. from ___honnan___
25. gave ___adott___
26. give ___ad___
27. going ___megy___
28. had ___vknek vmije volt___
29. has ___neki van___
30. her ___as ö___
31. him ___öt___
32. his ___as ö___
33. how ___hogyan___
34. if ___ha___
35. into ___bele___
36. just ___éppen___
37. know ___tud___
38. let ___enged___
39. long ___hosszu___
40. made ___csinált___

41. many ___sok___
42. may ___szabad___
43. much ___sok___
44. must ___kell___
45. never ___soha___
46. of ___-ból, -tól___
47. old ___öreg___
48. once ___egyszer___
49. open ___nyilt___
50. or ___vagy___
51. our ___miénk___
52. over ___fölött___
53. pretty ___csinos___
54. round ___kerek___
55. show ___mutat___
56. sing ___énekel___
57. sleep ___alszik___
58. soon ___nemsokára___
59. take ___vesz___

60. them ___öket___
61. there ___ott___
62. think ___gondol___
63. us ___minket___
64. very ___nagyon___
65. walk ___sétal___
66. were ___voltak___
67. when ___mikor___
68. who ___ki___
69. why ___miért___
70. wish ___kiván___

Second

1. always __mindig__	21. hold __tart__	41. small __kicsi__
2. any __bármely__	22. hot __forró__	42. start __kezd__
3. because __mert__	23. hurt __fáj__	43. tell __mond__
4. been __volt__	24. its __övé__	44. ten __tiz__
5. best __legjobb__	25. keep __tart__	45. their __as ö__
6. better __jobb__	26. kind __kedves__	46. these __ezek__
7. both __mindket__	27. light __könnyü__	47. those __azok__
8. bring __hoz__	28. live __el__	48. today __máma__
9. buy __vásárol__	29. myself __magam__	49. together __együtt__
10. carry __visz__	30. off __mellette__	50. try __próbál__
11. clean __tiszta__	31. only __csak__	51. under __alatt__
12. cut __vág__	32. own __saját__	52. upon __rajta__
13. does __tesz__	33. pick __felvesz__	53. use __használ__
14. done __készített__	34. pull __húz__	54. warm __meleg__
15. drink __iszik__	35. read __olvas__	55. wash __mos__
16. fall __esik__	36. right __jobbra__	56. well __jól__
17. full __tele__	37. seven __hét__	57. which __melyik__
18. goes __megy__	38. shall __fog__	58. would __volna__
19. got __kapott__	39. sit __ül__	59. write __ir__
20. grow __fejlödik__	40. six __hat__	60. draw __rajzol__
		61. eight __nyolc__

Dolch Basic Word List – Indonesian

Pre-primer

1. a _____
2. and ___dan-serta___
3. big ___besar___
4. blue ___biru___
5. can ___dapat bisa___
6. come ___datang___
7. down ___bawah___
8. for ___untuk bagi___
9. funny ___lucu___
10. get ___menerima___
11. go ___pergi___
12. green ___hijau___
13. have ___mempunyai-punya___
14. help ___tolong___
15. here ___disini___
16. I ___saya - aku___
17. in ___didalam___
18. is ___adalah___
19. it ___itu___
20. jump ___meloncat___
21. little ___kecil___
22. look ___melihat___
23. make ___membuat___
24. please ___marie - tolong___
25. my ___saya punya___

26. not ___tidak - bukan___
27. play ___bermain___
28. red ___merah___
29. ride ___naik___
30. run ___lari___
31. said ___berkata___
32. saw ___melihat___
33. see ___melihat___
34. the ___itu___
35. this ___ini___
36. to ___ke___
37. up ___naik___
38. want ___mau___
39. we ___kita-kami bersama___
40. with ___dengan___
41. work ___bekerja___
42. you ___kamu - anda___

Primer

1. all ___semua___
2. am _____
3. are _____
4. at ___ke - di___
5. away ___pergi___
6. black ___hitam___
7. but ___tetapi___
8. came ___datang___
9. did _____
10. do _____
11. eat ___makan___
12. fast ___cepat___
13. find ___mendapat___
14. good ___baik___
15. he ___dia - ia___
16. laugh ___ketawa___
17. like ___suka___
18. new ___baru___
19. no ___tidak - bukan___
20. now ___sekarang___
21. on ___di atas___
22. one ___satu___
23. out ___luar___
24. please _____
25. put ___meletakkan___

26. ran ___lari___
27. say ___berkata___
28. she ___dia - ia___
29. so ___jadi___
30. some ___berberapa___
31. stop ___berenti___
32. thank ___terima kasih___
33. that ___itu___
34. then ___pada waktu itu___
35. they ___mereka___
36. three ___tiga___
37. too ___juga___
38. two ___dua___
39. was _____
40. went ___pergi___
41. what ___apa___
42. where ___dimana___
43. white ___putih___
44. will ___akan___
45. yellow ___kuning___
46. yes ___ya___
47. your ___kamu punya___

First

1. about __tentang__	21. fly __terbang__	41. many __banyak__	60. them __mereka__
2. after __sesudah__	22. found __mendapat__	42. may __boleh__	61. there __disana__
3. again __lagi__	23. four __empat__	43. much __banyak__	62. think __memikir (kan)__
4. an _____	24. from __dari__	44. must __harus__	63. us __kita__
5. around __sekeliling__	25. gave __beri__	45. never __tidak pernah__	64. very __sangat - sekali__
6. as __seperti__	26. give __beri__	46. of __dari punya__	65. walk __barjalan__
7. ask __bertanyak__	27. going __pergi__	47. old __tua__	66. were __dimana__
8. ate __makan__	28. had __mempunyai__	48. once __sekali__	67. when __kapan__
9. be _____	29. has __mempunyai__	49. open __buka - terbuka__	68. who __siapa__
10. before __sebelumnya__	30. her __dia punya__	50. or __atau__	69. why __mengapa__
11. brown __coklat__	31. him __dia__	51. our __kita punya__	70. wish __ingin__
12. by __oleh__	32. his __dia punya__	52. over __atas__	
13. call __memanggil__	33. how __bagaimana__	53. pretty __indah__	
14. cold __dingin__	34. if __jikalau__	54. round __bulat - bundar__	
15. could __bisa - dapat__	35. into __kedalam__	55. show __melihatkan__	
16. can't __tidak bisa__	36. just __saja - cuma__	56. sing __menyanyi__	
17. every __setiap__	37. know __tahu-mengetahui__	57. sleep __tidur__	
18. far __jauh__	38. let __biarlah__	58. soon __cepat__	
19. first __pertama__	39. long __panjang - lama__	59. take __mengambil__	
20. five __lima__	40. made __dibuat__		

Second

1. always __selalu__
2. any __siapa-pun__
3. because __karena__
4. been _____
5. best __terbaik__
6. better __lebih baik__
7. both __keduanya__
8. bring __membawah__
9. buy __membeli__
10. carry __membawah__
11. clean __bersih - membersihkan__
12. cut __potong__
13. does _____
14. done __sudah selesai__
15. drink __minum__
16. fall __jatuh__
17. full __penuh__
18. goes __pergi__
19. got __dapat__
20. grow __timbul-timbuh__

21. hold __memegang__
22. hot __panas__
23. hurt __sakit__
24. its __kepunyaanya__
25. keep __memegang__
26. kind __macam__
27. light __terang__
28. live __hidup__
29. myself __saya sendiri__
30. off _____
31. only __hanya - saja__
32. own __diri-sendiri__
33. pick __memetik__
34. pull __menarik__
35. read __membaca__
36. right __benar - (correct) kanan - (direction)__
37. seven __tujuh__
38. shall __akan__
39. sit __duduk__
40. six __enam__

41. small __kecil__
42. start __mulai__
43. tell __mengata-ngatai__
44. ten __sepuluh__
45. their __mereka punya__
46. these __ini__
47. those __itu__
48. today __hari ini__
49. together __bersama-sama__
50. try __mencoba__
51. under __dibawah__
52. upon __diatas__
53. use __memakai__
54. warm __panas__
55. wash __mencuci__
56. well __baik__
57. which __yang mana__
58. would __akan__
59. write __menulis__
60. draw __menggambar__
61. eight __delapan__

Dolch Basic Word List -- Italian

Pre-primer

1. a un (masc), una (fem)
2. and e, ed (before vowel)
3. big grande
4. blue blu
5. can potere (verb)
6. come venire
7. down giù
8. for per
9. funny divertente
10. get ottenere
11. go andare
12. green verde
13. have avere
14. help aiutare (verb)
15. here quí
16. I Io
17. in in
18. is è (È)
19. it esso (masc)
20. jump saltare
21. little piccolo
22. look guardare (verb)
23. make fare
24. me me
25. my mio (masc)

26. not non
27. play giocare (verb)
28. red rosso
29. ride guidare (verb)
30. run correre
31. said detto
32. saw egli vide (he saw)
33. see vedere
    il, lo, la (sing)
34. the i, gli, le (plural)
35. this questo (masc)
36. to a
37. up sopra
38. want volere
39. we noi
40. with con
41. work lavorare (verb)
42. you tu-voi (you all)

Primer

1. all tutto
2. am sono
3. are essi sono (they are)
4. at a
5. away via
6. black nero
7. but ma
8. came egli venne (he)
9. did fece
10. do fare (verb)
11. eat mangiare
12. fast veloce (adj)
13. find trovare (verb)
14. good buono (adj)
15. he egli
16. laugh ridere (verb)
17. like piacere (verb)
18. new nuovo
19. no no
20. now adesso
21. on su
22. one uno (number)
23. out fuori
24. please per favore
25. put mettere (verb)

26. ran egli corse (he ran)
27. say dire (verb)
28. she ella
29. so così
30. some alcuni
31. stop fermarsi (verb)
32. thank ringraziare (verb)
33. that quello
34. then poi
35. they essi (loro)
36. three tre
37. too anche
38. two due
39. was egli era (he was)
40. went egli ando (he went)
41. what cosa (che cosa)
42. where dove
43. white bianco
44. will essere (future verb)
45. yellow giallo
46. yes sí
47. your tuo (masc)

First

1. about ___circa___	21. fly ___volare___	41. many ___molti___	60. them ___loro___
		maggio (month)	
2. after ___dopo___	22. found ___trovato___	42. may _potere (verb)_	61. there ___lì___
3. again ___di nuovo___	23. four ___quattro___	43. much ___molto___	62. think _pensare (verb)_
4. an ___un (masc)___	24. from ___da___	44. must _dovere (verb)_	63. us ___noi___
5. around ___intorno___	25. gave _egli dette (he)_	45. never ___mai___	64. very ___molto___
6. as ___come___	26. give ___dare___	46. of ___di___	65. walk _camminare (verb)_
7. ask _chiedere (verb)_	27. going ___andando___	47. old ___vecchio___	66. were _essi erano (they)_
8. ate _egli mangió (he)_	28. had _egli ebbe (he)_	48. once ___una volta___	67. when ___quando___
9. be ___essere (verb)___	29. has ___ha___	49. open _aprire (verb)_	68. who ___chi___
10. before ___prima___	30. her ___sua___	50. or _o, oppure_	69. why ___perchè___
11. brown ___marrone___	31. him ___lui___	51. our ___nostro___	70. wish _desiderare (verb)_
12. by ___attraverso___	32. his ___suo___	52. over ___sopra___	
13. call _chiamare (verb)_	33. how ___come___	53. pretty ___carino___	
14. cold ___freddo___	34. if ___se___	54. round ___intornóa___	
15. could _egli poté (he)_	35. into ___in-dentro___	55. show _mostrare (verb)_	
16. can't _non posso (I)_	36. just ___appena___	56. sing _cantare (verb)_	
17. every ___ogni___	37. know _sapere conoscere_	57. sleep _dormire (verb)_	
18. far ___lontano___	38. let ___lasciare___	58. soon ___presto___	
19. first ___primo___	39. long ___lungo___	59. take _prendere (verb)_	
20. five ___cinque___	40. made ___fatto___		

Second

1. always __sempre__	21. hold _tenere (verb)_	41. small __piccolo__
2. any __alcumo__	22. hot __caldo__	42. start _cominciare (verb)_
3. because __perchè__	23. hurt __fare male__	43. tell __dire (verb)__
4. been __stato__	24. its __suo__	44. ten __dieci__
5. best __migliore__	25. keep _tenere (verb)_	45. their __loro__
6. better __meglio__	26. kind __gentile (adj)__	46. these _questi (masc)_
7. both __entrambi__	27. light __luce__	47. those _quelli (masc)_
8. bring _portare (verb)_	28. live _vivere (verb)_	48. today __oggi__
9. buy _comprare (verb)_	29. myself _me stesso_	49. together _insieme_
10. carry _trasportare_	30. off __da__	50. try _provare (verb)_
11. clean _pulito (adj)_	31. only __solo__	51. under __sotto__
12. cut _tagliare (verb)_	32. own __proprio__	52. upon __sopra__
13. does __fa__	33. pick _scegliere (verb)_	53. use __usare (verb)__
14. done __fatto__	34. pull __tirare (verb)__	54. warm _caldo (tiepido)_
15. drink _bere (verb)_	35. read _leggere (verb)_	55. wash __lavare (verb)__
16. fall __cadere (verb)__	36. right _giusto (adj)_	56. well __bene (adv)__
17. full __pieno__	37. seven __sette__	57. which __che__
18. goes __va__	38. shall _essere (future verb)_	58. would _vorresti farlo (Would you do it?)_
19. got _egli ottenne (he)_	39. sit _sedere (verb)_	59. write _scrivere (verb)_
20. grow _crescere (verb)_	40. six __sei__	60. draw _disegnare (verb)_
		61. eight __otto__

Dolch Basic Word List – Japanese

PRE-PRIMER

1.a　ひとつの	29.ride　乗る	14.good　よい	42.where　どこへ、どこに
2.and　そして、また	30.run　走る	15.he　かれ	43.white　白い
3.big　大きい	31.said　言った	16.laugh　笑う	44.will　未来・意志
4.blue　青い	32.saw　見た（過去）	17.like　好き	45.yellow　黄いろい
5.can　できる	33.see　見る	18.new　新しい	46.yes　はい
6.come　来る	34.the　その	19.no　いいえ	47.your　あなたの
7.down　した	35.this　この	20.now　いま	FIRST
8.for　〜のため	36.to　〜へ	21.on　〜の上に	1.about　〜について
9.funny　おかしい	37.up　上に、上へ	22.one　ひとつ（の）	2.after　〜のあとに（で）
10.get　手に入れる	38.want　ほしい	23.out　外へ、外出して	3.again　また
11.go　行く	39.we　私達	24.please　どうぞ	4.an　ひとつの、ひとりの
12.green　緑色の	40.with　〜といっしょに	25.put　おく、入れる	5.around　まわりに、あたりに
13.have　持っている	41.work　働く	26.ran　走った	6.as　〜と同じくらいに
14.help　手伝う、助ける	42.you　あなた	27.say　言う	7.ask　きく
15.here　ここに	PRIMER	28.she　かのじょ	8.ate　食べた
16.I　わたし（女）、ぼく（男）	1.all　みんな、ぜんぶ	29.so　そのように	9.be　〜になる（命令形）
17.in　〜の中に	2.am　〜です　にいる	30.some　いくらか	10.before　〜の前に
18.is　〜です、にいる	3.are　二人称、複数	31.stop　止まる、止める	11.brown　茶色の
19.it　それ	4.at　〜で、〜に	32.thank　ありがとう	12.by　〜のそばに、近くに
20.jump　とぶ	5.away　あちらへ	33.that　それ、あれ	13.call　よぶ
21.little　少し、小さい	6.black　黒い	34.then　それから	14.cold　寒い
22.look　見る	7.but　でも	35.they　かれら	15.could　できた
23.make　つくる	8.came　きた	36.three　みっつ（の）	16.can't　できない
24.me　私を（に）	9.did　〜した（過去）	37.too　〜も	17.every　すべての
25.my　私の	10.do　する	38.two　二つ	18.far　遠くに
26.not　〜ない（否定）	11.eat　食べる	39.was　あった、いた	19.first　最初に、最初の
27.play　あそぶ	12.fast　速い、速く	40.went　行った	20.five　いつつ
28.red　赤い	13.find　見つける	41.what　なに	21.fly　とぶ

22. found 見つけた
23. four よっつ
24. from ～から
25. gave あげた
26. give あげる、くれる
27. going 行く
28. had 持っていた
29. has 持っている
30. her かのじょを(に)
31. him かれを(に)
32. his かれの
33. how どのようにして
34. if もし
35. into ～の中に
36. just ちょうど
37. know 知っている
38. let ～させる
39. long 長い
40. made 作った
41. many たくさんの
42. may ～してもよい
43. much たくさん
44. must ～しなければならない
45. never 決して～ない
46. of ～の
47. old 古い
48. once 一度、昔
49. open 開く、あける

50. or または
51. our 私達の
52. over ～の上に
53. pretty きれい(な)
54. round まるい
55. show 見せる
56. sing 歌う
57. sleep 寝る
58. soon すぐ
59. take 取る 連れて行く
60. them かれらを(に)
61. there そこへ(に)
62. think 思う、考える
63. us 私達を
64. very とても
65. walk 歩く
66. were ～にいた、あった
67. when いつ
68. who だれが(を)
69. why なぜ、どうして
70. wish ～したい

SECOND

1. always いつも
2. any 少しでも
3. because なぜなら
4. been ～のままで
5. best 一番よい
6. better ～よりよい

7. both 両方の
8. bring 持って来る
9. buy 買う
10. carry 運ぶ
11. clean そうじする
12. cut 切る
13. does する
14. done おわった
15. drink 飲む
16. fall 落ちる、秋
17. full いっぱい
18. goes 行く
19. got 手に入れた
20. grow のびる、育つ
21. hold 持つ、つかむ
22. hot あつい
23. hurt いたい
24. its それの
25. keep とっておく
26. kind 親切な
27. light 軽い、明るい
28. live 住む、生きる
29. myself 自分で
30. off はなれて
31. only ～だけ
32. own 自身の
33. pick ひろう
34. pull 引っぱる

35. read 読む
36. right 正しい、fiの
37. seven ななつ
38. shall 未来時制
39. sit すわる
40. six むっつ
41. small 小さい(な)
42. start はじめる
43. tell 話す
44. ten とお
45. their かれらの
46. these これらを(は)
47. those それらを(は)
48. today きょう
49. together いっしょに
50. try ～してみる
51. under ～の下に
52. upon ～の上に
53. use 使う
54. warm あたたかい
55. wash 洗う
56. well じょうずに
57. which どれ
58. would ～するだろう
59. write 書く
60. draw 描く
61. eight やっつ

Dolch Basic Word List – Korean

PRE-PRIMER

1. a 하나(의)
2. and 그리고
3. big 큰
4. blue 파란
5. can 할수있다
6. come 오다
7. down 아래로
8. for 위하여
9. funny 재미있는
10. get 얻다, 가지다
11. go 가다
12. green 초록의
13. have 가지다
14. help 돕다
15. here 여기(에)
16. I 나(는)
17. in 안에
18. is 이다, 있다
19. it 그것(은)
20. jump 뛰다
21. little 작은
22. look 보다
23. make 만들다
24. me 나를
25. my 나의
26. not 아닌
27. play 놀다
28. red 붉은(색)
29. ride 타다

30. run 달리다
31. said 말했다
32. saw 보았다
33. see 보다
34. the 그
35. this 이것(은)
36. to -에게로
37. up 위로
38. want 원하다
39. we 우리(들은)
40. with -와함께 가지고
41. work 일하다
42. you 너는

PRIMER

1. all 모두
2. am 이다, 있다
3. are 이다, 있다
4. at 에서, -에
5. away 떨어져서
6. black 검은(색)
7. but 그러나
8. came 왔다
9. did 했다
10. do 하다
11. eat 먹다
12. fast 빨리
13. find 찾다
14. good 좋은
15. he 그는

16. laugh 웃다
17. like 좋아하다
18. new 새로운
19. no 아니오
20. now 지금
21. on 위에
22. one 하나
23. out 밖에
24. please 부디-해주시오
25. put 놓다, 두다
26. ran 달렸다
27. say 말하다
28. she 그여자는
29. so 그렇게, 그래서
30. some 어떤, 약간의
31. stop 멈추다
32. thank 감사하다
33. that 저것(은)
34. then 그때
35. they 그들은
36. three 셋
37. too 역시, 또한
38. two 둘, 둘의
39. was 이었다
40. went 갔다
41. what 무슨, 무엇
42. where 어디에
43. white 흰

44. will 할것이다
45. yellow 노란(색의)
46. yes 네, 그렇습니다
47. your 너의, 당신의

FIRST

1. about 대략, -에하여
2. after 후에, 뒤에
3. again 다시
4. an 하나(의)
5. around 주위, 둘레에
6. as 때문에, 할때에
7. ask 묻다
8. ate 먹었다
9. be 이다
10. before 전에, 앞에
11. brown 갈색(의)
12. by 곁에, 옆에
13. call 부르다
14. cold 추운, 찬
15. could 할수있었다
16. can't 할수없다
17. every 각각의
18. far 멀리
19. first 먼저, 첫째로
20. five 다섯(의)
21. fly 날다
22. found 찾아내었다
23. four 넷(의)

24. from 로부터	53. pretty 예쁜	11. clean 깨끗한	40. six 여섯(의)
25. gave 주었다	54. round 둥근	12. cut 자르다	41. small 작은
26. give 주다	55. show 보이다	13. does 하다	42. start 시작하다
27. going 가고있다	56. sing 노래하다	14. done 했다	43. tell 말하다
28. had 갔었다	57. sleep 잠자다	15. drink 마시다	44. ten 열(의)
29. has 갖다	58. Soon 곧	16. fall 넘어지다	45. their 그들의
30. her 그 여자의	59. take 갖다	17. full 가득 찬	46. these 이것들(은)
31. him 그를	60. them 그들을	18. goes 가다	47. those 저것들(은)
32. his 그의	61. there 거기에	19. got 갔었다	48. today 오늘
33. how 어떻게	62. think 생각하다	20. grow 자라다	49. together 함께
34. if 만약에	63. us 우리를	21. hold 잡다	50. try 해보다
35. into 안으로	64. very 매우,대단히	22. hot 뜨거운	51. under 아래에
36. just 꼭, 바로	65. walk 걷다	23. hurt 다치다	52. upon 위에
37. know 알다	66. were 이었다	24. its 그 것의	53. use 사용하다
38. let 하게하다	67. when 언제	25. keep 지키다	54. warm 따뜻한
39. long 긴, 길다	68. who 누구	26. kind 친절한	55. wash 씻다
40. made 만들었다	69. why 왜	27. light 밝은, 가벼운	56. well 잘, 글쎄
41. many 많은	70. wish 하고싶다	28. live 살다	57. which 어느 것(이)
42. may 해도 좋다		29. myself 나 자신의	58. would 했을것이다
43. much 많이	SECOND	30. off 떨어져서	59. write 쓰다
44. must 해야한다	1. always 항상	31. only 겨우, 다만	
45. never 결코-아니다	2. any 어떤 것	32. own 자신의	60. draw 그리다
46. of 의	3. because 왜냐하면	33. pick 집다	61. eight 여덟
47. old 오래된	4. been 이었다	34. pull 당기다	1. 에게, 위하여, 왜냐하면
48. once 한번	5. best 가장 좋은	35. read 읽다	2. 재미있는, 이상하
49. open 열다	6. better 더좋은	36. right 오른쪽의	3. 공부하다
50. or 또는	7. both 양쪽 다	37. seven 일곱(의)	4. 소수의, 적은
51. our 우리들의	8. bring 가져오다	38. shall 할것이다	5. 얼마나, 몇이나
52. over 위로, 위에	9. buy 사다	39. sit 앉다	6. 나이가 많은, 연로한
	10. carry 가져가다		7. 오른쪽(의), 올 바른

1. To or For, Because
2. Funny 3. Study 4. Few
5. How many 6. Older, Elderly
7. Right

Dolch Basic Word List – Laotian

PRE-PRIMER

1. a (ເບິ່ງຄຳອະທິບາຍຢູ່ ໜ້າ ໒໑໘)
2. and ແລະ
3. big ໃຫຍ່
4. blue ສີຟ້າ
5. can ສາມາດ, ໄດ້
6. come ມາ
7. down ລົງ
8. for ເພື່ອ, ສຳລັບ
9. funny ໜ້າຫົວ
10. get ເອົາ, ໄດ້
11. go ໄປ
12. green ສີຂຽວ
13. have ມີ
14. help ຊ່ອຍ
15. here ຢູ່ນີ້
16. I ຂ້ອຍ
17. in ໃນ
18. is (ລາວ) ເປັນ, ແມ່ນ
19. it ມັນ (ສັດ, ສິ່ງຂອງ)
20. jump ເຕັ້ນ
21. little ນ້ອຍ
22. look ເບິ່ງ
23. make ເຮັດ
24. me ຂ້ອຍ
25. my ຂອງຂ້ອຍ
26. not ບໍ່ (ໜ້າກິຣິຍາ)
27. play ຫລິ້ນ
28. red ສີແດງ
29. ride ຂີ່
30. run ແລ່ນ
31. said ເວົ້າ (ອະດີດ)
32. saw ເຫັນ (ອະດີດ)
33. see ເຫັນ
34. the (ໃຊ້ໜ້າຄຳນາມ)
35. this ອັນນີ້
36. to ເຖິງ, ຫາ
37. up ຂຶ້ນ
38. want ຢາກ
39. we ພວກເຮົາ
40. with ນຳ, ກັບ
41. work ເຮັດວຽກ
42. you ເຈົ້າ, ພວກເຈົ້າ

PRIMER

1. all ທັງໝົດ
2. am (ຂ້ອຍ) ເປັນ, ແມ່ນ
3. are ເປັນ, ແມ່ນ
4. at ທີ່, ຢູ່
5. away ອອກໄປ
6. black ສີດຳ
7. but ແຕ່ວ່າ, ເທົ່ານັ້ນ
8. came ມາ (ອະດີດ)
9. did ເຮັດ (ອະດີດ)
10. do ເຮັດ
11. eat ກິນ
12. fast ໄວ
13. find ພົບ, ພໍ້, ຊອກຫາ
14. good ດີ
15. he ລາວ (ຜູ້ຊາຍ)
16. laugh ຫົວ (ຮາງ)
17. like ມັກ
18. new ໃໝ່
19. no ບໍ່, ບໍ່ແມ່ນ
20. now ດຽວນີ້
21. on ຢູ່ເທິງ, ເປີດ
22. one ນຶ່ງ, ຜູ້ນຶ່ງ
23. out ອອກ, ໝົດ
24. please ກະລຸນາ
25. put ເອົາໃສ່, ເອົາໄວ້
26. ran ແລ່ນ (ອະດີດ)
27. say ເວົ້າ
28. she ລາວ (ຜູ້ຍິງ)
29. so ດັ່ງນັ້ນ
30. some ບາງເລັກນ້ອຍ
31. stop ຢຸດ, ເຊົາ
32. thank ຂອບໃຈ
33. that ອັນນັ້ນ, ທີ່, ຊຶ່ງ
34. then ຕໍ່ (ມາ, ໄປ)
35. they ເຂົາເຈົ້າ
36. three ສາມ
37. too ຄືກັນ, ໂພດ
38. two ສອງ
39. was ເປັນ (ອະດີດ)
40. went ໄປ (ອະດີດ)
41. what ຫຍັງ, ທີ່
42. where ຢູ່ໃສ, ທີ່
43. white ສີຂາວ
44. will ຈະ
45. yellow ສີເຫລືອງ
46. yes ເອີ, ແມ່ນແລ້ວ
47. your ຂອງເຈົ້າ

FIRST

1. about ປະມານ, ກ່ຽວກັບ
2. after ຫລັງຈາກ
3. again ອີກ
4. an (ເບິ່ງຄຳອະທິບາຍໜ້າ ໒໑໘)
5. around ຢູ່ອ້ອມ, ປະມານ
6. as ດັ່ງ, ຄື, ເຊັ່ນ
7. ask ຖາມ, ຂໍ
8. ate ກິນ (ອະດີດ)
9. be ເປັນ, ແມ່ນ, ຢູ່
10. before ກ່ອນ, ແຕ່ກ່ອນ
11. brown ສີນ້ຳຕານ
12. by ໂດຍ, ດ້ວຍ
13. call ເອີ້ນ
14. cold ໜາວ
15. could ສາມາດ, ໄດ້
16. can't ບໍ່ສາມາດ, ບໍ່ໄດ້
17. every ທຸກໆ
18. far ໄກ
19. first ທີ່ນຶ່ງ
20. five ຫ້າ
21. fly ບິນ
22. found ພໍ້, ພົບ (ອະດີດ)
23. four ສີ່

24. from ຈາກ
25. gave ເອົາໃຫ້(ອະດີດ)
26. give ເອົາໃຫ້
27. going ກຳລັງໄປ
28. had ມີ(ອະດີດ)
29. has (ລາວ) ມີ
30. her ຂອງລາວ(ຜູ້ຍິງ)
31. him ລາວ(ຜູ້ຊາຍ)
32. his ຂອງລາວ(ຜູ້ຊາຍ)
33. how ແນວໃດ,ຢ່າງໃດ
34. if ຖ້າວ່າ
35. into ເຂົ້າໃນ
36. just ຫາກ,ພຽງແຕ່
37. know ຮູ້
38. let ປ່ອຍໃຫ້
39. long ຍາວ
40. made ເຮັດ(ອະດີດ)
41. many ຫລາຍ
42. may ອາດຈະ
43. much ຫລາຍ
44. must ຕ້ອງ
45. never ບໍ່ເຄີຍ...ເລີຍ
46. of ຂອງ
47. old ເກົ່າ, ແກ່
48. once ເທື່ອນຶ່ງ,ຄັ້ງດຽວ
49. open ໄຂ, ເປີດ
50. or ຫຼື
51. our ຂອງພວກເຮົາ
52. over ເທິງ,ຫຼາຍກວ່າ

53. pretty ງາມ,ສົມຄວນ
54. round ມົນ, ກົມ
55. show ສະແດງ,ໃຫ້ເບິ່ງ
56. sing ຮ້ອງເພງ
57. sleep ນອນ
58. soon ໃນບໍ່ຊ້າ
59. take ເອົາ,ເອົາໄປ
60. them ເຂົາເຈົ້າ
61. there (ຢູ່)ທີ່ນັ້ນ,ພຸ້ນ
62. think ຄິດ
63. us ພວກເຮົາ
64. very (ດີ,ຊົ່ວ...)ຫຼາຍ
65. walk ຍ່າງ
66. were ເປັນ(ອະດີດ)
67. when ເມື່ອ,ເມື່ອໃດ
68. who ທີ່, ໃຜ
69. why ເປັນຫຍັງ
70. wish ປະສົງ,ອວຍພອນ

SECOND
1. always ເລື້ອຍ
2. any... ໃດກໍໄດ້
3. because ເພາະວ່າ
4. been(ຄຳບອກອະດີດ)
5. best ດີທີ່ສຸດ
6. better ດີກວ່າ
7. both ທັງສອງ
8. bring ຖື,ເອົາມາ
9. buy ຊື້
10. carry ຖື

11. clean ສະອາດ
12. cut ຕັດ, ປາດ
13. does ເຮັດ(ລາວ)
14. done ເຮັດແລ້ວ
15. drink ກິນ
16. fall ຕົກ
17. full ເຕັມ, ອີ່ມ
18. goes (ລາວ) ໄປ
19. got ໄດ້(ອະດີດ)
20. grow ໃຫຍ່ຂຶ້ນ, ງອກ
21. hold ຖືໄວ້, ຈັບໄວ້
22. hot ຮ້ອນ
23. hurt ເຈັບ,ເຮັດໃຫ້ເຈັບ
24. its ຂອງມັນ
25. keep ຮັກສາໄວ້,ເກັບໄວ້
26. kind ຊະນິດ, ໃຈດີ
27. light ແສງ,ແຈ້ງ,ເບົາ
28. live ຢູ່, ອາໄສຢູ່
29. myself ຂອງເອງ
30. off ປິ່,ດັບ,ນອກ,ອອກ
31. only ເທົ່ານັ້ນ,ພຽງແຕ່
32. own ເປັນເຈົ້າຂອງ, ມີ
33. pick ເລືອກ,ຈັບເອົາ
34. pull ດຶງ
35. read ອ່ານ
36. right ຖອກ, ຖືກ
37. seven ເຈັດ
38. shall ຈະ
39. sit ນັ່ງ

40. six ຫົກ
41. small ນ້ອຍ
42. start ເລີ່ມ
43. tell ບອກ,ເລົ່າ
44. ten ສິບ
45. their ຂອງເຂົາເຈົ້າ
46. these ເຫຼົ່ານີ້
47. those ເຫຼົ່ານັ້ນ
48. today ມື້ນີ້
49. together ຮ່ວມກັນ,ພ້ອມກັນ
50. try ລອງ,ພະຍາຍາມ
51. under (ຢູ່)ກ້ອງ
52. upon ເທິງ
53. use ໃຊ້
54. warm ອຸ່ນ
55. wash ຊັກ , ລ້າງ
56. well ດີ
57. which ທີ່, ອັນໃດ
58. would ຈະ
59. write ຂຽນ
60. draw ແຕ້ມ,ລາກ,ດຶງ
61. eight ແປດ

ອັນບຸ໊ງ(ເປັນຄຳ
ທີ່ໃຊ້ຕົບປາສົບທີ່ພະຍັນຊະນະ
ຂຶ້ນກ່ອນ.

ອັນບຸ໊ງ(ເປັນຄຳ
ທີ່ໃຊ້ຕົບປາສົບທີ່ສະຫຼະຂຶ້ນກ່ອນ)

Dolch Basic Word List -- Blue Mong

Pre-primer

1. a _____

2. and ____thab____

3. big ____luj____

4. blue __xav (siv xav)__

5. can __muaj cuab kaav__

6. come ____tuaj, lug____

7. down __nqeg haav, nqeg taug__

8. for ____yog rua____

9. funny __lom zem__

10. get __muab, tau__

11. go ____moog____

12. green __ntsuab__

13. have ____muaj____

14. help __paab, cawm__

15. here __nuav qhov, nuav__

16. I ____kuv____

17. in ____huv____

18. is ____yog____

19. it __nwg (siv rua tsaj)__

20. jump __caws qa, txoom pwm__

21. little __miv ntsiv__

22. look ____saib____

23. make ____ua____

24. please __mog, yuad__

25. my ____kuv le____

26. not __tsi (tsi yog)__

27. play ____ua si____

28. red __lab (siv lab)__

29. ride __caij (caij neeg)__

30. run ____dla____

31. said __has (tau has)__

32. saw __kaw, pum lawm__

33. see ____pum____

34. the _____

35. this __nuav, qhov nuav__

36. to ____txug____

37. up __sau (nyob sab)__

38. want __xaavtau__

39. we ____peb____

40. with __nrug, sib xws, ua ke__

41. work __num, ua num__

42. you ____koj____

Primer

txhua tsaav taag,
1. all __huv tuab si__

2. am __yog (siv rua kuv)__

3. are __yog (siv rua koj)__

4. at __qhov (qhov ntawd)__

5. away __txaav dleb__

6. black ____dlub____

7. but __tuam sis (tag lug lawm)__

8. came __lug; tuaj (tag lug lawm lawm)__

9. did ____ua____

10. do __ua (ua dlej num)__

11. eat ____noj____

12. fast __ceev, nrawm, sai__

13. find __ntsib, pom, tau__

14. good ____zoo____

15. he __nwg (qua yawg)__

16. laugh ____luag____

17. like __nyam, sib xws, sib luag__

18. new ____tshab____

19. no ____tsi____

20. now __tam sim nua__

21. on ____sau____

22. one ____ib____

23. out __tawm, rhu, nrau__

24. please __mog, yuad__

25. put __ntsaws rua__

26. ran __dla (taag lug)__

27. say ____has____

28. she __nwg (qua puj)__

29. so __ib yaam le miv ntsiv, qee__

30. some ____tsaav____

31. stop ____nreg____

32. thank __ua tsaug__

33. that __ntawd, tod__

34. then __tom qaab ntawd__

35. they ____puab____

36. three __peb tuab yaam,__

37. too __sib npaug__

38. two ____ob____

39. was __yog (taag lug)__

40. went __moog (taag lug)__

41. what __dlaab tsi__

42. where __qhov twg__

43. white __dlawb__

44. will __yuav (tom ntej)__

45. yellow __dlaaj__

46. yes __yog, awj, wj__

47. your __koj le__

First

1. about _ntshig txug kwv yees_

2. after _tom qaab_

3. again _dlua thab_

4. an _____

5. around _ncig_

6. as _xws le_

7. ask _nug, thom_

8. ate _noj (taag lug)_

9. be _yog_

10. before _ua ntej_

11. brown _____

12. by _nrug, dlhau, ua ke_

13. call _hu_

14. cold _no, txag_

15. could _muaj cuab kaav_

16. can't _tsi muaj cuab kaav_

17. every _txhua txhua (tssav)_

18. far _dleb_

19. first _____

20. five _tsib_

21. fly _yaa_

22. found _ntsib, pum tau_

23. four _plaug_

24. from _ncaim, tuaj, lug_

25. gave _muab (taag lug)_

26. give _muab_

27. going _moog (taag tom)_

28. had _muaj (taag lug)_

29. has _muaj (nwg muaj)_

30. her _nwg (quaspuj)_

31. him _nwg (quas yawg)_

32. his _nwgle (quas yawg)_

33. how _yuav ua le caag_

34. if _yog tas_

35. into _huv, ncaaj nraim_

36. just _nyav qhuav (nyav qhuav, moog, kag)_

37. know _paub_

38. let _kua (kua nwg moog)_

39. long _ntev_

40. made _ua (taag lug)_

41. many _ntau ntau_

42. may _tej zag ntau (siv rua)_

43. much _tsaav suav tsitau_

44. must _yuav tsum_

45. never _tsi txeev_

46. of _yog, kws yog_

47. old _laug_

48. once _ib zag_

49. open _qheb_

50. or _los yog_

51. our _peb le_

52. over _dlhau lawm, hlaa_

53. pretty _zoo, zoo nkauj_

54. round _ncig_

55. show _qha, yaam_

56. sing _hu nkauj_

57. sleep _tsaug zug_

58. soon _tsi ntev, ti ti (tsi ntev sau ntej nuav)_

59. take _muab, nqaa_

60. them _puab_

61. there _tom, tod_

62. think _xaav_

63. us _peb_

64. very _ntau_

65. walk _moog kev, moog_

66. were _yog (taag lug lawm)_

67. when _thaum twg_

68. who _leej twg_

69. why _vim le caag_

70. wish _xaav tau_

Second

1. always   tuab yaam, sib kws, sib luag
2. any   tej tsaav
3. because   rua qhov
4. been   yog (tub yog) taag lug lawm)
5. best   zoo tshaaj plawg
6. better   zoo tshaaj
7. both   nkawm, ob tug ob tsaav
8. bring   coj, nqaa
9. buy   yuav (yuav them nyaj)
10. carry   nqaa, puag, tuav coj
11. clean   txhuam, so, cheb
12. cut   txav, ntuv
13. does   ua
14. done   tav, taag, ua laag lawm
15. drink   hau (hau dlej)
16. fall   quag, poob, dlog
17. full   puv
18. goes   moog (siv rua nwg)
19. got   tau, tub tau lawm
20. grow   luj, hlub

21. hold   tuav, nqaa, coj npaaj, txheem
22. hot   kub, ceev
23. hurt   mob
24. its   nwg le (siv rua tsaj hab tsaav tshaj xwm)
25. keep   khaws, ceev, tuav
26. kind   tsaav
27. light   teeb, pum kev
28. live   nyob
29. myself   kuv tug kheej
30. off   taag, tawm
31. only   xwb, tuab qhov
32. own   tug kheej le
33. pick   dle, luv
34. pull   nqug
35. read   (nyeem ntawv) nyeem
36. right   raug, yog, saab xis
37. seven   xyaa
38. shall   yuav (yuav moog)
39. sit   nyob tsawg
40. six   rau

41. small   miv, miv quav
42. start   cuab, chiv, pib
43. tell   gha
44. ten   kaum
45. their   puab le
46. these   tsaav nuav
47. those   tsaav ntawd
48. today   nub nua (nuav)
49. together   ua ke
50. try   xyum, sim
51. under   huv qaab
52. upon   saum, peg
53. use   siv
54. warm   suv
55. wash   xtxuav
56. well   zoo, yog
57. which   xws le
58. would   yuav (yuav ua)
59. write   sau
60. draw   zo dluab
61. eight   yim

Dolch Basic Word List – Navajo

Pre-Primer

1. a: *'a*
2. and: *dóó*
3. big: *tso; tsááz*
4. blue: *dootł'izh*
5. can: *yííłghą; haz'á*
6. come: *hágo*
7. down: *hadah; bidah; góyaa*
8. for: *bá; biká*
9. funny: *baa dlo hasin*
10. get: *ńdiiha*
11. go: *ti'*
12. green: *dootł'izh*
13. have: *naash'á*
14. help: *'áká'é'elgheed kodi; kodi*
15. here: *kwe'é; kwii; kodi; ná* (in handing something to a person)
16. I: *shi*
17. in: *góne'; bii'; bighi'*
18. is: *'at'é*
19. it: *'at'é*
20. jump: *dah niljíí*
21. little: *'ałts'íísi; 'ałch'iidi; yázhi; yáázh*
22. look: *dini'íí'*
23. make: *'ajiłįį*
24. me: *shi*
25. my: *t'áá shi*
26. not: *doo – da; doo'ajit'įįda* (one should not do that)

27. play: *nji né; deeshneeł*
28. red: *łichíí; halchii*
29. ride: *shił yilghoł*
30. run: *yilghol; ghoł* (as in, I will run away); *yóó'adeeshghoł*
31. said: *ní jiní*
32. saw: *yiiłtsą*
33. see: *yish'į*
34. the: _____
35. this: *díí*
36. to: *--jį́*
37. up: *deigo; hódah*
38. want: *nisin*
39. we: *nihi*
40. with: *bił*
41. work: *naalnish; njilnish*
42. you: *ni; ná* (for you)

Primer

1. all: *t'áá'ałtso*
2. am: *nishłį́*
3. are: *'at'e*
4. at: *di; --gi*
5. away: *bits'ąą jį́; yóó yiiyá*
6. black: *lizhin; diłhił*
7. but: *ndi*
8. came: *niiyá*
9. did: *'ííł'jid; 'ásdzaa; 'ánit'í; 'adaadzaa* (they did); *'ádaat' ínígíí; 'ádáát' jjid* (did something)
10. do: *'ádeesh nííł*
11. eat: *jiyá*
12. fast: *tsįįłgo*
13. find: *ha dínesh taał*
14. good: *yá'át'ééh łikan* (this is good food)
15. he: *bi*
16. laugh: *yidloo*
17. like: *bił yá'át'ééh; --gi 'át' éego*
18. new: *'ániidí*
19. no: *doo--da*
20. now: *k'ad*
21. on: *bikáá'*
22. one: *t'áá'ałaaí*
23. out: *tł'óo'di*
24. please: *t'áá'shoondi*
25. put: *nini'aah*
26. ran: *jiłghod; yideezgoh* (He ran into it)

27. say: *diní*
28. she: *bi*
29. so: *'ako*
30. some: *ła'*
31. stop: *niiltład*
32. thank: *'ahehe*
33. that: *'eii; 'éi; ńléí*
34. then: *'ako; 'ídáá'; 'índa*
35. they: *bi*
36. three: *táá'*
37. too: *dó'; 'ałdó'*
38. two: *naaki*
39. was: *nt'éé*
40. went: *ííyá*
41. what: *ha'át'íí; yááh*
42. where: *hąát'éegisha'; háadishą́*
43. white: *łigaii*
44. will: *dooleeł*
45. yellow: *łitso*
46. yes: *'aoo'; lą́'ąą'*
47. your: *nibi*

First

1. about: *baa*
2. after: *'áádóó; dóó bik'iji'*
3. again: *naana*
4. an: *'a*
5. around: *kó; binaagóó* (around it)
6. as: *–gi at'áo*
7. ask: *naabidiłkid nabideełkid* (I asked)
8. ate: *'ííyą́ą́'* (I ate, he ate); *da'ííyą́ą́'* (they ate); *dayooldeel* (they ate them)
9. be: *deeshłeeł*
10. before: *t'áá'doo*
11. brown: *yishtłizh*
12. by: *bíighahgi; baah; bee*
13. call: *ła'hodeeshni*
14. cold: *sik'as, it* (an object is cold); *disk'az*
15. could: *yiigha*
16. can't: *doo bíneeshą́ą da*
17. every: *t'áá'akwíí; t'áá'ákwíí jí* (every day)
18. far: *nízaad*
19. first: *'ałsé*
20. five: *'ashdla'*
21. fly: *tsé'édǫ́ii*
22. found: *bik'inatą́ą́*

23. four: *dįį'*
24. from: *-déé'; -dóó*
25. gave: *yeini'á*
26. give: *baqni'á*
27. going: *deíyá*
28. had: *beehóló̦ǫ́nt'éé*
29. has: *bee hóló̦*
30. her: *bi*
31. him: *bi*
32. his: *bi*
33. how: *hait'áo; ha'át'éegoshą'; haait'éegosha; haayit'éego*
34. if: *ládą́ą́'* (in case, if so)
35. into: *biih*
36. just: *t'óó; t'áá*
37. know: *bééhózin; bééhasin* (I know how); *yiishchįįh* (I know how)
38. let: *-ni' le'*
39. long: *neez, nineez*
40. made: *'áshłaa*
41. many: *la'í; t'óó'ahayóí; łání*
42. may: *shį́į́*
43. much: *t'óó'ahayóí*
44. must: *sha'shin; shį́į́*
45. never: *ts'ídá dooda*
46. of: *-déé'*
47. old: *sǫ'*
48. once: *t'ááłáhadi; łah* (once upon a time)

49. open: *'ąą'át'é; dínísh'íí'* (eyes open); *diich'ééh* (mouth open)
50. or: *doodaii'*
51. our: *nihi*
52. over: *báátis; bitis*
53. pretty: *nizhóní*
54. round: *nímaz; dijool; názbas; níghiz*
55. show: *dinííł'iił* (I will show you)
56. sing: *hataał; hodeeshtał*
57. sleep: *'iłhosh; 'iideeshhosh*
58. soon: *t'áadoo hodina'í; t'áadoo hodlina'í*
59. take: *nąą*
60. them: *bi*
61. there: *'áádi; 'ákwe'é*
62. think: *ntséskees*
63. us: *nihi*
64. very: *'ayóogo; t'áá-íighisíí; t'áá' íiyisíí*
65. walk: *na'adá*
66. were: *ńt'éé*
67. when: *hádą́ą́'sha'; hádą́ą́'* (in the past)
68. who: *hai; haisha; haish*

69. why: *ha'át'éego; ha'át'éegoshą'; ha'át'íísha'biniiyé*
70. wish: *nisin* (same as want)

Second

1. always: *t'áá'aɫaji';*
   hool'áágóó
2. any: *t'áábíhólníhí*
3. because: *háálá;*
   binninaa; 'éí baah;
   bee'at'é
4. been: *ńt'ę́ę́'*
5. best: *'agháadi;*
   yá'át'éhígíí
6. better: *yá'át'ééh*
7. both: *t'áá'ɫa*
8. bring: *yi'ááɫ*
9. buy: *nahiɫnii*
10. carry: *-'aaɫ;*
    hadeesh'ááɫ;
    didii'ááɫ
11. clean: *chin*
    baah'adin; nizhóní
12. cut: *deeshgish;*
    ahánígish;
    nihéɫgizh
13. does: *kojiiɫ'iihgo;*
    kójiiɫ'iih (one
    does this way)
14. done: *k'adę́ę;*
    'atsj'sit'é (as in,
    the meat is done)
15. drink: *yishdlą́ą́';*
    ashdlą́ada (I do
    not drink)
16. fall: *dégwo'*
17. full: *hadeezbin;*
    badéébiid; ná
    niichaad (I am full)

18. goes: *akǫ́ǫ́'yiilghooɫ*
19. got: *bee hóló*
20. grow: *neesséeɫ*
21. hold: *yinishta';*
    yíínta
22. hot: *sido; deesdoi;*
    honeezgai;
    hodínóogah
23. hurt: *neezgai; diniih*
24. its: *bi*
25. keep: *séɫtá*
26. kind: *jooshba';*
    baa jiinishbaɫeh
27. light: *'adinidíín;*
    'aszóli (in weight)
28. live: *kééhasht'íígo;*
    bii'shighan (I live
    in a hogan);
    kéédahoht'í (you
    live); *naaldeeh*
    (they live, exist)
29. myself: *t'áá shi*
30. off: *anáangéés*
31. only: *t'eiyá; t'éí;*
    'eiyá; t'áábízhání
32. own: *t'áá bí; shee*
    hóló
33. pick: *yíníshbé; ná*
    ńdideesh'ááɫ (I
    will pick up);
    shé'éts'ih (picks
    on me)
34. pull: *déɫts'óód*
35. read: *yíníshta';*
    ʾíínishta'

36. right: *t'áá'akót'é;*
    nishnáájí (direc-
    tion)
37. seven: *tsotsid*
38. shall: *dooleeɫ, ya'*
    (I shall)
39. sit: *nédá; sédá*
40. six: *hastą́ą́*
41. small: *'aɫtsisi*
42. start: *k'ad; nikiníyá;*
    disélts'ą́ą́'
43. tell: *bee niɫ*
    hodeeshnih;
    bidideeshniiɫ (I
    will tell him)
44. ten: *neeznáá*
45. their: *'áadi; 'ákwe'é;*
    bíɫ (theirs);
    daabí (theirs)
46. these: *díídí; díí*
47. those: *eíídi*
48. today: *diijj; jíídą́ą́';*
49. together: *'áɫah;*
    t'áá 'ahąąh
50. try: *yeigo;*
    bídínéeshtah
51. under: *biyaa*
52. upon: *bikáá'*
53. use: *chool'í*
54. warm: *hoozdo; sido*
55. wash: *ségis;*
    tááségiz; cháshk'eh
    (wash, arroyo)

56. well: *yá'át'ééhgo;*
    hózhǫ́; yá'át'ééh
    nísisdlį́į́' (I got
    well)
57. which: *háidíshą';*
    háidísh
58. would: *laanaanisin*
59. write: *'ak'e'elchí*
60. draw: *naɫtcha*
61. eight: *tseebíí*

Dolch Basic Word List -- Norwegian

Pre-primer

1. a ___en, et___
2. and ___og___
3. big ___stor___
4. blue ___blå___
5. can ___kan___
6. come ___komme___
7. down ___ned___
8. for ___for___
9. funny ___morsomt___
10. get ___få___
11. go ___gå___
12. green ___grønn___
13. have ___ha___
14. help ___hjelp___
15. here ___her___
16. I ___jeg___
17. in ___i___
18. is ___er___
19. it ___den___
20. jump ___hoppe___
21. little ___liten___
22. look ___se___
23. make ___gjøre___
24. me ___meg___
25. my ___min___
26. not ___ikke___
27. play ___leke___
28. red ___rød___
29. ride ___ri___
30. run ___løpe___
31. said ___jeg sa (I said)___
32. saw ___så___
33. see ___se___
34. the ___den___
35. this ___denne___
36. to ___til___
37. up ___oppe___
38. want ___vil ha___
39. we ___vi___
40. with ___med___
41. work ___arbeide___
42. you ___du___

Primer

1. all ___alt___
2. am ___jeg er (I am)___
3. are ___vi er (we are)___
4. at ___ved, i, på___
5. away ___bort___
6. black ___svart___
7. but ___men___
8. came ___kom___
9. did ___jeg gjorde___
10. do ___jeg gjør___
11. eat ___spise___
12. fast ___rask___
13. find ___finne___
14. good ___god___
15. he ___han___
16. laugh ___le___
17. like ___like___
18. new ___ny___
19. no ___nei___
20. now ___nu___
21. on ___på___
22. one ___en___
23. out ___ut___
24. please ___vennligst,* behage___
25. put ___sette___
26. ran ___jeg løpte___
27. say ___si___
28. she ___hun___
29. so ___så___
30. some ___nogen___
31. stop ___stoppe___
32. thank ___takke___
33. that ___den___
34. then ___da___
35. they ___de___
36. three ___tre___
37. too ___også___
38. two ___to___
39. was ___jeg var___
40. went ___gikk___
41. what ___hvad___
42. where ___hvor___
43. white ___hvit___
44. will ___vil___
45. yellow ___gul___
46. yes ___ja___
47. your ___din___

*Vær venniligst å rekke meg boken. (Pass me the book, please.)

First

1. about ___omkring___
2. after ___efter___
3. again ___igjen___
4. an ___en___
5. around ___rundt___
6. as ___likesom___
7. ask ___sporreom___
8. ate ___spiste___
9. be ___bli___
10. before ___for___
11. brown ___brun___
12. by ___ved siden av___
13. call ___kalle___
14. cold ___kold, kald___
15. could ___kunne___
16. can't ___kan ikke___
17. every ___enhver___
18. far ___fjern___
19. first ___først___
20. five ___fem___

21. fly ___flyr___
22. found ___fant___
23. four ___fire___
24. from ___fra___
25. gave ___ga___
26. give ___gi___
27. going ___gående___
28. had ___hadde___
29. has ___har___
30. her ___henne___
31. him ___ham___
32. his ___hans___
33. how ___hvordan___
34. if ___hvis___
35. into ___inni___
36. just ___bare___
37. know ___vite___
38. let ___la___
39. long ___lang___
40. made ___lave___

41. many ___mange___
42. may ___kan jag (I)___
43. much ___meget___
44. must ___må___
45. never ___aldri___
46. of ___av___
47. old ___gammel___
48. once ___engang___
49. open ___åpen___
50. or ___eller___
51. our ___vår___
52. over ___over___
53. pretty ___pen___
54. round ___rund___
55. show ___vise___
56. sing ___synge___
57. sleep ___sove___
58. soon ___snart___
59. take ___ta___

60. them ___dem___
61. there ___der___
62. think ___tenke___
63. us ___oss___
64. very ___meget___
65. walk ___spasere, gå___
66. were ___var___
67. when ___da___
68. who ___hvem___
69. why ___hvorfor___
70. wish ___ønske___

Second

1. always __alltid__
2. any __noen__
3. because __fordi__
4. been __vart__
5. best __best__
6. better __bedre__
7. both __begge__
8. bring __bringe__
9. buy __kjøpe__
10. carry __bære__
11. clean __ren__
12. cut __skjære__
13. does __han gjør (he)__
14. done __ferdig, gjort__
15. drink __drikk__
16. fall __falle__
17. full __full__
18. goes __han går (he)__
19. got __fikk__
20. grow __gro__

21. hold __holde__
22. hot __het, varmt__
23. hurt __skade__
24. its __dens__
25. keep __beholde__
26. kind __god__
27. light __lys__
28. live __leve__
29. myself __meg selv__
30. off __av, avsted__
31. only __eneste__
32. own __egen__
33. pick __plukke__
34. pull __trekke__
35. read __lese__
36. right __rett, riktig__
37. seven __syv__
38. shall __skal__
39. sit __sitte__
40. six __seks__

41. small __liten__
42. start __begynne__
43. tell __fortelle__
44. ten __ti__
45. their __deres__
46. these __disse__
47. those __de__
48. today __idag__
49. together __tilsammen__
50. try __prøve__
51. under __under__
52. upon __på__
53. use __bruke__
54. warm __varm__
55. wash __vaske__
56. well __vel__
57. which __hviklen__
58. would __ville__
59. write __skrive__
60. draw __tegne__
61. eight __åtte__

Dolch Basic Word List – Persian (Farsi)

PRE-PRIMER

1. a
2. and
3. big
4. blue
5. can
6. come
7. down
8. for
9. funny
10. get
11. go
12. green
13. have
14. help
15. here
16. I
17. in
18. is
19. it
20. jump
21. little
22. look
23. make
24. me
25. my
26. not
27. play
28. red
29. ride
30. run
31. said
32. saw
33. see
34. the
35. this
36. to
37. up
38. want
39. we
40. with
41. work
42. you

PRIMER

1. all
2. am
3. are
4. at
5. away
6. black
7. but
8. came
9. did
10. do
11. eat
12. fast
13. find
14. good
15. he
16. laugh
17. like
18. new
19. no
20. now
21. on
22. one
23. out
24. please
25. put
26. ran
27. say
28. she
29. so
30. some
31. stop
32. thank
33. that
34. then
35. they
36. three
37. too
38. two
39. was
40. went
41. what
42. where
43. white
44. will
45. yellow
46. yes
47. your

FIRST

1. about
2. after
3. again
4. an
5. around
6. as
7. ask
8. ate
9. be
10. before
11. brown
12. by
13. call
14. cold
15. could
16. can't
17. every
18. far
19. first
20. five
21. fly
22. found
23. four

#	English	Farsi	#	English	Farsi	#	English	Farsi	#	English	Farsi
24.	from	از	53.	pretty	زیبا	11.	clean	پاک	40.	six	شش (۶)
25.	gave	داد	54.	round	دور	12.	cut	قطع کردن	41.	small	کوچک
26.	give	دادن	55.	show	نشان دادن	13.	does	می‌کند	42.	start	شروع
27.	going	رفتن	56.	sing	خواندن	14.	done	انجام شده	43.	tell	گفتن
28.	had	داشت	57.	sleep	خوابیدن	15.	drink	نوشیدن	44.	ten	ده (۱۰)
29.	has	دارد	58.	Soon	بزودی	16.	fall	افتادن	45.	their	مال آنها
30.	her	به او (زن)	59.	take	گرفتن	17.	full	پُر	46.	these	اینها
31.	him	به او (مرد)	60.	them	به آنها	18.	goes	می‌رود	47.	those	آنها
32.	his	مال او	61.	there	آنجا	19.	got	گرفت	48.	today	امروز
33.	how	چطور	62.	think	فکر کردن	20.	grow	رشد کردن	49.	together	باهم
34.	if	اگر	63.	us	به ما	21.	hold	گرفتن	50.	try	کوشش کردن
35.	into	بطرف	64.	very	خیلی	22.	hot	داغ	51.	under	زیر
36.	just	فقط	65.	walk	قدم زدن	23.	hurt	صدمه	52.	upon	روی
37.	know	دانستن	66.	were	بودند	24.	its	مال او	53.	use	کار بردن
38.	let	گذاشتن	67.	when	کی	25.	keep	نگهداشتن	54.	warm	گرم
39.	long	دراز	68.	who	کی	26.	kind	مهربان	55.	wash	شستن
40.	made	ساخت	69.	why	چرا	27.	light	نور	56.	well	خوب
41.	many	بسیاری	70.	wish	آرزو	28.	live	زنده	57.	which	کدام
42.	may	ممکن		SECOND		29.	myself	خودم	58.	would	خواست
43.	much	بسیار	1.	always	همیشه	30.	off	جدا	59.	write	نوشتن
44.	must	باید	2.	any	هر	31.	only	فقط	60.	draw	کشیدن
45.	never	هرگز	3.	because	زیرا	32.	own	مال	61.	eight	هشت (۸)
46.	of	از	4.	been	بوده	33.	pick	چیدن			
47.	old	کهنه	5.	best	بهترین	34.	pull	کشیدن			
48.	once	یکبار	6.	better	بهتر	35.	read	خواندن			
49.	open	باز	7.	both	هردو	36.	right	درست			
50.	or	یا	8.	bring	آوردن	37.	seven	هفت (۷)			
51.	our	مال ما	9.	buy	خریدن	38.	shall	خواهم			
52.	over	روی	10.	carry	حمل کردن	39.	sit	نشستن			

Dolch Basic Word List – Polish

Pre-primer

1. a _____
2. and ____i____
3. big ___duży___
4. blue __niebieski__
5. can ___móc___
6. come ___przyjść___
7. down __na dole__
8. for _____dla_____
9. funny __śmieszny__
10. get ___dostać___
11. go ___iść___
12. green __zielony__
13. have ___mieć___
14. help ___pomoc___
15. here ___tutaj___
16. I ____ja____
17. in ____w____
18. is ___jest___
19. it ____to____
20. jump __skakać__
21. little __maly__
22. look __patrzeć__
23. make ___robić___
24. please __proszę__
25. my ___mój___

26. not ___nie___
27. play __bawić się__
28. red __czerwony__
29. ride __jechać__
30. run ___biec___
31. said __powiedział__
32. saw __zobaczył__
33. see __widzieć__
34. the _____
35. this ___ten___
36. to ____do____
37. up __w górę__
38. want __chcieć__
39. we ____my____
40. with ____z____
41. work __pracować__
42. you ____ty____

Primer

1. all __wszyscy__
2. am __jestem__
3. are ____sa____
4. at ____w____
5. away _____
6. black __czarny__
7. but ____ale____
8. came __przyszedł__
9. did __zrobił__
10. do __robić__
11. eat ___jeść___
12. fast __szybko__
13. find __znaleźć__
14. good __dobry__
15. he ____on____
16. laugh __smiać się__
17. like __lubić__
18. new __nowy__
19. no ___nie___
20. now __teraz__
21. on ____na____
22. one __jeden__
23. out __poza__
24. please __proszę__
25. put __położyć__

26. ran __biegł__
27. say __mowić__
28. she ___ona___
29. so ___więc___
30. some __niektóre__
31. stop __przestać__
32. thank __dziękować__
33. that __tamten__
34. then __potem__
35. they ___oni___
36. three __trzy__
37. too __także__
38. two ___dwa___
39. was __był__
40. went __poszedł__
41. what ____co____
42. where __gdzie__
43. white __biały__
44. will __będzie__
45. yellow __żólty__
46. yes ___tak___
47. your __twój__

First

1. about ___o___
2. after ___po___
3. again ___znowu___
4. an _____
5. around ___dokoła___
6. as ___jak___
7. ask ___pytać___
8. ate ___zjadł___
9. be ___być___
10. before ___przed___
11. brown ___brązowy___
12. by ___przy___
13. call ___wołać___
14. cold ___zimny___
15. could ___mógł___
16. can't ___nie nóc___
17. every ___każdy___
18. far ___daleko___
19. first ___pierwszy___
20. five ___pięć___

21. fly ___latać___
22. found ___znalazł___
23. four ___cztery___
24. from ___od___
25. gave ___dał___
26. give ___dać___
27. going ___idący___
28. had ___miał___
29. has ___ma___
30. her ___jej___
31. him ___nim___
32. his ___jego___
33. how ___jak___
34. if ___jeżeli___
35. into ___do, w___
36. just ___tylko___
37. know ___wiedzieć___
38. let ___pozwolić___
39. long ___długi___
40. made ___zrobiony___

41. many ___dużo___
42. may ___moze___
43. much ___wiele___
44. must ___musi___
45. never ___nigdy___
46. of _____
47. old ___stary___
48. once ___raz___
49. open ___otwierać___
50. or ___albo___
51. our ___nasz___
52. over ___nad___
53. pretty ___ładny___
54. round ___okrągły___
55. show ___pokazać___
56. sing ___śpiewać___
57. sleep ___spać___
58. soon ___wkrótce___
59. take ___brać___

60. them ___ich___
61. there ___tam___
62. think ___myśleć___
63. us ___nas___
64. very ___bardzo___
65. walk ___chodzić___
66. were ___byli___
67. when ___kiedy___
68. who ___kto___
69. why ___dlaczego___
70. wish ___pragnąć___

Second

1. always __zawsze__	21. hold __trzymać__	41. small __mały__
2. any __żaden__	22. hot __gorący__	42. start __zacząć__
3. because __ponieważ__	23. hurt __boleć__	43. tell __opowiadać__
4. been _____	24. its __tego__	44. ten __dziesięć__
5. best __najlepszy__	25. keep __trzymać__	45. their __ich__
6. better __lepszy__	26. kind __miły__	46. these __te__
7. both __oboje__	27. light __swiatło__	47. those __tamte__
8. bring __przynosić__	28. live __żyć__	48. today __dzisiaj__
9. buy __kupić__	29. myself __ja sam__	49. together __razem__
10. carry __nieść__	30. off _____	50. try __próbować__
11. clean __czysty__	31. only __tylko__	51. under __pod__
12. cut __krajać__	32. own __własny__	52. upon __na__
13. does __robi__	33. pick __wybierać__	53. use __używać__
14. done __zrobione__	34. pull __ciągnąć__	54. warm __ciepły__
15. drink __pić__	35. read __czytać__	55. wash __myć__
16. fall __spadać__	36. right __prawy__	56. well __dobrze__
17. full __pełen__	37. seven __siedem__	57. which __który__
18. goes __idzie__	38. shall __będzie__	58. would _____
19. got __dostał__	39. sit __siedzieć__	59. write __pisać__
20. grow __rosnąć__	40. six __sześć__	60. draw __rysować__
		61. eight __osiem__

Dolch Basic Word List -- Portuguese

Pre-primer

1. a __um, uma__
2. and ___e___
3. big __grande__
4. blue __azul__
5. can __poder__
6. come __vir__
7. down __em baixo__
8. for __para (por)__
9. funny __engraçado__
10. get __ganhar__
11. go __ir__
12. green __verde__
13. have __ter__
14. help __ajudar__
15. here __aqui__
16. I __eu__
17. in __dentro (em)__
18. is __ser, estar__
19. it __ele, ela aquilo__
20. jump __pular__
21. little __pequeño__
22. look __olhar__
23. make __fazer__
24. me __mim__
25. my __meu (minha)__

26. not __não__
27. play __brincar, jogar__
28. red __vermelho__
29. ride __passeio__
30. run __correr__
31. said __disse__
   serra = the tool
32. saw __viu__
33. see __ver__
34. the __o, a, os, as__
35. this __este, esta__
36. to __até para__
37. up __em cima__
38. want __desejar, querer__
39. we __nós__
40. with __com__
41. work __trabalho__
42. you __voçê__

Primer

1. all __todos__
2. am __sou (I am)__
      __são (they are)__
3. are __somos (we are)__
4. at __em__
5. away __ausente__
6. black __preto__
7. but __mas__
8. came __veio__
9. did __fiz, fez, fizeram__
10. do __fazer__
11. eat __comer__
12. fast __rápido__
13. find __achar__
14. good __bom, bôa__
15. he __ele__
16. laugh __riso__
17. like __gostar__
18. new __novo, nova__
19. no __não__
20. now __agora__
21. on __sobre__
22. one __um, uma__
23. out __fora__
24. please __por favor__
25. put __pôr__

26. ran __correu__
27. say __dizer__
28. she __ela__
29. so __então__
30. some __alguns, algumas__
31. stop __parar__
32. thank __agradecer__
33. that __aquele__
34. then __então__
35. they __eles__
36. three __três__
37. too __também__
38. two __dois__
39. was __eu fui, ele/ela foi__
40. went __foi__
41. what __o que__
42. where __onde__
43. white __branco__
44. will __será__
45. yellow __amarelo__
46. yes __sim__
47. your __seu, sua__

First

1. about ____sobre____	21. fly ____voar____	41. many ___muitos___	60. them ___eles___
2. after __depois__	22. found ___achou___	42. may ___poder___	61. there ___ali___
3. again __outra vez__	23. four ___quatro___	43. much ___muito___	62. think __pensar__
4. an ___um, uma___	24. from ___desde___	44. must ___deve___	63. us ___nós___
5. around ___arredor___	25. gave ___deu___	45. never ___nunca___	64. very ___muito___
6. as ___como___	26. give ___dar___	46. of ___de___	65. walk ___andar___
7. ask ___pedir___	27. going ___indo___	47. old ___velho___	66. were estavamos, eramos
8. ate ___comeu___	28. had ___teve___	48. once ___certa vez___	67. when __quando__
9. be ___ser, estar___	29. has ___ter, ten___	49. open ___abrir___	68. who ___quem___
10. before ___antes___	30. her ___a, ela___	50. or ___ou___	69. why __por que?__
11. brown __castanho__	31. him ___o, ele___	51. our ___nosso___	70. wish ___desejo___
12. by ___por___	32. his ___dele___	52. over ___sobre___	
13. call ___chamar___	33. how ___como___	53. pretty ___lindo___	
14. cold ___frio___	34. if ___se___	54. round ___redondo___	
15. could ___poder___	35. into ___em___	55. show ___mostrar___	
16. can't ___não pode___	36. just ___somente, justo___	56. sing ___cantar___	
17. every ___cada, todo___	37. know ___saber___	57. sleep ___dormir___	
18. far ___longe___	38. let ___deixar___	58. soon ___brevemente___	
19. first ___primeiro___	39. long ___comprido___	59. take ___levar___	
20. five ___cinco___	40. made ___fez___		

Second

1. always __sempre__
2. any __qualquer__
3. because __porque__
   __comó tem__
4. been __passado__
5. best __o melhor__
6. better __melhor__
7. both __ambos__
8. bring __trazer__
9. buy __comprar__
10. carry __carregar__
11. clean __limpo__
12. cut __cortar__
13. does __faz__
14. done __feito, fez__
15. drink __beber__
16. fall __cair__
17. full __cheio__
18. goes __vai__
19. got __tem__
20. grow __crescer__

21. hold __segurar__
22. hot __quente__
23. hurt __machucar__
24. its __é__
25. keep __guardar__
26. kind __tipo, bondoso__
27. light __luz__
28. live __viver__
29. myself __eu mesmo__
30. off __disligar__
31. only __somente__
32. own __próprio__
33. pick __escolher__
34. pull __puxar__
35. read __ler__
36. right __direito__
37. seven __sete__
38. shall __vai ser__
39. sit __sentar-se__
40. six __seis__

41. small __pequeno__
42. start __começo__
43. tell __dizer__
44. ten __dez__
45. their __deles__
46. these __êstes__
47. those __aqueles, aquelas__
48. today __hoje__
49. together __juntos__
50. try __tentar__
51. under __em baixo__
52. upon __sôbre__
53. use __usar__
54. warm __tépido, morno__
55. wash __lavar__
56. well __bem__
57. which __qual__
58. would __iria, faria__
59. write __escrever__
60. draw __desenhar__
61. eight __oito__

Dolch Basic Word List – Russian

Pre-Primer :

1. a –	26. not не	7. but но
2. and и	27. play играть	8. came пришёл, (а)
3. big большой	28. red красный	9. did сделал, (а)
4. blue голубой	29. ride ехать верхом	10. do делать
5. can могу	30. run бежать	11. eat есть
6. come приходить	31. said сказал	12. fast быстро
7. down вниз	32. saw видел	13. find находить
8. for за	33. see видеть	14. good хорошо
9. funny смешной	34. the –	15. he он
10. get получать	35. this этот, эта, это	16. laugh смеяться
11. go идти	36. to к	17. like нравиться
12. green зелёный	37. up вверх	18. new новый
13. have иметь	38. want хотеть	19. no нет
14. help помогать	39. we мы	20. now сейчас
15. here здесь	40. with с	21. on на
16. I я	41. work работа	22. one один
17. in в	42. you ты, вы	23. out из
18. is есть		24. please пожалуйста
19. it это	**Primer :**	25. put класть, положить
20. jump прыгать	1. all все, всё	26. ran бежал
21. little маленький	2. am –	27. say сказать
22. look смотреть	3. are –	28. she она
23. make делать	4. at возле, около	29. so так
24. please пожалуйста	5. away прочь, от	30. some некоторые, (ая,) (ое)
25. my мой, моя, моё	6. black чёрный	31. stop остановить, (ся)
	7. but но	

32. thank благодарить
33. that тот, та
34. then тогда
35. they они
36. three три
37. too тоже
38. two два
39. was был, (а, о)
40. went пошёл, ходил
41. what что
42. where где
43. white белый
44. will быть, (он, она будет)
45. yellow жёлтый
46. yes да
47. your твой, твоя, твоё

First :

1. about о, об
2. after после
3. again снова
4. an -
5. around вокруг
6. as как
7. ask спросить
8. ate ел, (а) съел, (а)

9. be быть
10. before перед, до
11. brown коричневый
12. by около, у
13. call звать
14. cold холодный
15. could мог, (могла)
16. can't не могу, (не может)
17. every каждый
18. far далеко
19. first первый
20. five пять
21. fly летать
22. found нашёл, (нашла)
23. four четыре
24. from из
25. gave дал, (а)
26. give дать
27. going идущий
28. had имел, (а)
29. has иметь
30. her её, ей
31. him ему
32. his его
33. how как

34. if если
35. into в, внутрь
36. just только
37. know знать
38. let позволять
39. long длинный
40. made сделал, (а)
41. many много
42. may можно
43. much много
44. must должен
45. never никогда
46. of от
47. old старый
48. once однажды
49. open открывать
50. or или
51. our наш
52. over через
53. pretty красивый
54. round круглый
55. show показывать
56. sing петь
57. sleep спать
58. soon скоро

59. take   взять, брать
60. them   их
61. there   вот, там
62. think   думать
63. us   нас, нам
64. very   очень
65. walk   ходить, гулять
66. were   ты,мы, вы, они были
67. when   когда
68. who   кто
69. why   почему
70. wish   желать

Second :

1. always   всегда
2. any   каждый, любой
3. because   потому что
4. been   будучи
5. best   лучший
6. better   лучше
7. both   обв, обе
8. bring   приносить
9. buy   покупать
10. carry   нести
11. clean   чистить
12. cut   отрезать

13. does   он,она, оно делает
14. done   сделано, сделав
15. drink   пить
16. fall   падать
17. full   полный
18. goes   идти
19. got   получил, (а)
20. grow   расти
21. hold   держать
22. hot   горячий
23. hurt   болеть
24. its   этому, ей, его, свой, своя
25. keep   держать
26. kind   1. добрый 2. сорт, род
27. light   1. лёгкий 2. свет
28. live   жить
29. myself   сам, (а)
30. off   с, со, от
31. only   только
32. own   собственный
33. pick   собирать
34. pull   тянуть
35. read   читать
36. right   правый, правильно
37. seven   семь

38. shall   я, мы будем
39. sit   сидеть
40. six   шесть
41. small   маленький
42. start   начинать
43. tell   рассказать
44. ten   десять
45. their   их
46. these   эти
47. those   тех, те
48. today   сегодня
49. together   вместе
50. try   пытаться
51. under   под
52. upon   на
53. use   пользоваться
54. warm   тёплый
55. wash   мыть
56. well   хорошо
57. which   который
58. would   он,она,ты,вы, они бы, было бы
59. write   писать
60. draw   рисовать
61. eight   восемь

Dolch Basic Word List -- Samoan

Pre-primer

1. a _____le, se_____
2. and _____ma_____
3. big _____tele-_____
4. blue _____lanumoana_____
5. can _____mafai_____
6. come _____sau_____
7. down _____lalo_____
8. for _____mō_____
9. funny _____mālie_____
10. get _____maua, 'aumai_____
11. go _____alu_____
12. green _____lanumea mata_____
13. have _____o i ai_____
14. help _____fesoasoani_____
15. here _____'i ī_____
16. I _____O a'u, 'Ou te_____
17. in _____totonu_____
18. is _____'ua_____
19. it _____mea_____
20. jump _____oso_____
21. little _____laitiiti_____
22. look _____vaai_____
23. make _____fai_____
24. me _____a'u_____
25. my _____la'u, lo'u_____
26. not _____lē, leai_____
27. play _____taalo_____
28. red _____mūmū_____
29. ride _____tietie_____
30. run _____tamóe_____
31. said _____faiane_____
32. saw _____sa vaai_____
33. see _____vaai_____
34. the _____le_____
35. this _____lea_____
36. to _____i-_____
37. up _____luga_____
38. want _____manaó_____
39. we _____tatou_____
40. with _____ma_____
41. work _____galue_____
42. you _____'oe_____

Primer

1. all _____'atoa_____
2. am _____ā'u_____
3. are _____'ua_____
4. at _____ià, i le_____
5. away _____mamao_____
6. black _____uliuli_____
7. but _____peitai_____
8. came _____sa sau_____
9. did _____sa, safaia_____
10. do _____faia, malie_____
11. eat _____'ai_____
12. fast _____saoasaoa_____
13. find _____maua, sué_____
14. good _____lelei_____
15. he _____o ia_____
16. laugh _____'ata_____
17. like _____mana'o, tusa_____
18. new _____fou_____
19. no _____leai_____
20. now _____nei_____
21. on _____luga_____
22. one _____tasi_____
23. out _____fafo_____
24. please _____faamolemole_____
25. put _____tuu_____
26. ran _____sa tamo'e_____
27. say _____fai mai, fai ane_____
28. she _____o ia_____
29. so _____'ona_____
30. some _____le isi nisi_____
31. stop _____faatali, tū_____
32. thank _____faafetal_____
33. that _____le_____
34. then _____pe'ā, 'ona_____
35. they _____latou_____
36. three _____tolu_____
37. too _____foi_____
38. two _____lua_____
39. was _____sa_____
40. went _____sa alu_____
41. what _____o se ā?_____
42. where _____o fea_____
43. white _____pa'epa'e_____
44. will _____o le'ā, loto_____
45. yellow _____samasama_____
46. yes _____ioe_____
47. your _____lau, āu_____

First

1. about ____e tusa____	21. fly ____lele____	41. many ____tele____	60. them ____latou____
2. after ____'uma, mavae____	22. found ____sa maua____	42. may __masalo atonu__	61. there ____'ō____
3. again ____toe____	23. four ____fā____	43. much ____tele____	62. think __mafaufau__
4. an ____o le____	24. from ____mai____	44. must ____tatau____	63. us __tatou, matou__
5. around __tusa, taá milo__	25. gave ____sa 'ave____	45. never __lē mafai__	64. very ____tele____
6. as ____faapei, tusa____	26. give ____'ave____	46. of ____o le____	65. walk ____savali____
7. ask ____fesili____	27. going ____alu____	47. old ____matua____	66. were ____sá____
8. ate ____sa' ai____	28. had ____sa iai____	48. once ____faatasi____	67. when ____anafea____
9. be ____fia____	29. has ____iai____	49. open ____tatala____	68. who ____o ai____
10. before ____aó léi____	30. her ____lona, ia____	50. or ____po o____	69. why ____aiseā____
11. brown ____'efu'efu____	31. him ____ia____	51. our __matou, tatou__	70. wish ____fia____
12. by ____talane____	32. his ____lona____	52. over __uma, luga__	
13. call ____valáau____	33. how ____faapefea____	53. pretty ____manaia____	
14. cold ____malulū____	34. if ____afai____	54. round __lapotopoto__	
15. could ____mafai____	35. into ____i totonu____	55. show ____faa áli____	
16. can't ____lē mafai____	36. just ____na'o le____	56. sing ____pese____	
17. every ____so'o se____	37. know ____iloa____	57. sleep ____moe____	
18. far ____mamao____	38. let ____tu'uina atu____	58. soon ____toeitiiti____	
19. first ____muamua____	39. long ____umī____	59. take ____'ave____	
20. five ____lima____	40. made ____na faia____		

Second

1. always _____soó_____
2. any ___soó se___
3. because _'a uā__
4. been _____sā_____
5. best __silisili__
6. better ___sili atu___
7. both ___'uma e lua___
8. bring ___'aumai___
9. buy __faatau mai__
10. carry _____'ave_____
11. clean __mamā__
12. cut _____tipi_____
13. does ___faia___
14. done __na faia__
15. drink _____inu_____
16. fall __pa'ū__
17. full __tumu__
18. goes ___alu___
19. got ___o i ai___
20. grow ____ola____

21. hold ___'u'u___
22. hot ___vevela___
23. hurt ____ti gā____
24. its ___o lona___
25. keep ___tausi___
     ituaiga
26. kind __lotoalofa__
27. light _molī malamalama_
28. live _____ōla_____
29. myself __a'u lava__
30. off __('ave) 'ese__
31. only ___na o'___
32. own __laù áu__
33. pick ____tau____
34. pull ___toso___
35. read ___faitau___
36. right _sa'o, taumatau_
37. seven ___fitu___
38. shall __o lè ā__
39. sit ___nofo___
40. six ___ono___

41. small ___laitiiti___
42. start ___'amata___
43. tell __ta'u faamatala__
44. ten ___sefulu___
45. their ___latou___
46. these __o 'ia__
47. those ___nā___
48. today __le asō__
49. together _faatasi 'uma_
50. try ___taumafai___
51. under __i lalo ifo__
52. upon __'ina 'ua__
53. use ___faa aogā___
54. warm _ma fanafana_
55. wash __fufulu, tatā__
56. well ___lelei___
57. which __le fea__
58. would _e mafai_
59. write ___tusi___
60. draw __tusi le ata__
61. eight ___valu___

Dolch Basic Word List – Spanish

Pre-primer

1. a   <u>un, una, uno(s)</u>
2. and   <u>y</u>
3. big   <u>grande</u>
4. blue   <u>azul</u>
5. can <u>puede, puedo</u> _{poder}
6. come <u>vengo, ven</u> _{venir}
7. down   <u>abajo</u>
8. for   <u>por, para</u>
9. funny <u>divertido</u> _{chistoso}
10. get <u>cojer, obtener</u>
11. go   <u>ve, vete, ir</u>
12. green   <u>verde</u>
13. have   <u>tener</u>
14. help <u>ayudar, ayuda</u>
15. here   <u>aquí</u>
16. I   <u>yo</u>
17. in <u>adentro, en</u>
18. is   <u>es, está</u>
19. it <u>eso, lo la</u>
20. jump <u>saltar, brincar</u>
21. little <u>chiquito, pequeño</u>
22. look   <u>mirar</u>
23. make   <u>hacer</u>
24. me   <u>yo</u>
25. my   <u>mio</u>

26. not   <u>no</u>
27. play   <u>jugar</u>
28. red <u>colorado, rojo</u>
29. ride <u>viojar, pasear</u>
30. run   <u>correr</u>
31. said   <u>dije, dijo</u>
32. saw   <u>vi</u>
33. see   <u>ver</u>
34. the   <u>el, la</u>
35. this   <u>este</u>
36. to   <u>a</u>
37. up   <u>arriba</u>
38. want <u>quiero, querer</u>
39. we   <u>nosotros</u>
40. with   <u>con</u>
41. work   <u>trabajar</u>
42. you   <u>usted, tú</u>

Primer

1. all   <u>todos</u>
2. am <u>soy, estoy</u>
3. are   <u>eres, son</u>
4. at   <u>a</u>
5. away   <u>lejos</u>
6. black   <u>negro</u>
7. but   <u>pero</u>
8. came <u>vino, venir</u>
9. did   <u>hizo</u>
10. do   <u>hacer</u>
11. eat   <u>comer</u>
12. fast <u>lijero, velóz</u> _{rápido}
13. find <u>hallar encontrar</u>
14. good   <u>bueno</u>
15. he   <u>él</u>
16. laugh   <u>reir</u>
17. like <u>gusta, gustar</u>
18. new   <u>nuevo</u>
19. no   <u>no</u>
20. now   <u>ahora</u>
21. on <u>encima, sobre</u>
22. one   <u>uno</u>
23. out <u>a fuera, fuera</u>
24. please <u>por favor</u>
25. put   <u>poner</u>

26. ran   <u>corrio</u>
27. say   <u>decir</u>
28. she   <u>ella</u>
29. so <u>así, entonces</u>
30. some <u>algo, algúnos</u>
31. stop <u>alto, deténgase</u>
32. thank   <u>gracias</u>
33. that   <u>ese, esa</u>
34. then   <u>entonces</u>
35. they   <u>ellos</u>
36. three   <u>tres</u>
37. too   <u>también</u>
38. two   <u>dos</u>
39. was   <u>estaba</u>
40. went   <u>fue</u>
41. what <u>que, lo que</u>
42. where   <u>dónde</u>
43. white   <u>blanco</u>
44. will <u>poder, voluntad</u>
45. yellow   <u>amarillo</u>
46. yes   <u>sí</u>
47. your   <u>tu, su</u>

First

1. about ___acerca de___
2. after ___después___
3. again ___otra vez___
4. an ___un, una, uno___
5. around ___alrededor___
6. as ___como___
7. ask ___preguntar___
8. ate ___comió___
9. be ___ser o estar___
10. before ___antes___
11. brown ___café___
12. by ___por, para___
13. call ___llamar___
14. cold ___frío___
15. could ___pude, poder___
16. can't ___no puedo___
17. every ___cada___
18. far ___lejos___
19. first ___primero___
20. five ___cinco___

21. fly ___volar___
22. found ___encontró___
23. four ___cuatro___
24. from ___de___
25. gave ___dió___
26. give ___dar___
27. going ___ir, va, voy___
28. had ___tuvo___
29. has ___tiene___
30. her ___ella___
31. him ___él___
32. his/hers ___su, de él/de ella___
33. how ___cómo___
34. if ___si___
35. into ___adentro de___
36. just ___exactamente, solamente___
37. know ___saber, conocer___
38. let ___deja, dejar___
39. long ___largo___
40. made ___hecho___

41. many ___muchos___
42. may ___puede, poder___
43. much ___mucho___
44. must ___debe, deber___
45. never ___nunca___
46. of ___de___
47. old ___viejo___
48. once ___una vez___
49. open ___abierto___
50. or ___o___
51. our ___nuestro___
52. over ___arriba, sobre___
53. pretty ___bonito___
54. round ___redondo___
55. show ___enseñar, mostrar___
56. sing ___cantar___
57. sleep ___dormir___
58. soon ___pronto___
59. take ___tomar___

60. them ___ellos___
61. there ___allá___
62. think ___pensar___
63. us ___nosotros___
64. very ___muy___
65. walk ___caminar___
66. were ___estaban, eran, fue___
67. when ___cuando___
68. who ___quien/quién*___
69. why ___por qué___
70. wish ___desear___

---

*Quien with no accent mark is a relative pronoun; quién has an accent over the *e* when it is a question.

Second

1. always __siempre__
2. any __algún, algunos, cualquier__
3. because __porque__
4. been __he estado / ha sido__
5. best __el mejor__
6. better __mejor__
7. both __los dos, ambos__
8. bring __traer__
9. buy __comprar__
10. carry __llevar a / transportar__
11. clean __limpio__
12. cut __cortar__
13. does __hace__
14. done __hecho__
15. drink __beber__
16. fall __caer__
17. full __lleno__
18. goes __va__
19. got __obtuvo__
20. grow __crecer__

21. hold __sostener, tener / aguantar__
22. hot __caliente__
23. hurt __doler__
24. its __su, sus__
25. keep __guardar / contener__
26. kind __tipo, clase__
27. light __luz__
28. live __vivir__
29. myself __yo mismo__
30. off __de fuera__
31. only __unico, solamente__
32. own __propio__
33. pick __escoger, cojer / selección__
34. pull __tirar, halar__
35. read __leer__
36. right __correcto__
37. seven __siete__
38. shall __voluntad, debe, debo, puedo__
39. sit __asiento, sentarse__
40. six __seis__

41. small __chico, pequeño__
42. start __comenzar, empezar__
43. tell __dicer__
44. ten __diez__
45. their __su, sus__
46. these __estos__
47. those __aquellos, esos__
48. today __hoy__
49. together __juntos__
50. try __procurar, tratar de__
51. under __debajo__
52. upon __sobre__
53. use __uso, usar__
54. warm __tibio__
55. wash __lavar__
56. well __pozo, bien__
57. which __cuál__
58. would __voluntad, puedo__
59. write __escribir__
60. draw __atraer, dibujar__
61. eight __ocho__

Dolch Basic Word List – Swedish

Pre-primer

1. a ___en, ett___
2. and ___och___
3. big ___stor___
4. blue ___blå___
5. can ___kan___
6. come ___komma___
7. down ___ner___
8. for ___för___
9. funny ___rolig___
10. get ___få___
11. go ___gå___
12. green ___grön___
13. have ___har, ha___
14. help ___hjälp___
15. here ___här___
16. I ___jag___
17. in ___i, inne___
18. is ___är___
19. it ___den, det___
20. jump ___hoppa___
21. little ___liten___
22. look ___titta___
23. make ___göra___
24. me ___mig___
25. my ___min, mitt___

26. not ___inte___
27. play ___leka___
28. red ___röd___
29. ride ___rida, åka___
30. run ___springa___
31. said ___sade, sa___
32. saw ___såg___
33. see ___se___
34. the ___denna, detta___
35. this ___den, det___
36. to ___till___
37. up ___upp___
38. want ___önska___
39. we ___vi___
40. with ___med___
41. work ___arbete___
42. you ___du___

Primer

1. all ___alla___
2. am ___är___
3. are ___är___
4. at ___vid, på, i___
5. away ___iväg___
6. black ___svart___
7. but ___men___
8. came ___kom___
9. did ___gjorde___
10. do ___gör, göra___
11. eat ___äta___
12. fast ___fort___
13. find ___finna___
14. good ___god, bra___
15. he ___han___
16. laugh ___skratta, scratt___
17. like ___tycka, tycker___
18. new ___ny___
19. no ___nej___
20. now ___nu___
21. on ___på___
22. one ___en, ett___
23. out ___ut___
24. please ___var snäll___
25. put ___sätta, lägga___

26. ran ___sprang___
27. say ___säga___
28. she ___hon___
29. so ___så___
30. some ___några___
31. stop ___stopp___
32. thank ___tacka, tack___
33. that ___att___
34. then ___då___
35. they ___de___
36. three ___tre___
37. too ___också___
38. two ___två___
39. was ___var___
40. went ___gick___
41. what ___vad___
42. where ___var vart___
43. white ___vit___
44. will ___vill___
45. yellow ___gul___
46. yes ___ja___
47. your ___din, ditt, dina___

First

1. about ___omkring___
2. after ___efter___
3. again ___igen___
4. an ___en, ett___
5. around ___omkring___
6. as ___som___
7. ask ___fråga___
8. ate ___åt___
9. be ___vara___
10. before ___före___
11. brown ___brun___
12. by ___av, vid___
13. call ___ringa, ropa___
14. cold ___kall, kallt___
15. could ___kunde___
16. can't ___kan inte___
17. every ___varje___
18. far ___långt___
19. first ___först___
20. five ___fem___

21. fly ___flyga___
22. found ___fann___
23. four ___fyra___
24. from ___från___
25. gave ___gav___
26. give ___giva, ge___
27. going ___skall gå___
28. had ___hade___
29. has ___har___
30. her ___henne, hennes___
31. him ___honom___
32. his ___hans___
33. how ___hur___
34. if ___om___
35. into ___inuti___
36. just ___bara, endast___
37. know ___veta___
38. let ___låt, låta___
39. long ___lång___
40. made ___gjorde___

41. many ___många___
42. may ___kan___
43. much ___mycket___
44. must ___måste___
45. never ___aldrig___
46. of ___av___
47. old ___gammal___
48. once ___en gång___
49. open ___öppen, öppna___
50. or ___eller___
51. our ___vår___
52. over ___över___
53. pretty ___vacker___
54. round ___rund___
55. show ___visa___
56. sing ___sjunga___
57. sleep ___sova___
58. soon ___snart___
59. take ___ta___

60. them ___de___
61. there ___där___
62. think ___tänk___
63. us ___oss___
64. very ___varje___
65. walk ___promenera, gå___
66. were ___vore, blev___
67. when ___när___
68. who ___vem___
69. why ___varför___
70. wish ___önska___

Second

1. always _alltid_

2. any _någon_

3. because _för att_

4. been _varit_

5. best _bäst_

6. better _bättre_

7. both _båda_

8. bring _komma med_

9. buy _köpa_

10. carry _bära_

11. clean _ren_

12. cut _skära_

13. does _gör_

14. done _gjort_

15. drink _dricka_

16. fall _falla_

17. full _full_

18. goes _går_

19. got _fått_

20. grow _växa_

21. hold _hålla_

22. hot _het, varm_

23. hurt _skadad_

24. its _dess_

25. keep _hålla_

26. kind _vänlig_

27. light _ljus_

28. live _leva_

29. myself _mig själv_

30. off _av_

31. only _endast_

32. own _egen, äga_

33. pick _plocka_

34. pull _draga_

35. read _läsa_

36. right _rätt, höger_

37. seven _sju_

38. shall _skall_

39. sit _sitt, sitta_

40. six _sex_

41. small _liten_

42. start _börja_

43. tell _berätta_

44. ten _tio_

45. their _deras_

46. these _dess de här_

47. those _dessa_

48. today _idag_

49. together _tillsammans_

50. try _försöka_

51. under _under_

52. upon _på_

53. use _använda_

54. warm _varm_

55. wash _tväta_

56. well _väl bra_

57. which _vilken_

58. would _skulle, kunde_

59. write _skriva_

60. draw _rita_

61. eight _åtta_

Dolch Basic Word List – Thai

Pre-Primer :

1.	a	–	26.	not	ไม่	7.	but	แต่
2.	and	และ	27.	play	เล่น	8.	came	มาแล้ว
3.	big	ใหญ่	28.	red	สีแดง	9.	did	ได้ทำ
4.	blue	สีน้ำเงิน	29.	ride	ขี่	10.	do	ทำ
5.	can	กระป๋อง	30.	run	วิ่ง	11.	eat	กิน
6.	come	มา	31.	said	ได้บอก, ได้พูด	12.	fast	เร็ว
7.	down	ลง	32.	saw	ได้เห็น	13.	find	เจอ, หา, พบ
8.	for	สำหรับ	33.	see	เห็น	14.	good	ดี
9.	funny	ตลก, น่าขัน	34.	the	–	15.	he	เขา (ชาย)
10.	get	ได้รับ	35.	this	นี้	16.	laugh	หัวเราะ
11.	go	ไป	36.	to	ถึง	17.	like	ชอบ
12.	green	สีเขียว	37.	up	ชี้ไป, ข้างบน	18.	new	ใหม่
13.	have	มี	38.	want	ต้องการ	19.	no	ไม่
14.	help	ช่วยเหลือ	39.	we	พวกเรา	20.	now	เดี๋ยวนี้
15.	here	ที่นี่	40.	with	ด้วย, กับ	21.	on	บน
16.	I	ฉัน	41.	work	ทำงาน	22.	one	หนึ่ง
17.	in	ใน	42.	you	คุณ	23.	out	ออก, ข้างนอก
18.	is	เป็น				24.	please	กรุณา
19.	it	มัน	**Primer :**			25.	put	วาง, ใส่
20.	jump	กระโดด	1.	all	ทั้งหมด	26.	ran	ได้วิ่ง
21.	little	เล็กน้อย	2.	am	เป็น	27.	say	บอก, พูด
22.	look	มองดู	3.	are	เป็น	28.	she	เขา (ผู้หญิง)
23.	make	ทำ	4.	at	ที่	29.	so	ดังนั้น
24.	please	กรุณา	5.	away	ไกลออกไป	30.	some	บางอัน
25.	my	ของฉัน	6.	black	สีดำ	31.	stop	หยุด
			7.	but	แต่			

32.	thank	ขอบคุณ
33.	that	นั้น , สิ่งนั้น
34.	then	เวลานั้น
35.	they	พวกเขา
36.	three	สาม
37.	too	ด้วย
38.	two	สอง
39.	was	เป็น
40.	went	ได้ไป
41.	what	อะไร
42.	where	ที่ไหน
43.	white	สีขาว
44.	will	จะ
45.	yellow	สีเหลือง
46.	yes	ใช่, ค่ะ, ครับ.
47.	your	ของคุณ

First :

1.	about	เกี่ยวกับ
2.	after	หลังจาก
3.	again	อีกที
4.	an	-
5.	around	รอบๆ
6.	as	เหมือนกับ
7.	ask	ขอ, ถาม
8.	ate	ได้กินแล้ว

9.	be	เป็น
10.	before	ก่อน
11.	brown	สีน้ำตาล
12.	by	โดย
13.	call	เรียก
14.	cold	หนาว
15.	could	สามารถ , ทำได้
16.	can't	ทำไม่ได้
17.	every	ทุกๆ
18.	far	ไกล
19.	first	ครั้งแรก, ที่หนึ่ง
20.	five	ห้า
21.	fly	บิน
22.	found	ได้พบ
23.	four	สี่
24.	from	จาก
25.	gave	ได้ให้
26.	give	ให้
27.	going	กำลังไป
28.	had	เคยมี
29.	has	มี
30.	her	ของเขา (ผู้หญิง)
31.	him	เขา (ผู้ชาย)
32.	his	ของเขา (ผู้ชาย)
33.	how	อย่างไร

34.	if	ถ้า
35.	into	ข้างใน
36.	just	เพียง
37.	know	ทราบ, รู้
38.	let	ให้
39.	long	ยาว, นาน
40.	made	ได้ทำ
41.	many	มาก , จำนวนมาก
42.	may	อาจจะ
43.	much	มาก
44.	must	ต้อง
45.	never	ไม่เคย
46.	of	ของ
47.	old	แก่, เก่า
48.	once	ครั้งหนึ่ง
49.	open	เปิด
50.	or	หรือ
51.	our	ของเรา
52.	over	ข้างบน
53.	pretty	สวย
54.	round	กลม
55.	show	แสดง
56.	sing	ร้องเพลง
57.	sleep	นอนหลับ
58.	soon	อีกไม่นาน

#	English	Thai		#	English	Thai		#	English	Thai
59.	take	เอาไป		13.	does	ทำ		38.	shall	จะ
60.	them	พวกเขา		14.	done	ทำเสร็จ		39.	sit	นั่ง
61.	there	ที่นั่น		15.	drink	ดื่ม		40.	six	หก
62.	think	คิด		16.	fall	ตก		41.	small	เล็ก
63.	us	พวกเรา		17.	full	เต็ม		42.	start	เริ่ม
64.	very	มาก		18.	goes	ไป		43.	tell	บอก
65.	walk	เดิน		19.	got	ได้แล้ว		44.	ten	สิบ
66.	were	เป็น,เคยเป็น		20.	grow	เติบโต,ปลูก		45.	their	ของเขา
67.	when	เมื่อ		21.	hold	จับ,ถือ		46.	these	อันเหล่านี้
68.	who	ใคร		22.	hot	ร้อน		47.	those	อันเหล่านั้น
69.	why	ทำไม		23.	hurt	เจ็บ		48.	today	วันนี้
70.	wish	ประสงค์,ปรารถนา		24.	its	ของมัน		49.	together	ด้วยกัน

Second :

#	English	Thai		#	English	Thai		#	English	Thai
1.	always	เสมอ		25.	keep	เก็บ		50.	try	พยายาม
2.	any	อันไหนก็ได้		26.	kind	ชนิด,แบบ		51.	under	ข้างใต้
3.	because	เพราะว่า		27.	light	แสง		52.	upon	ข้างบน
4.	been	เป็น		28.	live	อยู่อาศัย		53.	use	ใช้
5.	best	ดีที่สุด		29.	myself	ตัวฉันเอง		54.	warm	อบอุ่น
6.	better	ดีกว่า,ดีขึ้น		30.	off	ปิด,ถอด		55.	wash	ล้าง
7.	both	ทั้งสอง		31.	only	เพียง		56.	well	สบายดี
8.	bring	เอามา		32.	own	เป็นเจ้าของ		57.	which	อันไหน
9.	buy	ซื้อ		33.	pick	เก็บ,เลือก		58.	would	จะ
10.	carry	ถือ		34.	pull	ดึง		59.	write	เขียน
11.	clean	สะอาด		35.	read	อ่าน		60.	draw	วาดภาพ
12.	cut	ตัด		36.	right	ถูกต้อง,ขวา		61.	eight	แปด
				37.	seven	เจ็ด				

Dolch Basic Word List – Tongan

Pre-Primer

1. a/an: if quite indefinite, *ha;* if semidefinite, *e* (or *'a e*), or *he.*

2. and: *pea; mo; pea mo; 'o; mā; ka, kae;* or *kae'uma'a.*

3. big: *lahi; lalahi;* or *fuolahi.*

4. blue: *lanu-pulū* or *lanu-moana.*

5. can (be able): *lava.*
   can (tin): *kapa.*

6. come: *ha'u.*
   come about: *hoko.*
   come across: *'ilo; ma'u;* or *fetaulaki mo.*
   come away (become detached): *tō; mato'o; mahamu; manu'i;* or *matala.*
   come back: *foki mai.*
   come by (get): *ma'u.*
   come down: *'alu hifo.*
   come down on (reprove): *valoki'i* or *tafulu'i.*
   come in: *hu mai.*
   come in handy: *hoko 'o 'aonga.*
   come in two: *masī-ua; mafahi-ua; mavae-ua; mafoa-ua;* or *movete.*
   come on (sickness): *puke.*
   come open: *ava; mato'o;* or *matangaki.*
   come out with (say): *pehē.*
   come round (recover): *ake.*
   come short: *'ikai ke fe'unga.*
   come through: *'asi mai* or *hao mai.*
   come true: *hoko 'o pehe* or *hoko 'o mo'oni.*
   come up: *'alu hake.*

7. down: *hifo;* or *ki lalo.*
   down (fluff): *fulufulu'otua.*

8. for (conj.): *he*
   for (prep.): *ma'a; mo'o; ki;* or *mo.*
   for (duration): *'o; 'o fe'unga mo;* or *'i.*

9. funny: *fakaoli;* or *fakakata.*

10. get (obtain): *ma'u.*
    get (become): *faka'au.*

get (persuade): *fakaloto'i;* or *fakakouna.*
get (grasp, understand): *ma'u.*
   (There are as many, or more, of the many different possibilities of the word "get" as there are for the word "come" but the above will probably be enough.)

11. go: *'alu* (of clock or engine, etc.); *mo'ui.*
    (The note on No. 10 applies to the word "go" also.)

12. green (color): *lanu-mata.*
    green (unripe): *mata* or *mui.*
    green and healthy: *lau-ma'ui'ui.*

13. have (auxiliary verb): *kuo.*
    have (possess, etc.): *'i ai; 'i; taki;* or *ma'u.*
    (The note in No. 10 also applies to the word "have.")

14. help: *tokoni.*

15. here: *'i heni; ki heni; eni/'eni;* or ***ko eni/ko 'eni.***

16. I (preposed [before the verb] exclusive): *ou; ku; u;* or *kau;*
    (postposed [after the verb]): *au.*
    I (preposed, inclusive form): *te;*
    (postposed) *kita.*

17. in: *'i; 'i he loto.*

18. is (denoting identity): *ko.*
    (denoting existance/location/tense-sign): *'i ai.*
    (This also applies to *be, am, art, are, were, have been, will be,* etc.)

19. it: *ia; ne* or merely understood.

20. jump: *hopo; puna; tahopo;* or *topuna.*

21. little: *si'i/si'isi'i.*

22. look (see): *sio.*
    look (appear): *matamata; ngali; ngalingali;* or *ha.*
    (The note in No. 10 also applies to the word "look.")

23. make: *ngaohi; fa'u; 'ai; fakatupu; tufunga'i; fakakouna;* or *o'i.*
    (The note in No. 10 also applies to the word "make.")

2₄. me: *au.*

25. my: *he'eku; 'eku;* or *hoku.*
    (This note will apply to most pronouns: The pronoun "my" also has an exclusive definite, ordinary, emotional, and emphatic forms; and indefinite ordinary, emotional, and emphatic forms.)

26. not: *'ikai;* or *'oua.*

27. play (an instrument): *tā;* or *ifi.*
    play (a game): *va'inga.*
    play (drama, etc.): *fo'i faiva.*
    (The note in No. 10 also applies to the word "play.")

28. red: *kulokula.*

29. ride: *heka.*
    ride on the back: *fafa.*
    ride on the shoulders: *vakavaka'āhina.*
    ride roughshod: *fakaaoao.*
    ride on the breakers: *fānifo.*

30. run (intrance. verb): *lele.*
    run (flow): *tafe.*
    run (a business): *ngāue'i.*
    (The note in No. 10 also applies to the word "run.")

31. said: *na'a ne lea'aki.*

32. saw: *na'a ne sio/mamata.*

33. see: *sio.*

34. the: *he; e;* or *si'i.*

35. this: *ni* or *ko eni.*

36. to: *ki; kia;* or *kiate;*
    (indefinite) *ke.*

37. up: *hake;* or *ki 'olunga.*
    up (out of bed): *'ā.*
    (The note in No. 10 also applies to the word "up.")

38. want (be in want): *masiva.*
    want (want to get): *fie ma'u.*

39. we (dual, excluding you): *ma* or *kimaua.*
    we (plural, excluding you): *maua* or *kimautolu.*
    we (dual, including you): *ta* or *kitaua.*
    we (plural, including you): *tau* or *kitautolu.*
    (See note in No. 25.)

40. with (accompanying, etc.): *mo.*
    with (by means of): *'aki.*
    with (in charge of): *'i.*

41. work: *ngāue.*

42. you (singular): *koe;* or *ke.*
    you (dual): *kimoua;* or *mo.*
    you (plural): *kimoutolu;* or *mou.*
    (See note in No. 25.)

Primer

1. all: *kotoa; kātoa; fuli pē;* or *fua pē.*

2. am: (See No. 18, Pre-Primer.)

3. are: (See No. 18, Pre-Primer.)

4. at: *'i; ia;* or *'iate.*

5. away: *atu;* or *mama'o.*

6. black: *'uli'uli.*

7. but (adverb): *pē.*
    but (conjunction): *ka; kae; kae kehe; ka he;* or *ka ko.*
    but (preposition): *ngata pē 'i; ka ko;* or *tuku kehe.*

8. came: *na'a* (app. pronoun) *ha'u.*

9. did: *na'a* (app. pronoun) *fai* (Never say *fai* alone. It is a four-letter word meaning sexual intercourse. It always has to be used in a complete sentence.) *ngaohi;* or *'ai.*

10. do: *fai* (See caution on No. 9.) *ngaohi;* or *'ai.*

11. eat: *kai.*

12. fast (quick): *vave.*
    fast (firm): *ma'u; tu'u ma'u;* or *tauma'u.*
    fast (without food): *'aukai.*

13. find: *'ilo;* or *ma'u.*
    find (look for): *kumi.*

14. good: *lelei;* or *sai.*

15. he (no gender in Tongan to distinguish between "he" and "she", etc.): *ne;* or *ia.*
    (See note in No. 25, Pre-Primer.)

16. laugh: *kata.*

17. like (similar): *vāofi;* or *ngali.*
    like (transitive verb): *manako; sai'ia; ifo'ia; malie'ia;* or *lelei'ia.*

18. new: *fo'ou;* or *fo'ofo'ou.*

19. no: *'ikai.*

20. now: *eni; ni; ko eni; toki; leva; 'i he taimi ni; foki;* or *lolotonga.*

21. on (prep.): *'i ('i he funga tepile).*
    on (adv.): *atu.*
    (See note in No. 10, Pre-Primer.)

22. one (number): *taha.*
    one (pronoun): *te;* or *kita.*

23. out (outside): *ki tu'a;* or *atu.*
    out (fire or in game): *mate.*
    out (erroneous): *hala.*
    (See note in No. 10, Pre-Primer.)

24. please: *fakamolemole; kātaki;* or *mu'l (fakamolemole mu'a; kataki mu'a).*

25. put: *tuku;* or *'ai.*
    (See note in No. 10, Pre-Primer.)

26. ran (See No. 30, Pre-Primer — run — but tense and appropriate pronoun would be added.): These are the four past-tense forms used in Tongan: *Kuo; na'a; ne;* or *na'e.* (This will apply to all past tense.)

27. say: *pehē; lau; lea;* or *lea'aki.*

28. she: (Same as No. 15.)

29. so (thus): *pehē;* or *pehē fau.*
    so (therefore): *ai;* or *leva.*

30. some (quantity of): *ha.*
    some (number of): *ngaahi* or other dual or plural signs, or *ni'ihi.*

31. stop (intransitive verb): *tu'u; ma'u;* or *tuku.*
    stop (transitive verb): *ta'ofi.*
    stop (comma, etc.): *faka'ilonga malōlō.*
    stop (of an organ): *sitopa.*

32. thank: *fakamālō;* or *fakafeta'i.*

33. that (conjunctive): *ke.*
    that (who, whom, and which): *ia;* or *ha.*

34. then: *toki, leva; pea; pehē; ko ia; hili iā;* or *'osi ia.*

35. they: (dual) *naua* or *kinaua;* (plural) *nautolu* or *kinautolu.*
    (See the note in No. 25, Pre-Primer.)

36. three: *tolu.*

37. too (also): *foki.*
    too (excessively): *fu'u;* or *hulu.*
38. two: *ua.*
39. was: (See the note on tense signs in No. 26.)
40. went: (See the note on tense signs in No. 26; see also No. 11, Pre-Primer.)
41. what: *hā;* or *fē (ko e hā).*
42. where: *'i fē.*
43. white: *hinehina.*
44. will (document): *tohi tuku.*
    will (purpose, etc.): *loto.*
    will (decide/d): *fakapapau.*
    will (would): *te;* or *'e.*
45. yellow: *engeenga.*
46. yes: *'io.*
47. your (singular): *ho'o;* or *ho.*
    your (dual): *ho'omo;* or *homo.*
    your (plural): *ho'omou;* or *homou.*
    (See the note in No. 25, Pre-Primer.)

First

1. about (around): *holo.*
   about (roughly): *nai.*
   about (concerning): *ki; kau ki; 'o kau ki;* or *'i.*
2. after: *hili; 'osi;* or *kimui 'i.*
3. again: *toe.*
4. an: (See the note in No. 1, Pre-Primer.)
5. around (adverb): *holo;* or *takai.*
   around (preposition): *takatakai'i.*
6. as (like): *hangē.*
   as (because): *koe'uhi.*
7. ask (inquire): *fehu'i.*
   ask (request): *kole.*
8. ate: (See No. 11, Primer; see also the note in No. 26, Primer.)
9. be: (See the note in No. 18, Pre-Primer.)
10. before (adverb): *'anai; 'i mu'a; ki mu'a; mei mu'a; fuo fua, tomu'a;* or *sinaki.*
    before (preposition): *'i mu'a 'i;* or *kimu'a 'i.*
    before (conjunction): *te'eki;* or *toki.*
11. brown: *melomelo.*
12. by: *'i; 'e;* or *'aki.*
13. call: *ui; fākaui;* or *fangufangu.*
14. cold (adjective): *momoko.*
    cold (catarrh): *fofonu.*
15. could: (See first "can" in No. 5, Pre-Primer; see also the note in No. 26, Primer.)
16. can't: *'ikai lava.*
17. every: *kotoa;* or *kotoa pē.*
18. far: *mama'o.*
19. first: *'uluaki.*
20. five: *nima.*
21. fly (insect): *lango.*
    fly (intransitive verb): *puna.*
    fly (transitive verb): *fakapuna.*

22. found: (See No. 13, Primer; see also the note in No. 26, Primer.)

23. four: *fā.*

24. from: *mei.*

25. gave: (See the note in No. 26, Primer; see also the next number in this section.)

26. give: *foaki.*

27. going: (Same as go — see No. 11, Pre-Primer.)

28. had (See No. 13, Pre-Primer; see also the note in No. 26, Primer.)

29. has: (See No. 13, Pre-Primer; see also the note on No. 26, Primer.)

30. her: (See No. 15, Pre-Primer; see also the note in No. 26, Primer.)

31. him: (See note in No. 30, this page.)

32. his: (See note in No. 30, this page.)

33. how: *fēfē;* or *founga.*

34. if: *kapau; 'o kapau;* or *ka.*

35. into: *ki (hū ki loto).*

36. just (adjective): *totonu;* or *anga-tonu.*
    just (adverb): *pē; toki;* or *tonu.*

37. know: *'ilo.*

38. let (allow): *tuku;* or *fakangofua.*
    let (a house): *nofo totongi.*

39. long (intransitive verb): *faka'amu; faka'ānaua; 'unaloto;* or *holiholivale.*
    long (adjective): *lōloa;* (time): *fuoloa.*

40. made: (See No. 23, Pre-Primer; see also note in No. 26, Primer.)

41. many: *lahi* or *tokolahi.*

42. may: (Same as can.)

43. much: *lahi.*

44. must: *pau.*

45. never: *'ikai. . .teitei;* or *'oua. . .teitei.*
    (not yet): *te'eki.*

46. of: *'a;* or *'o.*

47. old: *motu'a; fuoloa;* or *mu'a.*

48. once: *tu'o taha.*

49. open (adjective): *ava; 'atā;* or *matangaki.*
    open (transitive verb): *fakaava; to'o; faka'atā; tangaki; huke; folahi; avangi; tatala hae;* or *fa'ai.*

50. or: *pe.*

51. our (exclusive): (dual) *he'ema;* or *homa;* (plural) *he'emau;* or *homau.*
    our (inclusive): (dual) *he'eta;* or *hota;* (plural) *he'etau;* or *hotau.*
    (See the note in No. 25, Pre-Primer.)

52. over (finished, past): *'osi;* or *hili.*
    over (above, upon, etc.): *'i* (as in *laka'i*).
    over (more than): *lahi hake 'i.*
    over (excessively): *fu'u;* or *hulu.*

53. pretty: *faka'ofo'ofa;* or *matamatalelei.*

54. round (adjective): *fuopotopoto.*
    round (adverb): *holo; takai.* (along): *ange;* or *hake.*
    round (preposition): *takai 'i.*
    round (noun): *takai* (song) *hiva taufetuli.*

55. show (intransitive verb): *e'a; 'ilonga;* or *mata'ā'ā.*
    show (transitive verb): *fakahā; fakahāhā; fakae'a; faka'ali'ali;* or *fakahinohino.*
    show (noun): *faka'ali'ali.*

56. sing: *hiva.*

57. sleep: *mohe.*

58. soon: *vave mai;* or *mei foki mai.*

59. take: *to'o;* or *'ave.*

60. them (dual): *kinaua.*
    them (plural): *kinautolu.*
    (See the note in No. 25, Pre-Primer.)

61. there: *ai; 'i ai; 'i hē; 'i hena;* or *ko.*

62. think: *fakakaukau; mahalo;* or *kohu.*

63. us (excluding you): (dual) *kimaua;* (plural) *kimautolu.*

us (including you): (dual) *kitaua;* (plural) *kitautolu.*
(See the note in No. 25, Pre-Primer.)

64. very (adverb): *'aupito; lahi;* or *lahi 'aupito.*
    very (adjective): *tonu.*

65. walk: *'alu (lalo); 'eva;* or *'eve'eva.*

66. were: (See No. 18, Pre-Primer; see also the note in No. 26, Primer.)

67. when (interrogative): *'anefē; 'afē;* or *fakakū.*
    when (conjunctive): *ka;* or *'o ka.*

68. who: *(ko) hai.*

69. why: *(ko e) hā.*

70. wish: *holi; faka'amu; fie; loto; taumaiā, pehē ange mai;* or *'amusiaange.*

Second

1. always: *ma'u ai pē;* or *taimi kotoa pē.*

2. any: *ha; ha. . .pē;* or *ha. . .moa pē.*

3. because: *koe'uhi.*

4. been: (See No. 18, Pre-Primer; see also the note in No. 26, Primer.)

5. best: *lelei taha.*

6. better: *lelei ange; sai ange;* or *sai hake.*

7. both: *fakatou'ose.*

8. bring: *'omai; mai;* or *fetuku mai.*

9. buy: *'i; 'e;* or *'aki.*

10. carry: *fua; to'oto'o;* or *fata.*

11. clean (adjective): *ma'a.*
    clean (transitive verb): *fakama'a.*

12. cut (verb): *hele; hifi; tofi; tafa; kosi; fahi; sipi; tu'utu'u;* or *tā.*

13. does: (See No. 10, Primer; see also the note in No. 26, Primer.)

14. done: (See No. 10, Primer; see also the note in No. 26, Primer.)

15. drink: *inu* (alcoholic liquor) *inu kava mālohi.*

16. fall (transitive verb): *tō; hinga; mape'e; holo; humu; ngangana;* or *mokulu.*
    fall (autumn): *fa'ahita'u fakatōlau.*

17. full: *fonu; pito;* or *'efi'efi.*

18. goes: (See No. 11, Pre-Primer; see also the note in No. 26, Primer.)

19. got: (See No. 10, Pre-Primer; see also the note in No. 26, Primer.)

20. grow (intransitive verb): *tupu.*
    grow (transitive verb): *tō.*

21. hold (of ship): *'ana.*
    hold (transitive verb): *puke;* or *kuku.*
    hold (capable of containing): *fe'unga mo.*
    hold (remain firm): *ma'u.*

22. hot: *vela; 'afu;* (pepper hot) *fifisi.*

23. hurt (transitive verb): *fakamamahi'i; fakalo-tomamahi'i;* or *ongovevela.*
    hurt (participle): *mamahi; lotomamahi; lavea; maumau; vevela;* or *vevela'ia.*

24. its: (See the note in No. 25, Pre-Primer.)

25. keep (transitive verb): *tauhi; malo; tuku;* or *'ai.*
    keep (intransitive verb): *nofo.*

26. kind (adjective): *anga-'ofa;* or *anga-lelei.*
    kind (sort): *fa'ahinga.*

27. light (not heavy): *ma'ama'a.*
    light (not dark): *maama.*

28. live (be alive): *mo'ui.*
    live (reside): *nofo.*

29. myself: *au.*

30. off (preposition): *mei.*
    off (distant): *mei ai;* or *mama'o.*
    off (forth): *atu.*

31. only: *pē; tofu pē; matematē pē; 'ata'atā pē;* or *ngata pē.*

32. own (transitive verb): *ma'u;* or *'a'ana.*
    own (adjective): *tonu; totonu;* or *pē.*

33. pick (choose): *fili.*
    pick (pluck): *toli; hu'i; faki; paki;* or *lohu.*
    pick (scoop): *vavao.*
    pick (teeth): *huhu.*
    pick (bones): *kai (hui).*

34. pull: *fusi; toho.*

35. read: *lau; laua; lau tohi;* or *lau konga.*

36. right (not left): *to'omata'u.*
    right (not wrong): *tonu; totonu;* or *mo'oni.*
    right (authority, privilege): *mafai; totonu;* or *ngofua.*
    right (transitive verb): *fakatonutonu.*

37. seven: *fitu.*

38. shall (futurity): *te; 'e;* or *ka.*
    shall (certainty): *pau.*

39. sit: *nofo (ki lalo);* or *tangutu.*

40. six: *ono.*

41. small: *si'i;* or *si'isi'i.*

42. start: *kamata.*

43. tell: *tala; fakahā; fakamatala'i; talanoa'i; faka'ilo;* or *talaki.*

44. ten: *hongofulu.*

45. their: (See the attached sheet on pronouns.)

46. these: (See No. 35, Pre-Primer.)

47. those: *na; ko ena; ko ē; or ko ia.*

48. today: *he 'aho ni; 'anenai;* or *'anai.*

49. together: *fakataha.*

50. try (test): *'ahi'ahi; feinga; feinga'i;* or *fakaangaanga.*
    try (judge): *fakamaau'i.*
    try (in Rugby football): *tata'o.*

51. under: *'i lalo 'i. . .*

52. upon: *'i he funga ('o e).*

53. use (noun): *'aonga; ngāue'aki; anga;* or *angafai.*
    use (transitive verb): *ngaue'aki; me'a ngaue'aki;* or *faka'aonga'i.*

54. warm (adjective): *māfana; mafana; pupuha;* or *velevela.*
    warm (transitive verb): *fakamāfana;* or *fakamafana.*

55. wash: *fufulu.*

56. well (noun): *vaikeli;* or *vaitupu.*
    well (in good health): *lelei;* or *mo'ui lelei.*
    well (adverb): *lelei.*

57. which: *fē.*

58. would (See the note in No. 26, Primer; see also No. 44, Primer.)

59. write (a letter): *tohi.*
    write (a book): *fa'u.*

60. draw (pictures): *tā; tā fakatātā; tā fakatataa'i.*
    draw (pull): *tohoaki; ta'aki; unuhi;* or *teteke.*
    draw (water): *'utu.*
    draw (tie in a game): *māhanga.*

61. eight: *valu.*

Dolch Basic Word List – Vietnamese

Pre-Primer

1. a ___ một
2. and ___ và
3. big ___ to
4. blue ___ maū xanh, biển
5. can ___ có thể
6. come ___ đến tới
7. down ___ xuống dưới
8. for ___ vì
9. funny ___ buồn cười
10. get ___ được
11. go ___ đi
12. green ___ mầu xanh lá
13. have ___ có
14. help ___ giúp
15. here ___ đây
16. I ___ tôi, ta
17. in ___ ở trong
18. is ___ là
19. it ___ nó, cái ấy
20. jump ___ nhảy
21. little ___ ít, nhỏ
22. look ___ nhìn
23. make ___ làm
24. me ___ tôi, ta
25. my ___ cuả tôi
26. not ___ không
27. play ___ chởi
28. red ___ mầu đỏ
29. ride ___ cưỡi ngựa, đi xe
30. run ___ chạy
31. said ___ đã nói
32. saw ___ đã thấy (to see) cửa (to saw)
33. see ___ thấy, nhìn
34. the ___ cái
35. this ___ cái nầy
36. to ___ tới
37. up ___ lên, trên
38. want ___ muốn
39. we ___ chúng tôi
40. with ___ với, cùng
41. work ___ làm việc
42. you ___ anh, ông

Primer

1. all ___ tất cả
2. am ___ là (sô ít)
3. are ___ là (sốnhiều)
4. at ___ ở
5. away ___ xa, khỏi
6. black ___ mầu đen
7. but ___ nhưng
8. came ___ đã tới
9. did ___ đã làm
10. do ___ làm
11. eat ___ ăn
12. fast ___ nhanh
13. find ___ tìm
14. good ___ tốt
15. he ___ nó
16. laugh ___ cười
17. like ___ thích
18. new ___ mới
19. no ___ không
20. now ___ bây giờ
21. on ___ trên
22. one ___ một
23. out ___ ngoài
24. please ___ làm ởn
25. put ___ để
26. ran ___ đã chạy
27. say ___ nói
28. she ___ cô ta, bà ta
29. so ___ vậy
30. some ___ một vài
31. stop ___ ngừng
32. thank ___ cảm ởn
33. that ___ cái ấy
34. then ___ rồi thì
35. they ___ chúng nó
36. three ___ ba
37. too ___ nửa, lắm, cũng
38. two ___ hai
39. was ___ đã là
40. went ___ đã đi
41. what ___ cái gì
42. where ___ ở đâu
43. white ___ mầu trắng
44. will ___ sẽ
45. yellow ___ mầu vàng
46. yes ___ dạ, phải
47. your ___ cuả anh

First

1. about _tứ phía, quanh_ khoảng chừng
2. after _sau_
3. again _nữa_
4. an _một cái_
5. around _xung quanh_
6. as _vì, mã,_ chũng như
7. ask _hỏi_
8. ate _đã ăn_
9. be _là_
10. before _trước_
11. brown _mầu nâu_
12. by _bởi_
13. call _gọi_
14. cold _lạnh_
15. could _có thể_
16. can't _không thể_
17. every _mỗi, một_
18. far _xa_
19. first _trước nhất_
20. five _năm_

21. fly _bay_
22. found _đã tìm_
23. four _bốn_
24. from _từ_
25. gave _đã cho_
26. give _cho_
27. going _đang đi_
28. had _đã có_
29. has _có_
30. her _của cô ta, cô ta_
31. him _nó_
32. his _của nó_
33. how _làm sao_
34. if _nếu_
35. into _ở trong_
36. just _đúng, ngay_
37. know _biết_
38. let _để, để cho_
39. long _dài_
40. made _đã làm_
41. many _nhiều_

42. may _có thể_
43. much _nhiều_
44. must _phải_
45. never _không bao giờ_
46. of _của_
47. old _già_
48. once _một lần_
49. open _mở_
50. or _hay là, hoặc_
51. our _của chúng ta_
52. over _qua_
53. pretty _đẹp, xinh_
54. round _tròn_
55. show _chỉ_
56. sing _hát_
57. sleep _ngủ_
58. soon _lập tức, tức thì, sớm_
59. take _lấy_
60. them _chúng nó_
61. there _đấy, kia đó_
62. think _nghĩ_

63. us _chúng ta_
64. very _rất_
65. walk _đi_
66. were _đã là_
67. when _khi nào_
68. who _ai_
69. why _tại sao_
70. wish _ước mong_

Second

1. always __luôn__
2. any __bất luận cái gì__
3. because __bởi vĩ__
4. been __đã là__
5. best __tốt nhất__
6. better __tốt hỏn__
7. both __cả hai__
8. bring __mang__
9. buy __mua__
10. carry __xách, mang, đem__
11. clean __sạch__
12. cut __cắt__
13. does __làm__
14. done __đá làm__
15. drink __uống__
16. fall __rỏi__
17. full __đầy__
18. goes __đi__
19. got __đã lấy__
20. grow __mọc lên__

21. hold __cầm__
22. hot __nóng__
23. hurt __đau, đốn__
24. its __cuả nó__
25. keep __giữ__
26. kind __tốt__
27. light __sáng__
28. live __sống, ở__
29. myself __chính tôi__
30. off __ở xa, lìa xa__
31. only __chỉ__
32. own __cua riêng, có__
33. pick __nhặt__
34. pull __kéo__
35. read __đọc__
36. right __phải, bên phải__
37. seven __bảy__
38. shall __sẽ__
39. sit __ngồi__
40. six __sáu__
41. small __nhỏ__

42. start __bắt đầu__
43. tell __nói__
44. ten __mười__
45. their __cuả chúng nó__
46. these __những cái kia__
47. those __cái kia__
48. today __hôm nay__
49. together __cùng nhau__
50. try __cố gắng, thử__
51. under __dưới__
52. upon __trên__
53. use __dùng__
54. warm __ấm__
55. wash __giặt, rửa__
56. well __tốt__
57. which __cái đó__
58. would __có thể__
59. write __viết__
60. draw __kéo, kẻ__
61. eight __tám__